THE *THINKING CLEARLY* SERIES

Series editor: Clive Calver

The *Thinking Clearly* series sets out the main issues in a variety of important subjects. Written from a mainstream Christian standpoint, the series combines clear biblical teaching with up-to-date scholarship. Each of the contributors is an authority in his or her field. The series is written in straightforward everyday language, and each volume includes a range of practical applications and guidance for further reading.

The series has two main aims:
1. To help Christians understand their faith better.
2. To show how Christian truths can illuminate matters of crucial importance in our society.

THE *THINKING CLEARLY* SERIES

Series Editor: Clive Calver

Thinking Clearly About Prayer

JOHN WOOLMER

MONARCH

EVANGELICAL ALLIANCE

British Library Cataloguing Data
A catalogue record for this book is available
from the British Library.

ISBN 1 85424 358 6

*Cover photograph of Victoria Falls
provided by the author.
See especially chapters 5 and 9.*

*'Many waters cannot quench love'
(Song 8:7)*

Co-published with

The Evangelical Alliance,
Whitefield House, 186 Kennington Park Road,
London SE11 4BT

SCB Publishers
Cornelis Struik House, 80 McKenzie Street,
Cape Town 8001, South Africa
Reg no 04/02203/06

Designed and produced by Bookprint Creative Services
P.O. Box 827, BN21 3YJ, England for
MONARCH PUBLICATIONS
Broadway House, The Broadway,
Crowborough, East Sussex, TN6 1HQ.
Printed in Great Britain.

Dedication & acknowledgements

To Brother Sam SSF, and the Hilfield Community with grateful thanks for their quiet inspiration.

Thanks to Jane, my wife, and to Rachel, Susie, Tim and Katy for their love and understanding, especially during my sabbatical period.

Thanks to Joyce Martin for her dedicated typing and preparation of the text, and to Janet Kiuison for preparing the initial submission.

To Mme Helène Stevens, and to Michael and Betty Feilden for the use of Valbourgès and Roquebrune during the writing period.

To Anne Goode and the Ammerdown Centre for providing regular spiritual places of retreat.

To the parishioners of St Peter & St Paul Shepton Mallet, St Aldhelm's Doulting, and St Bartholomew's Cranmore for their constant encouragement and many contributions to the text. To the many others who have shared part of their spiritual journey, and most especially to many friends in the Diocese of Northern Zambia.

To the Diocese of Bath & Wells, not least for the gift of a sabbatical.

To Tony Collins, and the staff at Monarch, for their help and encouragement.

Contents

Foreword

The saints throughout the ages have always wrestled with the dilemma of how you love God for who he is rather than for what he gives. Prayer presents us with similar paradoxes – can we get to the position where we pray because of who God is rather than what God gives? The time has come where many of us are hearing the call to live lives with deeper and more profound rhythms of communion with God. The paths we have been down have served us well, the food that has been served on our plate filled our stomachs, but the Spirit has urged us to the place where we long for more intimacy with God.

This is why *Thinking Clearly About Prayer* is so timely. It is not a 'How to…', a quick fix, a sweatless, tearless, bloodless formula for prayer. It is a book borne out of ministry among God's people, of personal experience of God's beckoning and opening out new depths of closeness, of sweat, tears and pain. John Woolmer is not one who stands removed, or one who is at the top of the mountain, his light blinding us and making us feel intimidated into following. Rather he honestly shares of his journey to deeper communion with the living God and encourages us to become fellow travellers. He encourages us to draw alongside and enter in.

Time and time again he encourages us to prayer – not to achieve some huge spiritual status, nor to impress others, but out of the simple response to the incredible love of God. Prayer is about response, trying to cope with God's goodness, and the wonder that God invites us to be part of what he is doing in the world. This frees John up to face many of the thorny questions that plague our Christianity.

In refreshing honesty this man faces questions of the spiritual wilderness – those times when God seems far away. He deals with the tension of God's sovereignty and our requests for forgiveness, evangelism, healing, guidance and praise. Each is treated with depth, sincerity and a genuine facing of the pain and agony of the Garden. Drawing on his experience and that of others he offers a distilled wisdom on many topics the like of which I have not come across. He weaves story in with Scripture, with practical guidelines and models and encouragements which mean you can do little else than spend the end of every chapter on your knees. There is testimony after testimony to the rich abundance of God's grace and goodness. There is invitation after invitation to enter more profoundly into life with and for God.

The call to prayer is unabating. It comes like wave after wave upon a beach. Or perhaps more like different dishes at the same feast. The feast is laid on by God, the necessary materials and utensils are found in the Bible. We are invited to taste new dishes, to experience new glories of the splendour of God's goodness which only the ones who strive for intimacy taste. I encourage you to feed on this book. To nourish your life and the life of the groups you belong to. Give this book to those who are struggling with prayer and to those who are called to be intercessors. Let it open up for you new paths of prayer into the heart of God. At such a time as this we must heed the prophetic call to know God and his ways with the world. So if you are prepared to pick this book up and read it, be prepared to travel the way of joy and praise, of forgiveness and healing, of witness and testimony, through the wilderness and up the mountain. But whatever you do you won't be able to just read it and do nothing.

J. John
Nottingham

1

The Great Promise and the Eternal Paradox

(Is prayer just a painkiller?)

In this opening chapter, we face the age-old question of the contrast between 'unanswered' prayer and the extraordinary encouragements that some have received.

In particular, we look at Jesus' wonderful promise to the penitent thief, alongside his own prayer, 'Father, if you are willing, take this cup from me.' We see how his drinking of this spiritual cup can bring salvation and hope in every situation, and forms the basis of all our praying.

The Great Promise and the Eternal Paradox

A young man, a lawyer called Aubrey Lekwane, was visiting a friend in Pretoria Central Prison. As he was being guided to the meeting, he saw a friend of long ago, his face ashen and stricken, being led along the corridor between two warders.

The man's face lit up. Tragically, he assumed that Aubrey was bringing him news of a stay of execution. Aubrey had to disillusion him. He tells[1] how his friend's face stiffened, and with head high and eyes cold he walked past, and without even a sideways glance continued his lonely walk to death.

Two contrasting deaths   By contrast, the *Gideon Magazine*[2] tells the story of a man called Lester Ezzell on death row in Florida. Lester was visited by his former Sunday School teacher, Curtis Oakes. Curtis had a real burden for Lester and, with great difficulty, visited him in prison. He was greeted by Lester with the words: 'You don't give up do you? You've been to my home. Now here you are, 750 miles away from home.' Still Lester didn't want to listen. Curtis left a Personal Worker Testament and asked him to read it. Eventually, Lester wrote letters to Curtis, first telling him of his conversion, and a final one which included the following words: 'By the time you receive this letter, my life will have been taken. I will have paid my debt to society for the wrong I have done. But I want you to know this, with that little Testament, and by the grace of God, I have led

12

forty-seven people to the saving knowledge of Jesus Christ. One of them happened to be a newspaper reporter who came to interview me. I just thank you for not giving up on me.'

Faith in a sea of mockery

Long ago, another young criminal faced judicial execution. His crime, in all probability, was more akin to Aubrey's friend than Lester Ezzell's. He was a rebel against the occupying power, his appointed means of execution more barbarous than theirs.

All around him, people waited and watched. The occupying soldiers were methodical and indifferent. Local religious leaders, usually conspicuously absent from such demeaning situations, watched and jeered. A fellow victim cursed, a silent group of onlookers maintained a dignified vigil. Beside him, an extraordinary young man, also being crucified, prayed for his executioners and comforted his friends. This young man, who apparently claimed to be King of the Jews, was causing an astonishing mixture of indifference, derision, and anger. The religious leaders were taunting him, the soldiers were dicing for his clothes, passers-by mocked, a small group of friends watched.

It made no sense. The criminal, in atrocious pain, had begun by cursing his strange companion. Slowly, as the agonising minutes ticked away, he found his attitude was changing. First, he rebuked his colleague, reminding him that they at least, by the brutal standards of their age, deserved death. Then he said: *A cry for help* 'Jesus, remember me when you come into your kingdom' (Lk 23:42).

He was certainly not the first, nor the last, to cry out for help when dying. He was the first to call on the name of Jesus. He stands at the head of myriads of people who, when faced with death, have called, in a mixture of hope and desperation, to Jesus.

Some scholars[3] question the veracity of the account, preferring to see that penitent thief's (to give him his traditional name) conversion as symbolic rather than historical.

It is curious how many people, like Lester Ezzell have, through Jesus, found peace at such times. This ought to encourage us to accept the original Lucan story at face value.

Luke tells that Jesus replied with the unbelievable promise: 'Today you will be with me in paradise' (Lk 23:43). This promise is a cornerstone of Christian hope.

Paradise promised

Either it was fulfilled (and essentially that depends on the truth of the Resurrection of Jesus), or it represents the cruellest hoax. If fulfilled, it rightly forms a basis for all ministry to the dying.

The condemned criminal who turns to Christ at the last moment, the dying cancer patient who seeks peace and forgiveness, the Christian martyr bravely bearing witness before a hostile crowd, the Christian saint dying painfully or peacefully, all share the same hope! That is the wonder of God's grace. The reality of Jesus' dying promise which has been the source of hope to millions in the last two millennia.

The penitent thief had scarcely time, or energy, to do more than breathlessly defend Jesus from the abuse of his partner-in-crime. He acknowledged his guilt and asked for help. This was more than enough to obtain from Jesus that beautiful promise of paradise which has inspired so many others.

Prayer at the end

Hope for the hypocrite

One such was the fashionable 18th-century preacher, Dr Dodd[4]. He, Dodd, despite having been discovered in 1774 trying to bribe the Lord Chancellor's wife to the tune of £3,000 (no small sum!) to obtain a wealthy living in Central London, was back in favour. By 1777 he was preaching successfully, and drawing large crowds at a chapel in Westminster. He busied himself with popular issues such as pamphlets attacking John Wesley and other early Methodists. Unfortunately for him, he was shown to have forged a bill for £4,200 in the name of Lord Chesterfield, a former pupil. He, too, was condemned to judicial death.

In his hour of need, he turned to John Wesley. Wesley went unwillingly to see him. He assumed Dr Dodd was trying to use him. To his surprise, he found that Dodd 'Entirely and calmly gave himself up to the will of God.'

Richard Wurmbrand,[5] who himself was imprisoned and

tortured for fourteen years in Romanian prisons, tells the chilling tale of Patrascanu, Minister of Justice, after the post-war coup in 1948.

Realism and hope for the atheist

Patrascanu was a victim of his own system. He and Wurmbrand shared a prison cell. Patrascanu, confident of release, joked about the communist system. He told the story of the Swiss Senator who wanted to be Navy Minister. 'But we have no navy,' said the Prime Minister. 'What does that matter,' the Senator replied, 'If Romania can have a Minister of Justice, why shouldn't Switzerland have a Minister of the Navy?'

Patrascanu, despite worsening treatment, continued to defend his idols Marx and Lenin. Wurmbrand tried to point him to Jesus. Their ways parted.

Six years later Patrascanu was given a rushed trial, appallingly tortured and executed. Just before his death, he met one of Wurmbrand's friends in his prison. He sent a final message 'If you meet Wurmbrand again, tell him he was right.'

Whether he was converted, or died a disillusioned Marxist, we don't know. Facing death, he certainly discovered the truth of the false god he had loyally served. We may hope he found mercy from the living Christ.

Many people find it difficult to turn to Christ even in such crises. Mistakenly, they feel that having denied him in their lifetime, it is hypocritical to turn at the last moment. Nevertheless, the penitent thief has inspired many others, and encourages us all, like Lester Ezzell's faithful Sunday School teacher, to pray at all times and without ceasing.

History has so many moving examples of Christian martyrs dying in hope, but one example will have to suffice.

Hope for the martyr

Polycarp,[6] Bishop of Smyrna (AD 69-155) faced martyrdom with incredible bravery. He refused to flee the city, despite the certainty of arrest. He gave those who came to arrest him food and drink, prayed for two hours(!), and then left with his captors. Given many opportunities to recant and deny Christ, he faced the hostile stadium and the Proconsul with the words, 'Eighty and six years have I served him, and he hath done me no wrong; how then can I blaspheme against my King who saved me?'

Equally powerful is the testimony of more normal Christian deaths. Jonathan Edwards writes, in a letter, of the death of David Brainerd, the first missionary to the Red Indians:[7]

Peace for the saint   A little before his death, he said to me, as I came into the room, 'My thoughts have been employed on the old dear theme, the prosperity of God's church on earth. As I waked out of sleep (said he) I was led to cry for the pouring out of God's Spirit and the advancement of Christ's kingdom, which the dear Redeemer died and suffered so much for: it is that especially makes me long for it.' But a few days before his death, he desired us to sing a psalm concerning the prosperity of Zion which he signified his mind was engaged in above all things, and at his desire we sang a part of the 102nd psalm. And when he had done, though he was then so low that he could scarcely speak, he so exerted himself, that he made a prayer, very audibly, wherein, besides praying for those present, and for his own congregation, he earnestly prayed for the reviving and flourishing of religion in the world.'

Sadly, there are all too many examples of those who seemingly die without hope in this world or the next.

One of my dearest friends, a staunch and resolute unbeliever, spent many hours trying to convince me of the absurdity of the Christian faith. We traversed the hills and meadows around Winchester; he even showed me the great religious paintings in Venice – accompanying his knowledgeable admiration of the

Some seem to die as they lived   paintings with the caustic comment, 'It's a pity that the subject is such rubbish.'

When he lay dying, I used to visit him. Unfortunately, he was able to do little except curse and rail against the God in whom he apparently didn't believe.

Part of the Eternal Paradox, which we must admit, is that Jesus died between two men – one apparently penitent, one apparently as hardened as ever. God's love was offered to both. God alone can judge them (or us).

Speculation about the nature of paradise can be pointless. Cynics talk of 'pie in the sky when you die'. My grandfather went a little further, declaring robustly that he didn't want to go to heaven. 'No bridge, no sex, and only music which I can't stand.'

But even he used to say his prayers at night. Apparently this was because he thought his own father might be right after all! My great-grandfather was a distinguished and humane Victorian clergyman. When Chaplain of Maidstone gaol, he draped a scaffold with velvet. The public were furious, as they couldn't see the execution properly. The resulting furore led to an end to the practice of public executions. My grandfather's lack of belief was deeply disturbed by his father's faith and humanity.

However, there have been enough 'deathbed' experiences to give us a glimpse beyond this life. Dorothy Kerin's[8] experience is well documented and very difficult to disbelieve.

In February 1911, at the age of twenty-two, she was blind and dying. Her well-documented illness was diagnosed as an advanced state of tuberculosis and diabetes. She was in great pain and grievously emaciated through lack of food. She spoke of hearing angels singing her favourite hymn. *Angels are* Then, to the utter astonishment of all onlookers, includ- *present* ing her doctor, she sat up and said: 'Do you not hear? I am well. I must get up and walk.' She did just that, demanding, and eating, a full meal.

Afterwards, she testified to hearing angels sing; seeing a beautiful vision of angels and the heavenly places, and of being called by name: 'Dorothy, your sufferings are over. Get up and walk!' She did and served Jesus for many years. She lived a normal lifespan and, among other notable works, founded the Christian House of Healing at Burrswood.

A biblical picture

For most of us, it will have to be sufficient to believe and trust that Jesus' promise is true. Paradise will be with him, in a spiritual realm beyond pain and suffering – a place of infinite beauty and glorious worship.

The biblical picture of paradise is clearest in the last chapter of the final book of the Bible:

> Then the angel showed me the river of the water of life, as *Paradise* clear as crystal, flowing from the throne of God and of the *regained* Lamb down the middle of the great street of the city. On each

side of the river stood the tree of life, bearing twelve crops of fruit, yielding its fruit every month. And the leaves of the tree are for the healing of the nations. No longer will there be any curse. The throne of God and of the Lamb will be in the city, and his servants will serve him. They will see his face, and his name will be on their foreheads. There will be no more night. They will not need the light of a lamp or the light of the sun, for the Lord God will give them light. And they will reign for ever and ever.' (Rev 22:1-5)

In this life, we get glimpses of this. Moments of spiritual reality that can be so intense that, like St Paul, we are lifted out of this world:

Paradise experienced

I know a man in Christ who fourteen years ago was caught up to the third heaven. Whether it was in the body or out of the body I do not know – God knows. And I know that this man – whether in the body or apart from the body I do not know, but God knows – was caught up to paradise. He heard inexpressible things, things that man is not permitted to tell. (2 Cor 12:2-3)

When we look at the wonder and beauty of our tired and flawed earth; despite the 'groanings of creation' (Rom 8:22), we catch sight of such beauty that paradise seems both probable and indescribable.

Walking through Kakemega Forest you can see, flitting in the sunlight, the glorious Mother of Pearl butterfly. Ordinarily, this great white butterfly glides around the edge of African woodland like an elegant silk handkerchief. Occasionally, if the sun catches its wings at just the right angle, it radiates a most glorious variety of iridescent colours – pink, pale violet, green – which grow in intensity as the angle changes.

Experience of God

In this life, we sometimes get glimpses of paradise, worship becomes transcendent, angels appear... we may, if God's grace allows, have experiences like Dorothy Kerin's, or St Paul's.

Without this hope, much of life seems a cruel jest. With it, believers can be inspired to great heights and comforted in great depths.

It is a very different hope from the Islamic concept which

seems to encourage a holy death in a holy war (Jihad); and totally different from the endless cycle of life suggested by religions which believe in reincarnation.

The cross – the gateway to paradise

The Christian hope is only possible through the cross. The penitent thief was, in a real sense, the first Christian. In his agony, he could never have seen it in such orthodox terms. True, he declared his faith, recognised his own sin, and sought help; but what mattered to him was the physical presence of Jesus – mutilated, bleeding, dying – but still full of compassion.

The mocking onlookers could neither see nor understand.

Go and tell this people: 'Be ever hearing, but never understanding; be ever seeing, but never perceiving.' *The* Make the heart of this people calloused; make their ears *blindness of* dull and close their eyes. Otherwise they might see with *unbelievers* their eyes, hear with their ears, understand with their hearts, and turn and be healed. (Is 6:9-10)

These prophetic words, used by Jesus during his explanation of the Parable of the Sower (Mk 4:12), and by Paul at the end of Acts (Acts 28:26) express the paradox of God's sovereignty and mankind's unbelief. We must pray for the veil of unbelief to be lifted (2 Cor 3:14, and see Chapter 8, p178). This appears to have happened to Patrascanu (see above) and it is our privilege and challenge to pray!

All this may seem quite straightforward. Either we believe, or we don't. 'Oh Vicar, I wish I had your faith', is a fairly constant cry. Yet it is not as simple as that. Nearly all believers know the bewildering uncertainty caused by times of spiritual darkness and unanswered prayer.

I do mean unanswered prayer. When the answer is 'yes', the signs, the coincidences, and the feelings are strong. *The problem* Sometimes, when the answer is 'no', or 'wait', it is *of* reasonably easy to hear, and even to understand. But *'unanswered* most of us, if we're honest, know those moments *prayer* when there seems to be a deafening silence.

We pray hard, in apparent faith, for a friend to be healed, and they die. At the same time others experience miraculous recoveries. We pray hard, with fervour, faith and hope, for a dear friend to be converted, and apparently they are unmoved. At the same time, others are dramatically converted. Therein lies one of the great prayer paradoxes.

A prayer not granted

One of my greatest spiritual helpers, Fred Smith, had an extraordinary ministry, especially in the area of healing. I have often witnessed the power of his ministry which had an 'apostolic' quality. I also saw people benefit from his prayers even when not physically healed.

In his book,[9] he writes movingly of his prayers for his eldest granddaughter who, aged twenty, was diagnosed as dying of leukaemia. She was a lovely girl, a deeply believing Christian. His prayers for her healing were not answered in the way that he hoped and believed:

> My granddaughter's death was, and still is, a cause of great sorrow to me. I do not understand why she was not healed. But I do trust in God's supreme victory and sovereignty, and ultimately I can say 'I do not understand, but I do believe.' Her death has not in any way prevented me from feeling compassion for those who are sick, and wanting to pray for them. Even if only one person was healed as a result of my prayers, it would still be worthwhile – one person healed is a lot better than no one.

Christians united in death

Some years ago, the leading evangelist, David Watson, and the radical theologian, Bishop John Robinson, both died of cancer. Both wrote movingly before their deaths of their faith and hopes. Many prayers were said for each of them. Yet, in each case, their friends and family had to go through the pain of a long-drawn-out illness and death.

What does one say, as a parish priest, or a visiting friend, to someone who is obviously dying, yet who is still believing fervently – supported by praying friends – for a miracle   ***Death is an*** that seems increasingly unlikely to happen? Sometimes   ***answer*** we must be very courageous, we must cease looking for a physical miracle, and prepare our friends and their family for the journey to paradise.

Recently, a young man was dramatically converted when visiting our church. He wanted to pray, and fast, for the recovery of his grandfather (whom I didn't know) who was dying of a stroke in a nursing home. Gently, I advised him to pray for a holy death rather than an earthly miracle. A few weeks later, he returned to see me; his grandfather had died, but his own new faith had been strengthened by the experience. Probably, if he'd continued fasting and praying for a miracle, his own spiritual journey would have been hindered and his grandfather would still have died.

I believe that we need to walk quietly and trustingly into the Garden of Gethsemane:

> Jesus went out as usual to the Mount of Olives, and his disciples followed him. On reaching the place, he said to them, 'Pray that you will not fall into temptation.' He withdrew about a stone's throw beyond them, knelt down and prayed, 'Father, if you are willing, take this cup from me; yet not my will, but yours be done.' An angel from heaven appeared to him and strengthened him. And being in anguish, he prayed more earnestly, and his sweat was like drops of blood falling to the ground. When he rose from prayer and went back to the disciples, he found them asleep, exhausted from sorrow. 'Why are you sleeping?' he asked them. 'Get up and pray so that you will not fall into temptation.' (Lk 22:39-46)

Jesus' great request

Whether or not verses 43 and 44 are part of the original text,[10] there is enough to make the tension of the spiritual battle very clear.

Jesus was willing to drink the cup – the cup of God's wrath. William Lane,[11] in his brilliant commentary on Mark's Gospel, describes this powerfully.

> The thought that the cup could be removed may have come from

Isaiah 51:17-23 where God, in a proclamation of salvation, summons Jerusalem to arouse from its drunken stupor and to recognise that 'the cup of staggering' has been taken away. Yet Scripture also speaks of those who 'Did not deserve to drink the cup (but) must drink it' (Jer 49:12). The tension between these alternative expressions of grace and judgement, respectively, seems to be reflected in Jesus' prayer with its confession of God's ability ('all things are possible to you'; cf Mk 10:27) and the firm resolve to submit to God's sovereign will. The metaphor of the cup indicates that Jesus saw himself confronted, not by a cruel destiny, but by the judgement of God.

The cup must be drunk

Jesus, willing to drink the cup, still prayed for its removal. The human Jesus shrank from the impending ordeal. He enquired, in agony of mind and spirit, whether there was another way. Most of us would seriously doubt his humanity without this passage. Deep down, Jesus knew that this was both Satan's hour and God's way.

Returning the third time, he said to them, 'Are you still sleeping and resting? Enough! the hour has come. Look, the Son of Man is betrayed into the hands of sinners. Rise! Let us go! Here comes my betrayer!' (Mk 14:41-42)

Jesus allowed himself to be handed over by the betrayer to the forces of darkness. Before that, there was one final display of his earthly power: 'When Jesus said, "I am he", they drew back and fell to the ground' (Jn 18:6).

The words used by Jesus, probably in Aramaic, using exactly the same name that God had given for himself to Moses, 'I am who I am' (Ex 3:14), felled the arresting party. Henceforward, Jesus, his will perfectly aligned to his Father's, allowed the opposition to do their work. 'That God was reconciling the world to himself in Christ, not counting men's sins against them. And he has committed to us the message of reconciliation' (2 Cor 5:19). Despite this, the paradox grows sharper.

Jesus' sacrifice

We may well, like former Archbishop Ramsey, feel uncomfortable with the Palm Sunday hymn 'Ride on! Ride on!' with its line 'The Father on his sapphire throne awaits is own anointed Son', which for all its beautiful imagery suggests a dangerously detached view of Jesus and his Father.

Yet, for the next long hours, Jesus is horribly alone – friends fail, opponents mock, soldiers flog, the judicial process continues on its cruel way and, finally, in the midst of it all, the sky darkens. He even refuses the offer of a humane painkiller (Mk 15:23).

St Luke doesn't record the mysterious cry, 'My God, my God, why have you forsaken me?' (Mk 15:34), but instead tells that Jesus spoke a word of total faith as he died, 'Father, into your hands I commit my spirit' (Lk 23:46).

The Resurrection is the answer

Only after the Resurrection does the full significance of what has happened become clear. The ancient rebellion in the first garden had brought death; Jesus' total submission in the Garden of Gethsemane and on Calvary, defeated the rebellion.

Jesus' death, and his dying promise to the dying thief, brings hope into every situation, however terrible. His victory means that the penitent thief's prayer was answered. His victory means that every honest prayer may be answered as the one who prays hopes. But the paradox of Jesus' own request in Gethsemane shows us that God is sometimes most powerfully at work when our deepest prayers are not answered in the way that we would hope.

When the psalmist (Ps 84:5-6), in the quaint language of the Prayer Book, says: 'Blessed is the man whose *The Christian* strength is in thee: in whose heart are thy ways, who *in difficulty* going through the vale of misery uses it for a well; and the pools are filled with water', he is expressing the same thought. The 'Vale of Misery'[12] has to be traversed many times in most Christian lives. Often Christian witness is at its most impressive in such circumstances. Recently, I met a Christian parent in a holiday discussion group. Her faith had been severely tested by the death, over a widely separated period of years, of two of her children. She still believed, and indeed radiated a confident, mature faith. But, like St Paul, in Philippians 1:23, she longed to be with Christ, in paradise, reunited with her much-loved children.

The paradox and the promise

Either we accept, live with, even welcome the paradox, or we shall be forced into one of two dangerous theological avenues.

We may twist the evidence, blaming others for lack of faith or vision, affirm that, despite all that has happened, God has answered favourably. Alternatively, we may lapse into a cynical agnosticism which effectively denies paradise and gives up on intercessory prayer.

I remember well a 1960's Theological College Vice-Principal preaching a sermon which effectively told us that such prayer was a waste of time. I spoke to him at great length afterwards just to make sure that I hadn't misunderstood. I'm told that subsequently he greatly changed his views. I'm afraid that I didn't wait to find out, that and other circumstances pointed to a change of college!

St Luke, evangelist and missionary, understood and accepted that the Father's 'no', and the deep spiritual turmoil of Jesus in the Garden, made possible the wonderful promise to the criminal at Golgotha.

St Luke, himself, knew this paradox. He had joined the apostolic team at just such a moment. The Holy Spirit (see Acts 16:6f) had just blocked Paul's plans, and directed them to Philippi – not exactly a pleasant experience!

Both the promise and the paradox are for us all. The practical question, which we shall look at throughout the following pages is, can we pray effectively – accepting the paradox, while rejoicing in the promise?

Notes

1. Michael Cassidy, *A witness for ever* (Hodder & Stoughton, 1995), p 80.
2. The Gideon Magazine, 'Saved on Death Row', Autumn 1995.
3. T. W. Manson, *The Gospel of Luke* (Moffatt NT Commentary, 1950), on Luke 23: 39-43.
4. Garth Lean, *John Wesley Anglican* (Blandford Paperbacks, 1964), p 73.

5. Richard Wurmbrand, *In God's Underground* (W. H. Allen, 1968) pp 31-34, 131.
6. 'Documents of the Christian Church' (OUP, 1967), pp 9-11.
7. Iain H. Murray, *Jonathan Edwards: a new biography* (Banner of Truth, 1987), p 304 and his original diaries.
8. Monica Furlong, *Burrswood – Focus of Healing* (Hodder & Stoughton, 1978), Chapter 1.
9. Fred Smith, *God's Gift of Healing* (New Wine Press, 1986), pp 137-138.
10. See, for instance, a long and inconclusive discussion in C. P. Evans, *St Luke* (SCM Press), pp 812-3.
11. William Lane, *Commentary on Mark's Gospel* (Marshall, Morgan & Scott, 1974), p 517.
12. See also John Bunyan, *Pilgrim's Progress* (Everyman, 1907), p 17, 'The Slough of Despond'.

2

Effective Prayer or Empty Words?

(Is prayer a waste of time and effort?)

This chapter gives examples of what St James calls 'The effective prayer of a religious man.'

We face Jesus' stern words on the true evidence of effective praying, and also his warnings about empty words.

We begin to discover the true purpose of prayer – a love relationship with the Father – all too easily blocked by unforgiveness, cynicism, idleness, and loss of our first love; yet amazingly restored by a gracious God who searches us out.

Effective Prayer or Empty Words?

Two examples of effective praying

(1) A bedridden woman

A bedridden woman[1] living alone with her sister in Victorian London, waited for her to return from church. Each Sunday she would ask about the service. Each Sunday, she would receive the same sort of disinterested reply about the deacons, the minister and the worship. On this occasion her sister continued, 'But it was a little different. We had a Mr Moody, a young man from America, to preach.'

'Ah!' said the bedridden one, 'I will have no lunch today, I must pray.'

Several years earlier, she had read an article written in a Christian newspaper by D. L. Moody. Since then she had been praying that God would bring him across the Atlantic to her sister's church.

Now her prayer had been answered, things were going to be different. Mr Moody was still a young man. His famous evangelistic career lay in an undreamt of future. He had been glad to be invited to England, but he hadn't found the morning's experience particularly edifying. A large congregation – typical of Victorian England – but singularly unresponsive. An atmosphere of spiritual deadness seemed to prevail.

In the evening, things were strangely different. The church seemed alive in the Spirit! Scores of people answered his evangelistic call. Puzzled, he made the challenge more decisive. To his astonishment, even greater numbers responded. He was asked to stay on, to preach and minister for several nights. A local revival seemed to have begun.

A revival begins

This had far greater consequences than for the congregation of one London church. Those evenings helped to launch D. L. Moody's evangelistic ministry. Moody was intrigued. Why had it been so different on the Sunday evening? He could have attributed it, quite properly, to the sovereignty of God. But he felt that there must also be a human reason. Eventually, he tracked down the bedridden woman and her church-going sister.

How easy it would have been for the ill woman to have lain in bed saying, 'It is so unfair! I'm too ill to do anything useful!' But instead of turning her face to the wall and giving up, she did her most effective spiritual work from her sick bed.

(2) A national crisis

It is much harder to believe that prayer can affect national matters, yet there is plenty of evidence that this is the case. Nehemiah (1:5ff) prayed fervently for his people, so did Daniel (9:4ff). During the last war, much prayer was offered, particularly during the remarkable evacuation from Dunkirk which saved the British Army from almost certain destruction. In 1991, many prayers were prayed for Zambia, for peaceful elections, and a proper transfer of power. The Anglican church, particularly Bishop Stephen Mumba, was much involved.

But in recent years, the extraordinary transition in South Africa which culminated in the elections on April 27th, 1994, is perhaps the most remarkable international event – and there was much prayer offered for many years.

In the Anglican Church, prayer led to spiritual renewal under Archbishop Bill Burnett, and then political renewal under his successor Desmond Tutu. African Enterprise, the organisation founded by Michael Cassidy,[2] worked tirelessly for peace. Some years earlier he had written quite hopefully *The Passing Summer* – everyone else prophesied doom, Cassidy saw some signs of hope. In *A witness for ever*, he tells the moving story of burgeoning prayer bringing unlikely people together to talk, to think, and sometimes to pray.

One of the unknown prayer warriors was a Mrs Sicwetch, who built up an extraordinary church in a tiny village called Lujizweni. Back in the 1950's they started praying, fasting, and expecting miracles. One passing visitor was a trainee pastor called Joseph Kobo.[3] He spent a few months there in 1957, then aged 22. She did much to help Joseph and he went on to work in the townships. But gradually he became disillusioned, took off his dog collar, and declared himself a Marxist. He joined the political, and then the military wing of the ANC. In the *A freedom fighter returns to Jesus* next twenty years he had many adventures, imprisonment on Robben Island, visits to the UN in New York, training by Russian and East Germans, acting as a courier bringing weapons into Namibia ... then he was arrested and in 1980 was imprisoned, in solitary confinement in a cold fortress in the Drakensberg mountains.

For two years, he was kept in complete silence. Then he received one piece of information, 'Your wife died, Kobo'. All he could do was to continue to watch the snake vulture catch its prey.

A while later, he heard a voice saying, 'Joseph, why are you here?' He was astonished. Was it a trick? But the voice wasn't in Xhoso, the language of the guards, nor English or Afrikaans.

It spoke again, 'Joseph, I called you to do a special thing. You don't need to be here. Why are you here?'

For ninety days Joseph, still unconvinced, kept hearing the voice. Eventually he broke down in tears and, after weeping for days, finally the hardened Marxist gave in. 'Lord, if you want me to serve you again...'

The result was extraordinary. The guards started talking, he was released, rejected by his family and local churches – far too dangerous, had a 2½ hour interview with the President, P. W. Botha, who was convinced of his change of heart, a torrid time with the ANC who were very unimpressed, and started preaching in the townships. Quickly, he was accepted and became a local leader. All this in the space of two years.

Then he was persuaded to return to Lijizweni. He found an

extraordinary church, full of prayer, fasting, praise, and miracles. They had called him to be their leader and to plant many new churches.

But why had it happened? Of course, it was a sovereign act of a gracious God. But there was a human link. For over twenty years Mrs Sicwetch and the congregation of Lujizweni had been praying that Joseph would recover his faith. And their prayers, like Elijah's, seemed to have remarkable effect!

The whole election process was fraught with danger. One friend of mine, Brian Blancharde,[4] had the privilege of being an official monitor for the elections. He tells of one incident from among many...

Vosloorus hears the silent voice

The local Peace Committee of Vosloorus, a violence-ridden black township in the East Rand, met some weeks before the election. One Party, IFP (Chief Buthelezi's party), had refused to join in the process. Tension in the township was rising to combustion point, hence the meeting to try and diffuse the situation.

About sixty people gathered representing the political parties, civic groups, the Army, the Police, the Church, and other organisations, including the International Church Peace Monitors. There were increasingly angry exchanges between the ANC and IFP local leaders. Some people started looking to the Church Peace Monitors as if expecting them to pacify the situation.

Then an African, a Baptist pastor, tiny in stature, but a giant in courage, stood up and in a quiet, gentle voice called for God's gift of wisdom on the meeting and bade the meeting pray.

Everyone bowed their heads as silence fell. After a while, the quiet was disturbed by urgent whispering and the rustle of paper as messages were exchanged.

Then the IFP representative stood up. He declared that he and his ANC counterpart had agreed a joint statement urging people to vote, to halt the violence, and to turn in the criminals. Both parties would sign the agreement, provided that the pastor would countersign it. Then it would be published!

These men, most of all the Baptist pastor, were risking their lives in that volatile situation. But it was the silent voice of God which relieved Vosloorus of much suffering in the next few weeks!

Friday, April 15th 1994

Michael Cassidy[5] tells of one incredible day. The previous few days had been times of unbearable tension. The elections were fixed, but chaos threatened. Chief Buthelezi, Chief Minister of KwaZulu, representing the Inkatha Freedom Party, was refusing to participate. Without his party, the elections would seem incomplete, and the whole post-election process would be fatally flawed. In addition, there would almost certainly be violence and heavy loss of life during the actual voting.

The international team of mediators, headed by veteran American statesman Henry Kissinger and former British Foreign Secretary, Lord Carrington (who had successfully brokered the Zimbabwe independence talks some years earlier), had failed. They were going home.

Professor Washington Okumu, a senior Kenyan diplomat, was appalled. He was in deep contact with Michael Cassidy and other prayer warriors. Okumu decided to make one last effort to contact Chief Buthelezi at Lanseria Airport early on the Friday morning.

Okumu dashed by taxi to the Airport. Unknown to him, Chief Buthelezi's plane had taken off. But something very strange happened. These are Buthelezi's own words:

An inexplicable problem

'We were hardly airborne when the pilot said there was something wrong with the plane. The compass was playing up. And this was a brand new plane! So we had to return to Lanseria. Okumu by now was in the manager's office, having just arrived. I said to him, "You know, my brother, God has brought me back, like Jonah (!), because there is something wrong with the plane, and it is obvious he wants us to meet."

'Washington Okumu then told me of a plan over which he had reflected very deeply during the night. He proposed to talk to Mr de Klerk, Mr Mandela and me to find out whether, in fact, we could still discuss how to make changes in such a way that I would be able to participate in the elections. The changes concerned the position of the

King and the Kingdom (Zulu King Goodwill Zwelithini and Kwa-Zulu). These were the main points. We talked at length and then decided to see each other on Sunday at the Royal Hotel in Durban on our way to the Jesus Peace Rally' (organised by Michael Cassidy and his team).

The Lanseria conversation was momentous 'in many ways a turning point' said Okumu later.

Just a coincidence?

Was it just a happy coincidence that turned the Chief's plane back? It seems unlikely. Consider these three facts! First, the instruments had been properly checked before take off; secondly, if they had gone wrong a few minutes later the plane would have diverted to a different airport; thirdly, when the plane was grounded, no errors in the compass system were found!

The managing director of Osprey Aerospace, whose pilots were on contract to the KwaZulu government commented, 'I believe it was an Act of God.'

As William Temple[6] used to say, 'When I pray, coincidences seem to happen…'

So much prayer was being offered in South Africa, and throughout the world, so much prayer was being answered! The Jesus Peace Rally which took place on the Sunday received messages of goodwill from State President F. W. de Klerk, Nelson Mandela, the Zulu King, and many others. Chief Buthelezi attended in person.

Effective prayer in Scripture

'The prayer of a righteous man is powerful and effective' (Jas 5:16b). While the immediate context is the healing ministry of the Christian church, James is also clearly thinking of wider issues as he cites, as his example, the great prophet Elijah. Elijah had been engaged in combatting a national drought brought about, and then ended, as a sign to the spineless King Ahab and his infamous wife, Queen Jezebel.

James is writing to encourage, actually to command (!), a sick person to summon the elders of the church for prayer. He clearly understood the necessity and the efficacy of prayer offered by a believing group of people.

The key to effective prayer
Jesus, too, taught much about the outcome of prayer. For the moment, one example will suffice: 'If you abide in me, and my words abide in you, ask whatever you will, and it shall be done for you' (Jn 15:7 RSV). The key to effective praying is abiding in Jesus. That is the only basis of the righteousness to which James refers. It was the basis of the bedridden sister's prayer. It was the basis of the great wave of prayer for South Africa organised by Michael Cassidy and others.

The first helped to launch one of the greatest of all evangelistic ministries, the second to bring about the most remarkable political transformation of the twentieth century. Even if, God forbid, South Africa should relapse into chaos, it would not invalidate the miracle.

The consequences of effective prayer

Effective prayer startles a complacent and largely unbelieving world. Some, sadly, are hardened in their unbelief. Jesus constantly faced this. Opponents attributed his signs to Beelzebub. 'And the teachers of the law who came down from Jerusalem said, "He is possessed by Beelzebub! By the prince of demons he is driving out demons."' (Mk 3:22).

Cities saw his signs and were unmoved. 'Woe to you, Korazin! Woe to you, Bethsaida! For if the miracles that were performed in you had been performed in Tyre and Sidon, they would have repented long ago, sitting in sackcloth and ashes. But it will be more bearable for Tyre and Sidon at the judgement than for you. And you, Capernaum, will you be lifted up to the skies? No, you will go down to the depths.' (Lk 10: 13-15).

Individuals received his ministry, often doing the exact opposite of what he had told them to, or taking what they had received for granted.

A man with leprosy came to him and begged him on his knees. 'If you are willing, you can make me clean.'

Filled with compassion, Jesus reached out his hand and touched the man. 'I am willing', he said, 'Be clean!' Immediately the leprosy left him and he was cured.

Jesus sent him away at once with a strong warning: 'See that you don't tell this to anyone. But go, show yourself to the priest and offer the sacrifices that Moses commanded for your cleansing, as a testimony to them.' Instead he went out and began to talk freely, spreading the news. As a result, Jesus could no longer enter a town openly but stayed outside in lonely places. Yet the people still came to him from everywhere.' (Mk 1:40-45)

Now on his way to Jerusalem, Jesus travelled along the border between Samaria and Galilee. As he was going into a village, ten men who had leprosy met him. They stood at a distance and called out in a loud voice, 'Jesus, Master, have pity on us!'

Effective prayer doesn't always produce spiritual fruit

When he saw them, he said, 'Go, show yourselves to the priests.' And as they went, they were cleansed.

One of them, when he saw he was healed, came back, praising God in a loud voice. He threw himself at Jesus' feet and thanked him – and he was a Samaritan.

Jesus asked, 'Were not all ten cleansed? Where are the other nine? Was no one found to return and give praise to God except this foreigner?' Then he said to him, 'Rise and go, your faith has made you well.' (Lk 17:11-19).

Of course, some, like the tenth leper, the Gadarene demoniac (see Mk 5:1-20, especially verse 20), Mary Magdalene (see Lk 8:1-3), and many others were wonderfully changed and became faithful disciples.

It is no different today. I know people who have been dramatically healed, who have received amazing answers to desperate prayers, who have even been used to pray for others, who now seem hardened and unmoved. Others have come into a new, deeper relationship with Christ as the result of effective ministry.

Occasionally the world sits up and takes notice. A Kenyan leader commented on the South African elections, 'The entry of the Inkatha Freedom Party to the elections was a diplomatic coup engineered by the Lord.'

Newspapers carried reports containing phrases such as: 'God stepped in to save South Africa' (*Durban Daily News*); 'History has thrown up an authentic miracle' (*Time* Magazine, USA); 'It was the Jesus Peace Rally that tipped the scales' (John Simpson, BBC). Reading Nelson Mandela's deeply moving autobiography,[7] I wonder who was praying for him when he was within a hairsbreadth of being sentenced to death at the notorious Treason Trial?

A warning from Jesus

Towards the end of the Sermon on the Mount, Jesus points us to the true evidence of effective prayer. He also warns us not to be deceived by spectacular results.

> Watch out for false prophets. They come to you in sheep's clothing, but inwardly they are ferocious wolves. By their fruit you will recognise them. Do people pick grapes from thorn bushes, or figs from thistles? Likewise every good tree bears good fruit, but a bad tree bears bad fruit. A good tree cannot bear bad fruit, and a bad tree cannot bear good fruit. Every tree that goes not bear good fruit is cut down and thrown into the fire. Thus, by their fruit you will recognise them.
>
> Not everyone who says to me, 'Lord, Lord,' will enter the kingdom of heaven, but only he who does the will of my Father who is in heaven. Many will say to me on that day, 'Lord, Lord, did we not prophesy in your name, and in your name drive out demons and perform many miracles?' Then I will tell them plainly, 'I never knew you. Away from me, you evildoers!' (Mt 7:15-23)

We live today, more than ever, in a culture which is looking for instantaneous results. Jesus' trenchant words warn us that in the matter of prayer, results don't prove anything.

The Christian gospel is based on justification by faith – not *Fruit is* justification by results, whether they be miracles, mega *what* churches, many missionaries, multi-media presentations... *matters* Jesus is interested in fruit, not spectacular results. 'Thus, by their fruit you will recognise them' (Mt 7:20).

The writer to the Hebrews, in the middle of a powerful passage on Christian ethics, puts it succinctly: 'Through Jesus, therefore, let us continually offer to God a sacrifice of praise – the fruit of lips that confess his name' (Heb 13:15).

Signs and wonders, direct answers to prayer, apparently effective prayer ministries may perhaps be cited to authenticate a ministry – but only one that bears Christlike fruit.

When John the Baptist was in prison, wondering if he had wasted his life, he sent a messenger to Jesus with a poignant question, 'Are you the one who was to come, or should we expect someone else?'

Jesus, instead of sending back a rebuke to someone whose faith was faltering, spoke eloquently of the fulfilment of Messianic prophecies and then turned to the crowd and among other things said, 'I tell you the truth: Among those born of women, there is not risen anyone greater than John the Baptist' (see Mt 11:1-19). Nevertheless, it is a sobering thought that Judas Iscariot must have cast out demons, healed the sick, and preached the gospel of the kingdom (see Mk 6:1-13).

Recently I read a book on the deliverance ministry which contained a sentence of breathtaking arrogance: 'We have cast out more demons than anybody else, except perhaps X and Y.' The implication for readers was clearly spelt out. We've done it! We've done it often!! So our theology must be right!!!

Now, it is perfectly possible, indeed probable, that those people may have helped many others. I am just making the scriptural point that 'results' don't prove the point.

Concentration on 'results' discourages other Christians

Many gracious Christians have a real and beautiful prayer life. Because it seldom, perhaps never, seems to lead to others being converted or healed, they get discouraged – especially if surrounded by 'successful' Christians, many of whom seem young and immature.

I remember speaking to a university group. I gave what I thought was an honest and fairly gentle account of a parish healing ministry. One young student was quite upset. She said, 'My Dad's a Vicar. Nothing like this happens in his parish. Is there something wrong with him?'

I have been greatly moved by reading Patricia St John's[8] auto-biography. Her wonderful children's books are well known. My own children have benefited from them, and more than one has made a first profession of faith through reading *Treasures of the Snow* or *The Tanglewood Secrets*. She writes movingly of her work, and that of her brother and other faithful missionaries, in Tangier and Morocco. They saw some amazing answers to prayer, they were given extra-ordinary insights into the difficulties of prayer and the need for persistence, but they saw little fruit in evangelism, which was their greatest desire.

Faithfulness not success

The true nature and purpose of prayer

True prayer is God's chosen means of grace. In prayer, God meets us and we build up a living relationship with him. St Paul puts it with great clarity: 'For through him (Jesus) we both have access to the Father by one Spirit' (Eph 2:18). A good verse, inciden-tally, to offer prayerfully to marauding Jehovah's Witnesses who apparently believe the Scriptures, but deny the doctrine of the Trinity!

True prayer means learning to abide in Christ (see again John 15:1-8). True prayer leads us to discover the wonderful truth that our Saviour is also our friend: 'I no longer call you servants, because a servant does not know his master's business. Instead I have called you friends, for everything that I learned from my Father I have made known to you' (Jn 15:15).

Not only are we friends, but we are even privileged to know something of the Father's business. And the purpose of it all is re-emphasised in the next verses (vv 16,17): 'You did not choose me, but I chose you and appointed you to go and bear fruit – fruit that will last. Then the Father will give you whatever you ask in my name. This is my command: Love each other.'

Varied fruit, character, consistency, and evangelism

There will be fruit – fruit of character (Gal 5:22-23); fruit of lips that confess his name (Heb 13:15, see above); and fruit of evangelism (Rom 1:13): 'I do not want you to be unaware, brothers, that I planned many times to come to you (but have been prevented from doing so until now) in order that I might have a harvest among you, just as I have had among the other Gentiles'.

The Greek word translated 'harvest' in the above, is the same word used for fruit in the previous passages.

Such prayer leads us to understand something of the Fatherhood of God. It is the work of a spiritual lifetime. It requires a mixture of faith, time, and effort. Living as we do in the age of the quick fix ('Come forward and you will receive...'), it is hardly surprising that many try to short circuit the discipline involved. The fruits, or lack of them, are all too apparent.

Sometimes there is a brief honeymoon, when prayers do seem to be heard, followed by steady disillusionment. Prayer, as in our chapter subtitle, seems a waste of time and effort. With which sentiment Jesus, at times seems to agree!

What makes prayer a waste of time?

Evelyn Waugh, in his amusing book *Decline and Fall*,[9] causes the despairing new schoolmaster to set his unruly class an essay for which there will be a prize 'for the longest essay irrespective of merit.'

Sadly, many leaders of intercessions, well rehearsed prayers at prayer meetings, and preachers, fall into this trap. By contrast, a medieval classic[10] pleads for succinct prayer:

A man or woman, suddenly frightened by fire, or death, or what you will, is suddenly in his extremity of spirit driven hastily and by necessity to cry or pray for help. And how does he do it? Not, surely, with a spate of words; not even in a single word of two syllables! Why? He thinks it wastes too much time to declare his urgent need and his agitation. So he bursts out in terror with one little word, and that of a single syllable: 'Fire!' it may be, or 'Help!'

Just as this little word stirs and pierces the ears of the hearers more quickly, so too does a little word of one syllable, when it is not merely spoken or thought, but expresses also the intention in the depth of our spirit. Which is the same as the 'height' of our spirit, for in these matters height, depth, length and breadth all mean the same. And it pierces the ears of Almighty God more quickly than any long psalm churched out unthinkingly. That is why it is written 'Short prayer penetrates heaven.'

John Bunyan, as so often, has some sharp words:

> …there are two things that provoke to prayer. The one is a detestation of sin and the things of this life: the other is a longing desire after communion with God in a holy and undefiled state and inheritance. Compare but this one thing with most of the prayers that are made by men, and you shall find them but mock prayers, and the breathings of an abominable spirit: for even the most of men either do not pray at all, or else only endeavour to mock God and the world by so doing: for do but compare their prayers and the course of their lives together, and you may easily see that the thing included in their prayers is the least sought after by their lives. O sad hypocrites![11]

If we find Bunyan's words too negative (and he was suffering imprisonment for, amongst other things, refusing to use the form of prayer in the 1662 Book of Common Prayer) we will find, as ever, that Jesus' are sharper:

We are not heard for much speaking   And when you pray, do not be like the hypocrites, for they love to pray standing in the synagogues and on the street corners to be seen by men. I tell you the truth, they have received their reward in full. But when you pray, go into your room, close the door and pray to your Father, who is unseen. Then your Father, who sees what is done in secret, will reward you. And when you pray, do not keep on babbling like pagans, for they think they will be heard because of their many words. Do not be like them, for your Father knows what you need before you ask him.' (Mt 6:5-8)

Jesus is objecting to prayer which is done for show, prayer which uses an unending babble of words, and prayer which is full of self-righteous pride. Such prayer achieves nothing. Indeed, it may be far worse, it may achieve a further hardening of impenitent and unbelieving hearts.

Patricia St John[12] has a delightful story of a lady who had a dream about prayer. The dream was of a church were five people were kneeling in prayer, and in front of each sat a bird with folded wings. An angel was watching them.

The first was a beautifully dressed woman kneeling in the front of the church, the second a man deep in apparently sincere prayer, the third a woman in tears, the fourth a tramp, and the fifth a small boy.

The smart woman's bird was large and very white – and quite dead. The angel explained sadly that the woman, a regular churchgoer, was quite insincere and more concerned about the cost of her neighbour's hat than the words she was saying.

The man's praying enabled his bird to soar up through the roofless church, up into the sky. Suddenly the man's face changed. His devout expression became very bitter, and he muttered something under his breath. His bird plummeted as though transfixed by an arrow. The angel commented, 'His prayers started well, then he remembered a wrong done against him. He cannot forgive. See, he is hurrying out to plan some revenge, that's why his prayers never reached the Father.'

The third prayer, a very sad young lady, was having a great struggle. The bird kept rising and falling, but eventually, with much beating of its wings, it reached the clear blue sky and disappeared. Again, the angel explained. 'The woman has had a great sorrow. She has only just returned to pray after many years of doubting that God loved or cared for her. As she prayed, her doubts returned, but she confessed her doubts and persisted praying to believe God's promises. Her prayer reached the Father. He has drawn near to her, to comfort her. See! She is smiling.'

The fruit of prayer depends largely on our spiritual state

The tramp's prayer bird was weak and dingy. The man didn't even seem to be speaking, but the bird suddenly rose and flew into the sunshine. The angel laughed for joy. 'That man doesn't know how to pray at all,' said the angel. 'He has never prayed in his life. He doesn't know what words to use. But his heart is heavy with sin and needs. His thoughts are crying out for mercy and forgiveness. And just at this moment all the angels of God are rejoicing because another sinner has come home.'

The final prayer, the little boy, had a tiny spotless bird. He folded his hands, and said he was sorry that he had slapped his sister, asked God to make his mother well, and to help him with his sums. He thanked God for the football that he had on his birthday, and the bird flew straight upwards with a song of joy, and the child jumped up and ran out into the garden to kick his ball, laughing up into the face of the angel as he passed by.

That lovely dream illustrates both effective ways of praying which maintain or establish a relationship with God, and some of the blocks which make such a relationship virtually impossible.

I say virtually, because within the providence of God there are many examples of God meeting and transforming the most unlikely prayers.

Examples of useless praying

Jesus attacked the 'vain repetitions' of the Pharisees. He had no time for conceited self-righteous prayers.

> To some who were confident of their own righteousness and looked down on everybody else, Jesus told this parable: 'Two men went up to the temple to pray, one a Pharisee and the other a tax collector. The Pharisee stood up and prayed about himself. "God, I thank you that I am not like other men – robbers, evildoers, adulterers – or even like this tax collector. I fast twice a week and give a tenth of all I get."
>
> But the tax collector stood at a distance. He would not even look up to heaven, but beat his breast and said, "God, have mercy on me, a sinner."
>
> 'I tell you that this man, rather than the other, went home justified before God. For everyone who exalts himself will be humbled, and he who humbles himself will be exalted.' (Lk 18:9-14)

There is a wonderful anthem by Glück on these words, where the glorious self-righteousness of the Pharisee is beautifully contrasted with the humility of the tax collector.

True prayer needs humility Jesus' teaching about prayer was given to his disciples. The tax collector in the parable began a life of discipleship when he truly sought forgiveness. If we feel that all our praying has been useless, or we are counselling somebody who feels that, we had better face the possibility that it may be true!

Bad news usually precedes good in the gospel of Jesus. We

don't enter the kingdom by being nice, kind, decent people, we enter the kingdom when we discover something of the meaning of repentance and how it applies to us – personally.

Jonathan Edwards,[13] writing about the revival in his parish of Northampton, USA, before 1736, is at pains to show how frequently the Holy Spirit first convicted members of his congregation of their sinful state. They often couldn't pray, and could only cry to God for mercy. At times of revival, people seem generally much more aware of the holiness of God, and the futility of self-righteous prayer.

Unforgiveness, cynicism and idleness

Jesus taught more about the need to forgive others than almost any other issue (except perhaps the equally unpopular teaching about money and possessions!). We shall devote much of Chapter 7 to this key issue. Suffice it to say here that a failure to forgive others is one of the quickest ways of rendering our prayers useless.

We live in a very cynical age. After I had been ordained deacon, and just before I was made priest, my headmaster put up a notice in the staff common room: 'John Woolmer is made school chaplain with immediate effect.' 'What effect?' laughed my colleagues. Most meant it kindly! What they didn't know was that the very next day a short period of mission was beginning in the school. A mission, outwardly unsuccessful, which paved the way for something quite unusual a few years later.

'Susanna, you are idle!' was a regular cry to my, then, seven-year-old daughter who liked to avoid helping with the chores. One day she replied, 'Then you ought to bow down and worship me!'

There is a great connection between idleness and idolatry. Idleness paves the way to idolatry. Idolatry relies on others to solve our spiritual problems. Idolatry looks to the spiritual guru, or the spiritual experience, for a quick fix. Idolatry can (and I speak cautiously) exalt the Spirit – contrary to Scripture. 'He will bring glory to me by taking from what is mine and making it known to you' (Jn 16:14). Idolatry exalts human beings; leaders who command, and often demand, absolute spiritual obedience.

Idleness, called sloth in the seven deadly sins, is very relevant in many churches, particularly in regard to any sort of disciplined prayer. 'Pray continually,' says St Paul (1 Thess 5:17). 'We always thank God, the Father of our Lord Jesus Christ, when we pray for you, because…' (Col 1:3), he says to a church that he has *never* met. 'Do not be anxious about anything, but in *everything*, by prayer and petition, with thanksgiving, present your requests to God' (Phil 4:6) he says to his friends in Philippi. 'Pray in the Spirit on *all occasions* with all kinds of prayers and requests. With this in mind, *be alert* and *always* keep on praying for all the saints' (Eph 6:18), is how he concludes the great passage on spiritual warfare.

'The end of all things is near. Therefore be *clearminded and self-controlled* so that you can pray,' says St Peter (1 Pet 4:7). 'Dear children, keep yourselves from idols' (1 John 5:21 – the concluding words of his great epistle).

Prayer requires discipline   True prayer requires discipline, determination, and hard work. Of course it needs the inspiration and leading of the Holy Spirit, but the first prayer battle is in the will.

A great friend of mine for some years has got up early to pray and to meditate. Tim was a remarkable, and very reluctant convert. He was brought unwillingly to church by his teenage son, who argued that his schoolfellows, Hindu and Muslim, took their religion seriously, and so should they. The result was a Sunday afternoon visit by the Rector. Tim and his wife were just entering their back gate when they saw my car draw up. They decided to hide Tim behind the dustbins! After knocking and getting no answer, I tried the back door. As I was attacked by their dogs, an embarrassed Tim emerged. This unpropitious beginning has led to a great friendship!

For some months, after a hesitant profession of faith, adult confirmation, and faithful attendance at the Parish Prayer Meeting, he felt he was making little progress. Then on Good Friday, while hoovering the house, God gave him the first three verses of this poem, and the tune. Self-discipline was rewarded with inspiration.

Dark was my life till the Lord spoke to me.
Hard was my heart and no point could I see:
Jesus spoke clearly to me, glory be!
'Lay down your burdens, come follow me.'
                              Now there's
Love in my heart for the light of my life,
Peace in my soul now my Saviour is near.
Love everlasting and peace evermore,
O how I wish I'd listened before.
                              I know
Pray'rs will be answer'd and all sins forgiv'n,
Doubts are dispelled and my future is clear.
Now I will worship and serve him with joy:
Gladly I'll follow Jesus the King.
                              And so,
If you're alone and your heart's full of care,
If darkness rules in your life, don't despair.
Seek, look, and listen, and soon you will see
He will say clearly 'Come, Follow Me.'

Tim didn't know that 'Come Follow Me' was the recently chosen title of our forthcoing Parish Festival. Soon he added the fourth verse to round off the Festival theme.

Eight years later, God had led Tim (who used to have little time for religion, and none at all for the Church of England) to become Bath & Wells Diocesan Registrar.

As for all of us, there have been disappointments amidst many answers to prayer and encouragements.

Tim has been a particular encouragement to me. Early in our friendship, he *insisted* that I took time away from the parish to pray and to listen. The result has been a regular monthly day of Retreat, and more recently, a weekly morning for prayer, preparation and planning, in a parishioner's quiet and prayerful house.

In November 1995, Tim testified to his faith at a supper at Cranmore in a local pub. Nothing very remarkable in that, you might say, except that when Tim's father ran the pub, it was felt to be so haunted that a succession of landlords, until the very successful present one, had a series of miserable experiences. It was the last place on earth that the youthful Tim, who in younger days had tape recorded the sounds of the ghost (!), would have expected to speak about the Risen Christ. The pub, which certainly used to disturb sensitive people, now seems quiet and peaceful.

Forsaking our first love

The last block to effective praying that we shall consider here is the all too common one – 'losing our first love'. The Risen Christ (see Revelation 2:1-7) charged the once great Ephesian Church with this failing.

Prayer is in essence a love relationship with God through Jesus. That is why the great mystic writers, like St John of the Cross,[14] and great Puritan writers like John Bunyan and Jonathan Edwards, turn quite naturally to the Song of Songs.

Our generation reads the Song, if at all, as a remarkable love poem (and at one level that is quite proper). But the great writers of old saw a far deeper meaning. The restless searching of the human soul caught up and satisfied by the romantic spiritual love of the Father.

We must rekindle our first love. Do you remember the day of your conversion? Do you remember the first few times that God spoke to you? Do you remember the thrill of answered prayers? Do you remember first praying for the sick?

Prayer needs rekindled love Those of us who are married will remember when we first met our future partners. Life's priorities changed. Hope (and despair!) alternated.

So it should be on our spiritual journey. We need a 'time of refreshing' (Acts 3:19). One thing almost certain is that as we recover our certainty about the priority and practice of prayer, God the loving Father will meet us with arms outstretched.

Here is a testimony, from a clergy widow, to the sort of rekindling that God longs to bring:

'Three years after the death of my husband I felt led by God to make a fresh start, and I moved to Shepton Mallet. Eighteen months later I knew without doubt that I was in the right place, but not really why I was there. My faith was rather jaded, the joy, though not the peace, had gone.

'One morning I received a letter with 'Women of God Ministries' on the envelope. I was intrigued by the opening sentence of the letter... 'We have a mutual friend, Virginia Tracy...' – this friend I had met in Saudi Arabia and she now lived in the USA. There was an invitation to attend the first Women of God International Conference to be held in Scotland. I decided to go, and visited friends on my journey to and from Scotland.

'The Conference was a truly wonderful weekend. There was much laughter throughout and even the excellent teaching sessions had us all laughing at the many anecdotes and illustrations. The main emphasis of the teaching was "Chosen, Beloved and Special to God." The many worship times were uplifting and inspiring as over 200 women praised God, and the ministry was powerful and a great blessing to me. There was no doubt that the Holy Spirit's presence was felt and seen at work in the lives of those there.

'God moves in a mysterious way – a letter from an unknown lady in Scotland – a friend in the States and a rekindled Christian in England. The joy had returned.' A fruitful time of service had really begun.

Just occasionally, God first leads us deeper into the wilderness, deeper into darkness, so that we may learn to trust him more. We shall return to this theme later. (See end of Chapter 4). The purpose of this 'pruning' is always to make us more fruitful.

Notes

1. S. D. Gordon, *Quiet Talks on Prayer* (Revell, c.1900), pp 141-7.
2. Michael Cassidy, *The Passing Summer* (Hodder & Stoughton, 1989).
3. Joseph Kobo, *Waiting in the Wings* (Word Publishing, 1994), p 202ff.
4. Brian Blancharde, who jointly with his wife, Hilary, works for USPG in the South West of England. He had the privilege of being asked to be one of the International Peace Monitors before and during the 1994 elections. (See also Chapter 7, p 5 on forgiveness).
5. Michael Cassidy, *A Witness for Ever* (Hodder & Stoughton, 1995), p 163ff.
6. Often attributed to Archbishop William Temple.
7. Nelson Mandela, *Long Walk to Freedom* (Abacus, 1994), especially pp 443-450.
8. *Patricia St John tells her own story* (OM Publishing, 1993).
9. Evelyn Waugh, *Decline and Fall* (Penguin, 1937), p 38.
10. Unknown author of *Cloud of Unknowing* (Penguin Classics, 1961), from Chapter 37.
11. John Bunyan, *Prayer* (Banner of Truth, 1965), p 47.
12. Patricia St John, *Would you believe it?* (Pickering & Inglis, 1983), p 91.
13. Jonathan Edwards, *On Revival* (Banner of Truth, 1984), throughout.
14. Sister Eileen Lyddon, *Door through Darkness* (New City, 1994), for a clear introduction to the writings and thoughts of St John of the Cross (1542-1591).

3

The Wilderness and the Mountain

(Do I really have to go to absurd places to pray?)

We examine prayer in the wilderness – the place of spiritual testing. We also visit the mountain – the lonely place set aside for prayer.

The Wilderness and the Mountain

The wilderness

> The Spirit immediately drove him out into the wilderness. And he was in the wilderness forty days, tempted by Satan; and he was with the wild beasts; and the angels ministered to him. (Mk 1:12-13 – RSV)

Mark is intrigued by the wilderness. He quotes Isaiah's prophecy: 'A voice of one crying in the wilderness.' John the Baptist comes out of the wilderness (1:4). Jesus is drawn by the Spirit into the wilderness (1:12). The wilderness is the place of spiritual testing; while it is often the place of spiritual failure, it is also the place of spiritual opportunity and growth. In the wilderness, the Israelites had received many blessings – protection, food, water, the direct leadership of the Lord – yet it had been a place of grumbling, rebellion, lack of faith, and immorality. Eventually, they came through. Under the leadership of Moses, followed by Joshua and Caleb, the next generation emerged into the Promised Land. Yet worse was to follow. Grumbling about God became insisting on their own way (as in the matter of a King – see 1 Sam 8:5); rebellion became schism which sowed the seeds for the destruction of the Northern Kingdom (as in the matter of Jeroboam the son of Nebat who caused Israel to sin, see 1 Kings

The wilderness, the place of spiritual testing

15:34 etc.); lack of faith became a slavish following of the Law, (see Hos 6:6), immorality became cult prostitution and Baal worship (see Is 57 etc).

Yet the wilderness remained a place of hope, as in Isaiah's wonderful vision:

> The desert and the parched land will be glad;
>   the wilderness will rejoice and blossom.
> Like the crocus, it will burst into bloom;
>   it will rejoice greatly and shout for joy.
> The glory of Lebanon will be given to it,
>   the splendour of Carmel and Sharon;
> they will see the glory of the LORD,
>   the splendour of our God.   (Is 35:1-2)

This continues with a vision of the King's highway, the joy of the redeemed, and protection from the wild beasts, shows that the prophets saw the wilderness as a place of encounter. Moses and the burning bush, Elijah sulking under his juniper bush, and perhaps Jeremiah in front of his almond tree, all encounter the living God in wilderness situations.

Jesus goes out in the wilderness to pray and to fast, tested by Satan, amidst the wild beasts, yet attended by angels. *Jesus in the* There lies the heart of the spiritual battle. Jesus must *wilderness* have prepared for this during the first hidden thirty years of his life. Now it was for real. We cannot begin to imagine what this encounter meant to Jesus.

Prayer we find difficult; fasting, even for half a day, taxes most of us grievously. Satan's attacks are so subtle that we *Satan's* usually fail to notice them: temptation to doubt – 'Did God *subtle* really say?'; temptation to indulge – 'A little of what you *attacks* fancy won't do you any harm'; temptation to work, work and more work – 'Surely you want to be a success?'; temptation to stray from God's commandments – 'Everyone else is doing it – even some in the church – so why shouldn't you?'; temptation to climb the ecclesiastical or some other ladder – 'If you don't, someone much worse will!' And so it goes on. Satan chips away at our beliefs, our standards, our hopes. It all happens so subtly that we don't notice it.

For Jesus, the first real assault was much more direct. Doubtless he'd received all the subtle temptations in the previous thirty years. Now Satan attacked with all his might; Jesus prevailed because he was prepared. He was already uniquely committed to prayer, and to his Father's way. The Holy Spirit's baptism, received just before in the Jordan, was the sign that the battle was now to be joined in earnest.

Just occasionally, we may catch a glimpse of that battle – particularly if we are called to new ministry or new prayer. Sometimes we get caught up in the battle, particularly when God releases places and people.

The Village of the Severed Chicken's Head

In May 1992, I made a second visit to Zambia. I was accompanied by my wife Jane, Martin Cavender – a great friend who had recently moved from the sober post of Diocesan Registrar to the spiritual maelstrom of being Administrative Director of Springboard, the Archbishops' Initiative on Evangelism – and his son Henry.

We arrived in Mutwe Wa Nkoko (the Village of the Severed Chicken's Head) late one Monday evening. We were accompanied by Archdeacon Tobias Kaoma, priest-in-charge of the nearby Chipili Mission Station, Agnes Mupeta, the leader of the Mothers' Union for the Luapula province (whose husband Douglas, a lawyer who showed great courage defending local opposition party members before the change of government in the previous year), Martha Zulu, a formidable prayer warrior, and that time leading youth work in the province. We were driven along miles of dusty tracks by the Bishop's faithful driver, Jonas. En route we called on the local chieftain, to obtain permission to enter his territory and to pray for his daughter who was about to go into labour. On the way back, we were able to pray for his two-hour-old granddaughter, and to be given that greatest of Zambian honours – a live chicken – which attacked Martin's trousers with the persistence of the widow in Jesus' parable.

We received a traditional Zambian welcome. Hundreds of dancing, smiling faces. Garlands of flowers, and endless singing of 'Sangalale, Sangalale' (Let's be joyful!). We left our vehicle and joined in the fun. The village was quite small. A little church, a good deep well, a few houses; and, in the distance, a school whose roof had been blown off eighteen months earlier.

We washed in blazing hot water, in a little stockade, under the light of the Southern Cross and the other African stars. There was a camp fire. Much singing, much laughter. There was a clever sketch about a man who tried to steal from his neighbour, but first he had to steal a bone to silence the dog. (All a bit safer than the fire eater that I met in another village two years later, who sent a jet of flame towards the Bath & Wells Diocesan Missioner who, despite the most rapid evasive action, still emerged with singed eyebrows. That, apparently, was illustrating the destruction of Sodom and Gomorrah!)

The next morning, a crowd of about 500 gathered. We held a service in the open air, in front of the little church. It was all very quiet, and good natured. I spoke from Isaiah 12, especially verse 3: 'With joy you will draw water from the wells of salvation'. *A good beginning*

Their infectious joy, and their deep, clean well, were obvious illustrations. Blue Charaxes butterflies danced across from one great tree to another, providing me with a pleasant distraction. Before lunch, we started to pray for the sick. Even by the standards of ministry in the Luapula province, a ferocious battle erupted, mainly centred around the Venerable Tobias Kaoma.

Two years earlier, Tobias had enlivened a rather desultory afternoon session of a clergy conference at Kitwe. In the middle of a very sound exposition of the 'Gifts of the Spirit', he had started singing, dancing, and crying out in several different languages. I didn't know Tobias yet. I must confess that I thought, with echoes of Acts 2:13, that he might be drunk. Knowing him as I do now, a very upright citizen, a former headmaster ordained late in life, I realise the absurdity of the thought. The Holy Spirit had fallen on him with great power! Immediately, he was used in prayer of deliverance and healing.

The battle in Mutwe was very strong. We only had to start praying for people and many of them shook, fluttered their eyelids, collapsed on the ground (sometimes doing a *The battle erupts* passable imitation of a local snake) and screamed. In the midst of this maelstrom one spirit voice spoke to me – in perfect Oxbridge English – 'Go away, I'm not leaving this person.'

In the afternoon, after a quick lunch and a moving visit to a maize field where we saw the devastating effect of the drought on their crops, I found myself speaking about choices.

I challenged the congregation to choose Christ and to put away the charms, fetishes, and other signs from the witch doctors.

Choose this day!   There was laughter – not the friendly laughter of the morning, but hollow, mocking laughter. I asked Tobias, who was a brilliant interpreter, what was happening. He said, 'They are saying – we have so little, and now you are asking us to give things up!' Suddenly I felt something terrible. For almost the only time in my life, I felt the anger of God. Even now, I find it quite awesome to write about. I spoke, I know not what, firm, hard words. It was not my normal manner. When I had finished, I felt quite shattered.

Like the great prophet, I would gladly have slunk away under a juniper bush. I had failed, going way over the top. I don't remember much about the rest of the day. We had a session with Father James, the local priest, and his healing team who were helping in the ministry. (I always insisted on having one, and preferably two or three, Zambians to help me when I was praying. It's scriptural (Jas 5:14), it's good for training, and it's vital to have people who know what's really going on across the barriers of language, culture etc.). I think that I was so shattered that Martin addressed them.

Had I gone too far?   The next morning we began with a Eucharist in the church. This part of Zambia has a High Church Anglican tradition, which means there's great dignity and order amidst the freedom that the charismatic gifts can bring. I tried not to notice a substantial hornet busying itself with building a nest behind the altar. Eventually, about 300 people crowded into the small church. I was about to continue with some teaching, very uncertain how it would be received, when a Zambian woman of about thirty-five (a grandmother!) came forward. Could she say something? It is very unusual for anyone to give a testimony in Zambia. It is even more unusual for a woman, unknown and unasked, to intervene, especially when visitors were present.

As she spoke, in Bemba, her face lit up. It was obvious that her words were making a great impression. A few moments later I heard the gist of her story from Tobias.

She had walked towards the church in the half-light of the early morning. She, and her companion, noticed a figure dressed in white following them. Intrigued, she went round one side of the church and waited. Then she went around to the back of the little church, where the ground is very *Divine intervention* open, near the well, expecting to meet the person dressed in white. No one was there. Zambians do not wear pure white clothes – indeed the women always wear highly coloured chitengas (long skirts) and the men dark trousers.

Her face glistened as she told her story. The leader of the Mothers' Union leapt up and gave her a scarf and enrolled her on the spot! (The M.U. is a very powerful spiritual agency in Zambia, and it is significant that the woman was not even a member of that group).

After that, we could do no wrong. There was a huge response to an evangelistic message – men coming forward just as freely as women. Prayer became much easier. One of the village elders committed his life to Jesus. We were very sad to leave after lunch, with the Blue Charaxes butterflies still dancing in the trees.

Two years later, part of a SOMA[1] (Sharing of Ministries Abroad) team that I was leading, visited Mutwe. It was still hard going – but the lady who'd seen the angel was a very visible part of the church.

I talked to a remarkable priest in Luansha, a copper belt mining town, who at the age of eighty was still building new churches and evangelising new areas. He said he'd had some fierce spiritual battles with demons in his younger days at Mutwe. Clearly it's a place that lives up to its name.

We all felt greatly exhausted by this visit. The spiritual wilderness had been a place of fierce encounter, but we had witnessed the Lord's overruling and presence in a dramatic way. None of us would ever forget the face of the lady testifying to her spiritual encounter. The wilderness had truly rejoiced!

After the wilderness, the mountain

The mountain is the place of deep spiritual blessing. Jesus had special places of prayer – the Mount of Olives was one (see Lk 21:37 and 22:39). We, too, will find special places (quiet places, not necessarily literally mountains!), where it is easier to forget the world, and to turn our attention to God. But it will need an act of the will. We will need to decide that it is really important.

The example of Jesus is clear – he spent much time in prayer. This may seem obvious, but you have to read the Gospels carefully to see what a major part of his earthly life it was. St Luke, particularly, highlights his times of prayer.

Mark opens his account of Jesus' ministry (Mk 1:14-34) with a hectic period involving proclamation of the kingdom, evangelism 'Come Follow Me', exorcism 'Be quiet, come out of him!', healing, personal ministry to Peter's mother-in-law, and more healing far into the night. What happens next day?

The importance of solitary prayer Very early in the morning, while it was still dark, Jesus got up, left the house and went off to a solitary place, where he prayed. Simon and his companions went to look for him, and when they found him, they exclaimed: 'Everyone is looking for you!' Jesus replied, 'Let us go somewhere else – to the nearby villages – so that I can preach there also. That is why I have come.' So he travelled throughout Galilee, preaching in their synagogues and driving out demons.' (Mk 1:35-39)

Very early in the morning, Jesus gets up, goes to a solitary place and prays. It is a decisive time of prayer. The question appears to have been – 'What are the priorities?' Peter, characteristically, searches him out, and bursts in on his time of quiet with the pejorative statement, 'Everyone is looking for you.' In other words, there is another great crowd building up outside mother-in-law's house, and why on earth don't you come and sort the situation out?

Jesus is unimpressed. His lengthy, early morning prayer vigil has underlined that his priority is not healing, but preaching the kingdom. Healing and deliverance will follow the preaching. The message must be proclaimed in many places.

Luke, who alone tells us that Jesus was praying at his baptism, then tells us: 'Jesus *often* withdrew to lonely places and prayed' (Lk 15:16).

Before the choosing of the twelve, Luke tells us, 'One of those days Jesus went out to a mountainside to pray, and spent *the night* praying to God' (Lk 6:12).

St John tells that after the feeding of the five thousand, 'Jesus, knowing that they intended to come and make him king by force, withdrew again to the hills by himself' (Jn 6:15).

The mountain, the place where God meets his servants

St Luke also records Jesus praying (Lk 9:18) before the decisive question at Caesarea Philippi (Who do you say I am?). Before the Transfiguration (Lk 9:28-36), Luke mentions that Jesus went up the mountain to pray, and that as he was praying, the appearance of his face changed.

Quite incidentally, we discern a clear message about the priority of prayer in Jesus' life. No Gospel writer concentrates on proclaiming it – it happens quietly, secretly, almost untouched by a casual reader. Yet it is clearly the essential spiritual priority for our Lord.

We would love to know how he prayed, what was said, what was heard, how much was in total silence. But we are not told. What is clear is that, if it is not the priority of our life, and the life of our churches, we shall fail.

Even the results of Jesus' prayer life present us with at least one great mystery. Why, after a full night of prayer, did he choose Judas? It is a mystery to which many answers, mostly inadequate, have been given. Perhaps for our purposes it might underline the message of the previous chapter – don't judge the quality of prayer by results, but by fruit. Judas was, in a deep sense, a necessary part of God's plan. Doubtless he could have repented before handing Jesus over.[2] Afterwards, perhaps he did. But sadly, his final action speaks more of worldly sorrow than genuine repentance. This important distinction is clearly made in 2 Corinthians 7:10. For our part, we should marvel at the restraint of the four Gospel writers – who have few bad words and realise that, but for the grace of God, any of us could do the same.

For God alone my soul waits in silence (Psalm 62:1, RSV)

Evangelicals and charismatics, and I'm glad to count myself one, like words. Prayer meetings, praise meetings, prophecies – all are important, all have their place, but the scriptural priority seems elsewhere.

The need for silence and the pull of the world

Where and when did David compose most of his psalms? Where did Elijah gather his spiritual strength for his onslaught on Queen Jezebel and her false priests? Where did Moses encounter God? Where and how did Jesus spend precious time before the great moments of his life? What did Paul do immediately after his conversion? (see Gal 1:17).

It's what my godly mother would have called 'a glimpse of the obvious' to say that we live in a busy, stressful world. In the busy West, men and women seem either over-employed or unemployed. I know many good men and women whose family life is suffering – or in some cases has been shattered – by the demands of modern employment.

Many Christians, ordained and lay, are equally caught up in this busy whirlpool. Priests, with a touch of pride, recite the ridiculously long hours that they work. And what does it achieve? The author of Ecclesiastes, in one of his more despairing moments, writes:

I denied myself nothing my eyes desired;
I refused my heart no pleasure.
My heart took delight in all my work,
   and this was the reward for all my labour.
Yet when I surveyed all that my hands had done
   and what I had toiled to achieve,
everything was meaningless, a chasing after the wind;
   nothing was gained under the sun. (Eccles 2:10,11)

Yet even he, writer of many words, knew his limitations!

Guard your steps when you go to the house of God. Go near to listen rather than to offer the sacrifice of fools, who do not know that they do wrong.
Do not be quick with your mouth,

do not be hasty in your heart
to utter anything before God.
God is in heaven and you are on earth,
so let your words be few.
Much dreaming and many words are meaningless. Therefore stand in
awe of God. (Eccles 5:1,2 & 7)

Stand in awe of God! That is a great purpose of prayer; and it requires few words. To learn the way of silent prayer requires great courage and great discipline. Paul wasn't frightened of either:

Do you not know that in a race all the runners run, but only one gets the prize? Run in such a way as to get the prize. Everyone who competes in the games goes into strict training. They do it to get a crown that will not last; but we do it to get a crown that will last for ever. Therefore I do not run like a man running aimlessly, I do not fight like a man beating the air. No, I beat my body and make it my slave so that after I have preached to others, I myself will not be disqualified for the prize. (1 Cor 9:24-27)

I am writing these words while staying for a month at Hilfield Friary in Dorset. The house is run by a community of Anglican Franciscans. All sorts and conditions of men are welcome equally. Wayfarers and retreating priests; visiting bishops and ex clergy; young men trying to rediscover a direction in life; disillusioned people trying to scrounge a few days' hospitality... All are welcomed, all eat the same food, all are offered the same discipline.

The value of discipline in our prayer life

The routine of the house (which actually varies quite a lot from day to day) revolves around four services – Morning Prayer at 7 a.m., Midday Prayer and Holy Communion at 12, Evening Prayer at 5.45 and Night Prayer at 9 p.m. Two things stand out – a varied and beautifully prayed liturgy involving much use of Scripture, especially the Psalms, and the use of silence. Extempore prayer takes place, but the real presence of God seems felt in the half hour of silent prayer before breakfast – and at other times. To sit, or kneel, amidst a group of twenty or so men (women visitors do come, especially for the midday services) who are all quietly and silently praying, listening, adoring, interceding is deeply moving. Curiously, it is easier (for me, anyway) to manage such prayer amidst the company of others than alone. The corporate silence brings a fellowship of its own.

In the past, God has from time to time greatly blessed silent times of prayer. I was reminded today of a deep experience of years ago. I was sitting on some bales of straw in the middle of a large field of recently cut corn. Praying and thinking about an important talk I was to give that evening at the end of a parish house party. Suddenly the Lord seemed to point out that the field was in the shape of a great capital 'L'. A dark wood nestled in the crook of the L. Minutes earlier I had been walking in that wood, trying to escape into the cornfield. One small track petered out at a great thorn hedge on the edge of the field, another led into an active wasps' nest; eventually a meandering path, took me out of the lighter deciduous woodland back into bleak, dark evergreens, and then led me to a little gate (like Bunyan's wicket gate)[3] into the field. For a while, I had clung to the edge of the field, enjoying the shade of some tall oak trees. Eventually, I left their shadows and strode boldly towards the bales of straw.

And the Lord continued to point things out. It seemed that the field was a 'type' for Christian discipleship. We were all learners; and there were many ways of entering it. I, like most others, assumed 'my way' was 'the way'. Actually, there were a large number. I had wandered through the dark wood, searching for a way out, glimpsing a better place (the cornfield seen through the trees), I had made several false starts, then had accepted the need for real darkness (conviction of sin) and found the gate. Quietly and decisively I had been led through. For a while, I had preferred the safety of the shade, but eventually had been led right out into the sunlight.

Christ has many different ways to find him

Other routes included one that involved a desperate scramble over, or through, the thorn hedge. This represents the many bruised and broken people who come to Christ from desperate circumstances. They are often helped by the prayers and support of the all too few Christians living, working, and praying at the increasingly uncomfortable edge of our society.

All too many are left wandering in the wood amidst the wasps. Some turn for comfort to the psychadelic red fungi that are common in such woods, seeking New Age experiences, to find hope and to distance themselves from the pain of an unfriendly and hostile world.

There was a simple way, in the N.W. corner, which involved climbing a fence and crossing a shallow stream. It was a very long way from there to where I was sitting! This seemed to correspond to those who appear to grow gradually from a Christian childhood into a mature adult faith.

A more difficult route, in the N.E. corner of the L, involved coming out of a copse which adjoined the main wood, scrambling down a steep bank, wading a deep part of the stream, and emerging into the safety of the field.

That seemed to correspond to those who, after an adult crisis, come through the waters of baptism, probably by immersion, and then make their way quite quickly along the thorn hedge to the bales.

In the S.E. corner of the L there was a way which involved a circuitous route across miles of green meadow. The journey was long and meandering. It seemed possible to enter the field that way without fully realising the special significance of the journey.

That corresponded to those whose spiritual journey is gentle and undirected. Some of whom, often in Anglican churches, only realise the significance of their journey when they become aware of other pilgrims entering by a different way.

Today, the Lord added something to the picture. All around the field, as well as pilgrims making their way towards the centre (and, in reality, I'm still near the edge), were other pilgrims kneeling. Some, facing outwards, interceding for those trapped in the wood, or meandering in the meadow; others facing inwards with hands uplifted in silent adoration. With them, too, were some of the angels playing their mysterious part in the spiritual battle.

The result of the picture

I should add that while my parish house party talk may not have been brilliant, there were some remarkable consequences. A small group of us gathered in 'an Upper Room' to pray and wait upon the Holy Spirit.

None of us was used to this approach. When we started to pray at least four significant things happened. An Indian lady started to sing 'blessed' choruses – but it sounded all wrong. Lacking Paul's patience (or time – see Acts 16:16-18), I told her quietly but firmly 'to shut up in the name of the Lord.' Not unnaturally, she left the room somewhat distressed. After she had returned

The battle and the blessing home, she discovered a deep spiritual problem connected with Hindu ancestors, was released, and went on her way rejoicing. More positively, a very musical lady started to pray in tongues. That, too, was just a beginning. Not only did she begin to receive physical healing, but a wonderful ministry of music was released. Eventually, she was ordained. Her husband, a senior health care executive, felt no strange phenomena, but received a clear, later tested, call to ordination. He and his wife have just finished a long ministry in a difficult area of Reading. A fourth person, a young woman, also heard a call to full-time service.

Perhaps for those of us privileged to pray, the consequences were even greater. We discovered that if we don't try to do too much, the Holy Spirit works much more powerfully around us!

A trying anniversary

I find it useful to keep a spiritual diary. I only write up mine about once a month. It is wonderful to look back to see both the prayers that God has answered and the messes that he has released one from. To puzzle over the things that didn't work out, and to remember the people, the experiences, and the scriptures that were so important at earlier stages of the journey. But we must beware looking back in anger, bitterness, or sorrow. It's too easy to wallow in the past, to become like the Israelites in one of their worst moods.

The danger of spiritual nostalgia The rabble with them began to crave other food, and again the Israelites started wailing and said, 'If only we had meat to eat! We remember the fish we ate in Egypt at no cost –

also the cucumbers, melons, leeks, onions and garlic.

But now we have lost our appetite; we never see anything but this manna!' (Num 11:4-6)

It hadn't been all that wonderful in Egypt, and now they were eating God's special food. But that wasn't good enough! Let's go back to Egypt. It's easy for us to fall into this trap. There was one period of deep depression after an operation which left me high on anaesthetics one moment, and deeply confused and full of panics at another. I would cheerfully have gone back to school-teaching. It was easy to idealise the former delights of mathematics, forgetting the limitations. Anyway, even if Egypt was better, it was no longer where God wanted the Israelites, and they had enough miraculous evidence to make that clear.

A few years ago today, I was awaiting the result of an interview. It was not the only job which I've applied for (and failed to get!), but it was the only one I've ever really coveted. I only applied because of a strange coincidence which led to someone asking me to consider applying. Certainly it seemed both a real challenge and something that I could tackle. One or two people were very encouraging.

By the start of the day, I was fairly certain of the answer; by the end of the day, despite no communication, I knew it. In all probability, I wasn't even close to being chosen – but it hurt. Why had God led me to apply – before it seemed right to think of moving?

God knows best, but we struggle to accept it!

It took a long time for God to show me in many ways why the answer was 'No', apart from that simple fact of better candidate(s) (who would also have prayed hard and felt a certain leading). He has greatly blessed me in unexpected ways since that day. Gradually, as I came to accept his will, I became happier than I ever remember.

I should have known better. God's NO has, time and time again, blessed me. The only times that hasn't been the case is when the NO has involved a desperate intercession for other people. Some of these negative answers remain a real puzzle.

And that brings me back to silence. If we will learn to be still before God, we shall offer less desperate, hopeless, faithless prayers which get rejected – how on earth did the mother of James and John expect her stupid prayer to be answered (Mt 20:20-28)? If we learn to 'abide in Christ' then precisely because we are abiding, we shall understand his will, and learn to ask effectively. We will also accept more readily that there are many things which we cannot understand, many things which we cannot know, many secret things which God alone knows.

We see things which angels long to look into (1 Pet 1:12), and we should be content with that!

While wilderness experiences of testing and spiritual battle seem necessary for our growth, the mountain top experiences keep us spiritually in tune and refreshed.

Notes

1. SOMA – an international charismatic organisation designed to bring small teams to share their experience of the Holy Spirit. It has been particularly blessed in many Third World dioceses. The Bishop of North Zambia said publicly, 'The first SOMA trip transformed my diocese.'
2. See especially W. H. Vanstone, *The Stature of Waiting* (Darton, Longman & Todd), for an unusual and enlightening discussion of Judas.
3. John Bunyan, *Pilgrim's Progress* (Everyman, 1907).

4

The Generous Father

(If God knows – why pray?)

This chapter explores the biblical picture of God – the paradox of the loving Father and the immortal, invisible, only wise God. It considers the danger of a distorted, man-made, picture of God, asks how God shows himself to us through prayer and faces four common objections to prayer: (1) it is just for the feeble minded; (2) what is needed is active goodness, not passive prayer; (3) it is an intellectual absurdity; (4) it doesn't work.

Finally, we look at a variety of people's experiences of the presence of God in prayer.

The Generous Father

'What does God look like?' We had just celebrated an open air communion, deep in the forest, about an hour's drive from the Chipili Mission Station in Zambia. Most of the villagers were present: a visit from a priest was rare enough, a party of white people unheard of.

We had invited a short question time before splitting up to pray for the sick and to teach the church leaders. Most of the questions had been routine.

'What does God look like?' Not much use quoting Moses' experience (Ex 34:23), even less use quoting a bishop who, in a peculiarly uninspired moment, said, 'When I think of God, I think of someone like my Headmaster, only bigger.'

'What does God look like?' It's an important question, because we shall pray better if we have understanding of whom we are praying to. My own, inadequate answer was to produce a camera. Even in the deepest bush they knew what a 'snap' was. Jesus is God's snap! When we see Jesus, when we hear Jesus, when we read about Jesus, we begin to get a picture of God.

The biblical picture of God

The Bible gives at least two quite different pictures of God. We need to, indeed we must, live with this tension and accept another

66

paradox. First, we have the picture of the distant, almost un-knowable, majestic Creator. Two quotations from among many must suffice – from Nehemiah's great prayer of penitence offered on behalf of himself, his family and his nation: 'O *God, distant,* LORD, God of heaven, the great and awesome God, *holy, and* who keeps his covenant of love with those who love *unapproachable* him and obey his commands (Neh 1:5); and Paul's great paean of praise: '…God, the blessed and only Ruler, the King of kings and Lord of lords, who alone is immortal and who lives in unapproachable light, whom no-one has seen or can see. To him be honour and might for ever. Amen (1 Tim 6:15b & 16).

Secondly, and in great contrast, we have the picture of the intimate, father and mother figure. A God so personal, so loving, so concerned with the details of life that he knows every bird, every hair on our head (see Mt 10:30).

Isaiah, often writing of the awesome holiness of God, also pictures his great intimacy: 'But Zion said, "The *God, intimate,* LORD has forsaken me, the Lord has forgotten me." *loving, and* Can a mother forget the baby at her breast and have *experienced* no compassion on the child she has borne? Though she may forget, I will not forget you!' (Is 49:14-16).

Like Jeremiah,[1] Paul prays for the Ephesian church to have a very personal experience of God: 'I keep asking that the God of our Lord Jesus Christ, the glorious Father, may give you the Spirit of wisdom and revelation, so that you may know him better' (Eph 1:17); and of his love shown in Christ:

> For this reason I kneel before the Father, from whom his whole family in heaven and on earth derives its name. I pray that out of his glorious riches he may strengthen you with power through his Spirit in your inner being, so that Christ may dwell in your hearts through faith. And I pray that you, being rooted and established in love, may have power, together with all the saints, to grasp how wide and long and high and deep is the love of Christ, and to know this love that surpasses knowledge – that you may be filled to the measure of all the fulness of God. (Eph 3:14-19).

Oscar Cullman[2] makes the valuable point that God's hiddenness, which is so often a stumbling block for faith, is a part of God's holiness. But this leads to God revealing himself where we least expect him, in secret!

Elijah, in 1 Kings 19:11f, finds God not in the strong wind, but in the still small voice. In Matthew 6:5f, Jesus tells his hearers to go into a remote room, shut the door, and to pray alone.

Here is a striking contrast, another paradox; the holy, and often hidden God, meets his children as their loving Father.

Jesus' teaching about the nature of God

Jesus not only teaches that God is his Father, but he is also the disciples' Father, and he can be prayed to in a most intimate way.

This is how you should pray:

> Our Father in heaven, hallowed be your name, your kingdom come, your will be done on earth as it is in heaven.
> Give us today our daily bread.
> Forgive us our debts, as we also have forgiven our debtors.
> And lead us not into temptation, but deliver us from the evil one.
> For if you forgive men when they sin against you, your heavenly Father will also forgive you. But if you do not forgive men their sins, your Father will not forgive your sins. (Mt 6:9-15)

The familiar words of the Lord's Prayer assume that God is close and intimate.

'If you then, though you are evil, know how to give good gifts to your children, how much more will your Father in heaven give the Holy Spirit to those who ask him! (Lk 11:13). God's intentions for us are good and generous. The key phrase is 'how much more' showing that God longs to meet our deepest need.

'Father, if you are willing, take this cup from me; yet not my will, but yours be done. (Lk 22:42). I have discussed this very intimate request in the opening chapter.

'Jesus said, "Father forgive them, for they do not know what they are doing".' ... 'Jesus called out with a loud voice, "Father, into your hands I commit my spirit." When he had said this, he breathed his last' (Lk 23:34 & 46). These final two examples, prayers prayed during the actual crucifixion, show that even in this ultimate crisis, Jesus still trusts God as his Father and prays to him in a very personal way.

When Jesus prays 'Abba Father,'[3] it is certainly a very intimate form of address – the very opposite of the 'great and terrible' God prayed to by Nehemiah, Daniel, and others.

God is our Father

It is not just a contrast between Old and New Testaments. The New Testament often presents God as distant and majestic – see, for instance, the Revelation of St John, the glorious accounts of Jesus' Transfiguration, (Lk 9:28-36) and the terrifying accounts of the end of the world (Mk 13), all of which reinforce an understanding of a majestic distant God.

Living with the paradox

This paradox appears in our worship. Intimate choruses like *Abba Father*:

> Abba Father, let me be
> Yours and Yours alone.
> May my will for ever be
> evermore Your own.
> Never let my heart grow cold,
> never let me go,
> Abba Father, let me be
> Yours and Yours alone.[4]

Intimate choruses and distant hymns

are often put alongside hymns, with majestic imagery, like:

> Immortal, invisible, God only wise,
> In light inaccessible hid from our eyes,
> Most blessed, most glorious, the Ancient of Days,
> Almighty, victorious, thy great name we praise.[5]

The paradox appears much in the writings of the Mystics. Mother Julian's oft-quoted hazelnut[6]: 'He showed me a little thing, the size of a hazelnut, in the palm of my hand, and it was as round as a ball. I looked at it with my mind's eye and I thought, "What can this be?" And answer

A mystic's view of the paradox

came, "It is all that is made." I marvelled that it could last, for I thought it might have crumbled to nothing, it was so small. And the answer came into my mind, "It lasts and ever shall because God loves it." And all things have being through the love of God.

In this little thing I saw three truths. The first is that God made it. The second is that God loves it. The third is that God looks after it.

'What is he indeed that is maker and lover and keeper? I cannot find words to tell. For until I am one with him I can never have true rest nor peace. I can never know it until I am held so close to him that there is nothing in between.'

This beautiful insight comes in the midst of tremendous visions of the majesty of God and the sufferings of Christ. Her point is that even so insignificant a thing, the size of a hazelnut, is deep within the creation, love and protection of God – and more importantly, it is a profound pointer to the nature of God's relationship with us.

Modern science can make the same point. The creator God of the universe, far beyond all black holes, is also the God of the atom. The mathematical theory of chaos – despite its name – throws up patterns of great beauty and suggests a deep order in the created universe.[7]

Christians find it harder to live with this tension. We lapse into casual chatter, or we decide that God is too distant to pray to. On the one hand, we expect God to find a parking place for us, and on the other, we cry out 'Can anyone pray after Auschwitz?'[8] or indeed after Rwanda?

I remember the anger of an English doctor who visited South Africa in the late 1970's. At the height of the apartheid situation, she was struck by the awful contrast of the lack of basic medicine in the African townships and hospitals, and the testimonies of rich white Christians, who had plenty of medicine, to God's healing. 'Why does he heal the backs of the rich and not lift the burden from the backs of the poor?' It didn't make sense to her. She was a strong Christian who had suffered her own personal tragedy, but kept her faith.

It seems to me that this is another part of the paradox of prayer. The healings which occurred, particularly after the charismatic renewal of the Anglican church under Archbishop Burnett, helped to renew the white church. This prepared the way for the deep repentance necessary which made the miracle of 1994 possible.

David Prior,[9] writing in 1985 says, 'In South Africa, for several decades most Christians have spoken out clearly, indeed stridently, against the injustice and evil of apartheid. These criticisms are accurate and apposite, but the sad fact was that the Christian church revealed nothing different, let alone better, in its community lifestyle. As a result, the emphasis among Christians in the 1970's began to veer towards ensuring that, specifically in the community lifestyle of the church, there was more justice; no discrimination; truth, righteousness, love and compassion.

A mathematical diversion

It is vital that we retain the biblical picture of God. We distort it at our peril. Let me offer you a simple mathematical illustration, and a mathematical warning. Perspective drawing depends on simple mathematics. Suppose you wish to draw a series of railway carriages in perspective – how do you begin?

Stage 1

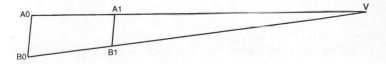

A0 A1 B1 B0 represents one side of the first carriage. A0 B0 and A1 B1 are vertical (no perspective). The 'parallel' lines A0 A1, B0 B1 meet at a vanishing point V. How do we proceed?

Stage 2

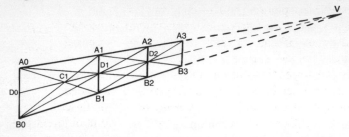

Join the diagonals A0 B1 and A1 B0 to meet at C1. Draw VC1 to meet A0 B0 at D0 and A1 B1 at D1. Draw B0 D1 to meet A0 A1 V at A2 and A0 D1 to meet B0 B1 V at B2. Miraculously A2 B2 is vertical! (This can be proved by higher mathematics).

Continue by drawing A1 D2 to cut B0 B1 B2 V at B3 and B1 D2 to cut A0 A1 A2 V at A3. Miraculously A3 B3 is vertical!!

Stage 3

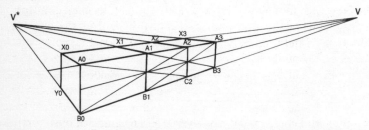

Repeat Stage 2. Draw a vertical line X0 Y0 to complete end of the first carriage, so that A0 X0, B0 Y0, meet at V* (a second horizontal vanishing point). Join V* A1, V* A2, V* A3, and where these lines intersect VX0 at X1, X2, X3, the carriages are complete!

Perspective drawing gives us an artistic, mathematically accurate way of representing three dimensional figures on two dimensional paper! We have great freedom (the vanishing points can be far or near).

Similarly, the Bible represents God for us on its pages! The best representation is the life and work of Jesus, but all the other pages add to the picture.

But, and there is an important but, it is possible to produce extraordinary pictures and distortions.

Max Escher,[10] a famous mathematical artist, used to produce remarkable pictures in which an ascending staircase would appear in all parts of his picture. Everywhere people were walking upwards – yet eventually they arrived back at their starting point. This is *not* a mathematical paradox![11] It is a brilliant use of false perspective. Different vanishing lines were used in different parts of the picture, enabling Escher's trick to look totally convincing.

False mathematics lead to impossible results

This may be harmless, and even attractive, in art, but in theology it is deadly.

False images of God

The book of Judges, a bloodthirsty book which mainly records the spiritual and ethical failings of Israel and its leadership, ends with the words 'Everyman did what was right in his own eyes'(RSV). In other words, they made God in their own image! The theology of the New Age movment – attractive as it is with its deep concerns for creation and the environment, for healing and for therapy, for community, and for care for the individual, almost inevitably, and sometimes proudly, makes God to fit the needs and aspirations of each individual. Interestingly, Ruth Gledhill[12] made the same sort of comment after visiting a Buddhist meeting. She implied that Buddhists were taught to accept what they could from the readings, and contrasted this with the rigid teaching of the church.

Freemasonry, by contrast, worships a distant, impersonal God – 'The Universal Architect.' Deep impersonal understandings of God usually seem to require special rituals, special knowledge by which the initiated can look down on the uninitiated.

The danger of a free for all

Each, in very different ways, (and remember Christians often do the same) distorts the biblical revelation of God.

How does God show himself to us?

The deepest, clearest revelations of God come to us as those of a loving Father. They come to us in moving passages of Scripture, and they come to us in the intimacy of worship and prayer.

> Because you are sons, God sent the Spirit of his Son into our hearts, the Spirit who calls out, 'Abba, Father.' So you are no longer a slave, but a son; and since you are a son, God has made you also an heir. (Gal 4:6,7)

God shows himself as a loving Father in Scripture and in prayer

> ...because those who are led by the Spirit of God are sons of God. For you did not receive a spirit that makes you a slave again to fear, but you received the Spirit of sonship. And by him we cry, 'Abba, Father.' The Spirit himself testifies with our spirit that we are God's children. Now if we are children, then we are heirs – heirs of God and co-heirs with Christ, if indeed we share in his sufferings in order that we may also share in his glory. (Rom 8:14-17)

Here lies a deep revelation which can transform our prayer life. It can also give us such an experience of God that some of the common objections to prayer, which we will shortly consider, seem relatively unimportant.

First, we must try and understand what is happening. We note again Luke 11:9-13 (cf Mt 7:7-11 and note v12). Jesus teaches us, with great confidence, that God, the Father, wants to give the Holy Spirit to us. That is his gift – and our means of conversion. Without the Holy Spirit, we are not Christians.

> You, however, are controlled not by the sinful nature, but by the Spirit, if the Spirit of God lives in you. And if anyone does not have the Spirit of Christ, he does not belong to Christ. (Rom 8:9)

With the gift of the Spirit, we can begin to pray.

> In the same way, the Spirit helps us in our weakness. We do not know what we ought to pray for, but the Spirit himself intercedes for us with groans that words cannot express. And he who searches our hearts knows the mind of the Spirit, because the Spirit intercedes for the saints in accordance with God's will (Rom 8:26,27).

Of course, God hears our prayers before we are Christians. Often he answers them – both in great matters (like the penitent thief's desperate request – see Chapter 1), and in smaller matters (many are healed before any real commitment to Christ). It was the same in the Gospels.

Before conversion we are even more inclined to use God, and to expect him to be at our beck and call. There is a nice incident, which illustrates this attitude, recorded in the early life of Hilfield Friary[13]

God generously responds to prayers of non-Christians but he is not available on demand

> Work with Brother Douglas was always a priority even over formal prayer, for his soul was truly his cell, and he had the great gift of being able to be recollected in God, and to intercede for others while hard at it in the garden. Like St Francis, his one antipathy was 'Brother Fly', the lazy brother who refused to work. These would inevitably 'get their sandwiches' (being sent on their way with sandwiches for the journey); but Brother Douglas hated this, and would endure a great deal and pray much before finally deciding to dismiss a wayfaring brother.
>
> Some departed of their own accord, but with others persuasion was necessary. One man asked if he might join the Confirmation class, and added that he had already been confirmed twice, at Malta and Gibraltar, but he thought it would do him good to be confirmed again. He certainly was in need of grace, for taking a violent dislike to another brother he struck him on the head with a hoe. Brother Douglas had to ask him to leave, but in order that the man might perhaps take away a happy impression, he walked with him along the road for a mile. Explaining with his gracious tact why it had been necessary to ask him to go, Brother Douglas said that he hoped he would try to put into practice some of the things he had learnt at the home, but the man replied:
>
> 'I came to God's house, and God took me in; now God turns me out and that puts the tin hat on God.'

Many much more sophisticated people put 'the tin hat on God' because he doesn't turn out to be the sugar daddy who meets all their needs. After conversion, indeed throughout discipleship, we still struggle. Many experience a honeymoon period when prayers are remarkably answered, only to experience later times of darkness and uncertainty.

Now we turn to some of the basic theological and practical objections to prayer.

Objection 1: Prayer is just for the feeble minded

Oscar Cullman[14] quotes some of Nietzsche's mocking comments on Christianity in particular, and religion in general.

> 'We have grown pious again' – thus these apostles confess; and many of them are too cowardly to confess it. I look into their eyes, then I tell them to their face and to the blushes of their cheeks: 'You are those who again pray! But it is a disgrace to pray! Not for everyone, but for you and me... You know it well: the cowardly devil in you who would like to clasp his hands and to fold his arms and to take it easier – it is this cowardly devil who persuaded you "There is a God".'

Occasionally I meet, or read, other robust opponents of any sort of revealed religion. Professor Dawkins, writer of *The Selfish Gene* and many other popular and learned books, is another avowed apostle of atheism. Such people have an evangelical fervour against religion. It is important to take their criticism seriously. They, at least, are not guilty of the polite indifference which is so hard to pray through.

One charming friend of mine, a former Professor of English Literature, was very shocked by my evangelical faith. He would walk me around the Winchester water meadows fulminating against any belief in God. He would listen to no arguments – he knew that they were absurd.

In exasperation one day, I retorted, 'I know that it is true, because of what I've experienced.'

Ojbection that prayer is a walking stick for the feeble minded

Intellectually untenable, yet it did have some effect. From then on I was given a hearing! As I mentioned in Chapter 1, when my poor friend was dying I used to visit him in a home. In his more lucid moments, he was cursing the God in whom he didn't believe. But what answer do we give to Nietzsche and others? Yes! we plead guilty – prayer is for the weak and feeble minded – and we are glad to be numbered among them.

St Paul, by any reasonable account one of the world's great intellectuals, wrote in 1 Corinthians 1:18: 'The message of the cross is foolishness to those who are perishing, but to us who are being saved it is the power of God.' He continues with the thought, 'Has not God made foolish the wisdom of the world?' (v20).

Yes, prayer for the weak! But God's weakness exceeds men's strength

Worldly wisdom will never understand prayer, only a mind and spirit redeemed by the cross will be able to make any sense of it.

Mankind, flawed and sinful, does need spiritual support. Mankind, despairing at the process of ageing and impending death, does need a spiritual hope. Mankind, struck dumb by some new tragedy,[15] does need a God who suffered hell and was crucified.

Deep tragedies have a double-edged effect on people's beliefs. Those very close to them, who have suffered personal loss, often seem to draw closer to God. They accept that in a flawed world, God is not a universal policeman. Through prayer, through practical love received, through forgiveness, their spiritual life is often deepened. Those more on the edge tend to blame God and draw further away from belief. Of course, this is only a general observation, and will not hold true in all situations and with all people. Look carefully at Jesus' sharp words in Luke 13:1-5.

We feeble-minded children are loved, sustained, and nurtured by our generous Father. This gives us hope, and can bring us thorugh any darkness.

Objection 2: What the world needs is active goodness, not passive prayer

Cullman[16] writes of Brecht's play *Mother Courage*. In the midst of preparation for a surprise attack on the neighbouring town, the farmers pray helplessly to God, whereas the dumb heroine, Kaltrin, leaves the prayer and beats her drum, to warn the city. Her life is lost, the city is saved.

Of course, no one in their right mind sees the two as alternatives. Nehemiah rebuilds and defends the walls of Jerusalem with a combination of hard work, swords at the ready, and spiritual preparation: 'Remember the Lord, who is great and awesome, and fight for your brothers...' (Neh 4:14).

True prayer and good practice go hand in hand

A Christian surgeon will doubtless pray before an

operation, may even launch an arrow prayer at a crisis point, but he (or she) will use his (God given) skill to the best of his ability. Once or twice in a lifetime, he will find that an operation is unnecessary and attribute this to prayer and/or a spontaneous remission – but his prime duty is to operate with all the skill that he has been given.

My contention is that prayer greatly increases active goodness. Here in the Friary, there is much that is simply good. Wayfarers, ex-prisoners, broken clergy, are given rest, time, work, dignity. They are not expected to join in the rhythm of prayer and worship. This may occupy the brothers for 3-4 hours a day – but they still get a great deal of work done, and work of the highest quality.

John Wesley, arguably the world's most successful evangelist, whose main concern was to see disciples with honest, useful, changed lives, spent many hours a day in prayer.

Jackie Pullinger,[17] whose extraordinary ministry behind the Walled City in Hong Kong, saw so many miracles amongst heroin and opium addicts that the authorities took notice of her methods, spent hours in prayer and taught her teams to pray for the release of addicts through direct Spirit-led prayer. She achieved far more than an army of well intentioned social agencies could ever have managed. Why? Partly because she lived the life of the poor, and primarily because she believed in the power of prayer and knew that God would act through her, as he had called her so clearly to her task.

Normal Christian goodness needs prayer to sustain it   The world doesn't need either active goodness or passive prayer – it needs both. Always there will be people called to be at either end of the scale. A few Christians working very long hours may need to live mainly off the prayer of others; a few may be called to a total ministry of prayer (like the bedridden sister in Chapter 2). Normal Christian life will be both. Goodness will flow out of true prayer. Quality time spent in prayer is repaid a thousand times.

Frequently, my morning of preparation completes a seemingly impossible mountain of talks and administration and reading – because it's been preceded by good quality prayer. Allow the prayer to disappear and chaos returns. God's arithmetic, whether it be on time or money, is strangely different from ours.

The generous Father short circuits many practical difficulties when we trust him.

Here is a story which shows that the right combination and social action can produce the most beautiful results. Patricia St John[18] recounts how she and Fatima, her Moroccan Christian friend, set off early for a visit which involved medicine and mission in Morocco. They caught a bus – quite an answer to prayer – and after a while asked the bus driver to let them out at a fork in the road. Their village was just up the road.

The bus driver, a surly, unpleasant man, refused. He said he was going on to the next bridge. 'You can walk from there.'

Patricia was distressed. It would take them miles out of their way, and leave them with a very steep walk in the heat of the day. She cried out to God, 'O Lord, we need to get home – please make him stop.' She became very cross.

Trust God despite the circumstances

Fatima, a recent convert, remained very calm. She said, 'We prayed this morning that all should be well. We shall get back sometime. Let us be patient.'

Patricia didn't feel at all patient when, at last, the bus stopped and put them down at the foot of a steep hill – seven miles from home! She was so distressed that she never heard a woman with a baby in her arms approach.

'Is that the English nurse?' the woman demanded. She was a strong, dark-eyed country woman, her neck covered with charms to protect her from evil spirits, her legs covered in gaiters to protect her from thorns and snakes. Her baby was appallingly ill – eyelids swollen like great grapes, eyes beneath obviously infected.

She told Fatima, 'Last night, I knew my child was getting worse. She was burning with a heavy fever. I slept with a heavy heart, and as I slept, I dreamt. A man came to me in white, he said to me, "Take that child to the English nurse." I said in my dream, "I do not know where she lives, nor do I know her." And the man in white answered, "Rise at dawn and go down to the main road *by the bridge*, and there you will find her waiting for you. She will tell you what to do." So here I am!'

The child, after a few penicillin injections, made a rapid recovery. Patricia and Fatima returned many times to the village to share the news of their Saviour's love. Patricia thanked her heavenly Father many times that he had *not* answered her prayers for the bus to stop.

Objection 3: Prayer is an intellectual absurdity – even the Bible says God knows what you want – so why pray?

> And when you pray, do not keep on babbling like pagans, for they think they will be heard because of their many words. Do not be like them, for your Father knows what you need before you ask him. (Mt 6:7,8)

That seems clear! Surely we should spend our precious prayer time in contemplation, meditation, adoration, worship, thanksgiving, confession. Intercession (which is the prayer most people use most of the time) is at best unimportant and at worst faithless. The problem is that elsewhere Jesus encourages us to do just that! We have already noted Luke 11:9-13; add to that Mark 11:22-25; Matthew 18:19-20; John 15:7; John 16:23; Acts 4:23-31; Philippians 4:4-7; James 4:2; and countless other texts, and we see that Scripture insists that we pray *specifically* for ourselves and others.

It is obvious then that the generous Father (who produces a gift of a coin in an emergency – see Mt 17:24-7), who knows our needs and those of others, expects us to pray about them.

The Bible encourages specific prayer Earthly parents like their children (sometimes) to ask for things. It is a way of knowing what children really want. Children may like surprises, but they appreciate even more receiving what they have pleaded for.

Spiritually, if we pray for something, and it happens, we are excited. It seems more like a God-incident than a coincidence. Our faith grows! But that is only part of the story.

Has God limited his power at this stage of history?

The famous analogy from World War II is of the decisive victory of D Day. At that point, an Allied victory was certain. But there was a great deal of unpleasantness to follow. In particular, the Allies had no control over Hitler's ability to launch V rockets and possibly to invent nuclear weapons.

Taking the analogy of the binding of Satan in the book of Revelation, perhaps we may join Cullmann in saying,[19] 'The devil is bound to a line which can be lengthened even to the point that for a while Satan can make himself independent and has to be fought against by God.

'Going slightly beyond the Revelation of St John, this means that the whole fearful character is to be attributed to the evil which temporarily looses itself from these bonds. If this event is taking place within the divine plan, then God himself has limited his omnipotence for this interim period. Evil cannot ultimately prevail, but we can choose evil and greatly hinder God's purpose.'

What this means is that God enjoins our help – our prayers – in the battle against evil. The ultimate victory is assured, but the intensity of the battle may vary as we pray.

To me, this makes perfect pastoral sense. A little while ago, I went to pray in a house where a visiting Christian (the past youth worker) couldn't sleep. It turned out that his hostess, and her children, were seeing ghosts and other strange happenings. A quick prayer released the youth worker into sleep. A return visit with a prayer partner led to prayer throughout the house.

The hostess experienced a severe attack; it turned out that she had some previous occult involvement, but soon she, and the house, felt quite different. She herself wrote: 'I have prayed and felt God's presence, yet had no real answer to my prayer until Friday, 19th January 1996 – the day that my house was exorcised and my soul spring-cleaned.

God routs the dark powers in the name of Jesus

'Soon afterwards I leapt in the bath and found the excitement and truth of Christianity more than I could bear! I felt for a moment that I would have to turn my back on this new world because of the emotion of happiness, wonder, and my responsibility as a Christian.

'But despite this I turned to the Bible for advice! I first picked up the book *Listening to God*. Out dropped a bookmark, given me

by Joyce, who helped you pray in my house. It directed me to
John 9:4 and Acts 4:20. My Bible was already open there, I had
been reading this the night before, "While daylight lasts, we must
carry on the work of him who sent me, night comes when no one
can work." It struck me immediately that in my enthusiasm, I had
missed out on a lot of sleep, now God was telling me to rest and
learn to be more effective.

'Acts 4:20 says, "We cannot possibly give up speaking of the
things that we have seen and heard." God was telling me to share
what I've heard and seen – after twenty-nine years I've finally
heard God speak. It has reaffirmed my belief, and brought me
past the point of no return.'

Sue first came to church because she felt her daughter, aged
four, should discover something about religion. This set a chain
of events in motion. Our youth worker lodged there for a year. He
felt uneasy in the house and asked for prayer. Sue shared strange
things that she, and her children, had seen. We prayed, and light
came! Since then many things in Sue's life have made sense and
the Holy Spirit has brought a wonderful peace, new relationships
with Christians, and a new confidence at work – especially in the
local prison. It was very like Charles Wesley's great hymn:

> My chains fell off, my heart was free
> I rose, went forth, and followed Thee.[20]

Of course, God could have routed the darkness in that house at
any time. But he chose to use the wisdom of the youth worker in
seeking help, and the prayers of the local church. My humble
guess is that otherwise the situation would still be unresolved.
Prayer was needed.

Another quite dramatic occasion was in a little village church.
Sometimes the Sunday School came in during the service, before
the talk. On this occasion they were late and I had to give an adult,
rather than a children's talk. We had just sung the song 'I will
sing, I will sing a song unto the Lord.'[21] This was the favourite
song of Bob, a lovely older member of our main church, who had
moved away. I mentioned his testimony – in particular a very
nasty encounter that he had with a fortune teller, who had

accurately predicted the date of a serious accident to his mother (which led to her death), some fifty years earlier. This had held him back from faith for many years.

I never would have mentioned this story without the double catalyst of the children being late and the singing of Bob's favourite song. It had an electric effect. One longstanding member of the congregation admitted a past serious spiritual difficulty and needed some quite difficult ministry.

Obviously, God could have brought freedom in other ways. But he didn't! He chose to use the strange combination of coincidence, spiritual insight, and confession to bring about an important victory.

We have, I believe, a huge responsibility to pray with faith. Extraordinary spiritual results take place when we do, they seldom happen when we don't!

God uses ordinary people to pray

When the disciples couldn't help the epileptic boy, they very sensibly asked Jesus why they had failed. He replied, 'This kind can come out only by prayer' Mark 9:29 ('and fasting' in some manuscripts). In other words, believing, hardworking, faithful (see parallel passage in Matthew 17:19ff) prayer was required. God needed effective prayer to accomplish this sign.

Ours is not to reason why – but prayer is an essential part of every Christian's spiritual work.

Objection 4: Prayer doesn't work – for me

You will remember the old story of Robert the Bruce and the spider – the message was, try, try and try again. That, I think, is not the message for those who find prayer difficult. I prefer the approach of a former maths teacher who, when we failed to solve some complex problem, would say, 'Think, think again, and think differently!'

Too often we have a 'Thomas'-like mentality in our approach to prayer. St Thomas makes a memorable and brief appearance on the gospel stage. First, he is full of pessimism when hearing of the death of Lazarus:

So then he told them plainly, 'Lazarus is dead, and for your sake I am glad I was not there, so that you may believe. But let us go to him.' Then Thomas (called Didymus) said to the rest of the disciples, 'Let us also go, that we may die with him.' (Jn 11:14-16)

We must beware a pessimistic negative attitude
Then he offers a wonderfully negative comment when Jesus starts to teach about his own departure:

'You know the way to the place where I am going'. Thomas said to him, 'Lord, we don't know where you are going, so how can we know the way?' (Jn 14:4-5)

After the Resurrection, almost inevitably he is the one of the Twelve, apart from the unfortunate Judas, who is missing: 'Now Thomas (called Didymus), one of the Twelve, was not with the disciples when Jesus came' (Jn 20:24). Thomas had the ability not to be in the right place at the right time. He missed the great spiritual blessing of the first encounter with the risen Lord. As we all know, for Thomas, it came right in the end and Jesus closed the encounter with words of particular importance for our problem: 'Blessed are those who have not seen and yet have believed' (Jn 20:29b).

Many people's spiritual experiences are like those of Thomas. Other people's prayers get answered, other people's partners get converted, other people have godly children, other people see miracles, other people witness effectively... The result is that they become spiritually depressed, purveying a mixture of cynicism (there go the holy people whose prayers God hears), of superiority (my faith doesn't need the rent a miracle crowd), of despair (Lord, why don't you ever help me?), of anger (Lord, I'm giving up on your impossible church – and you).

It can all seem so unfair. Probably it is! There is nothing in Scripture to suggest that answers to prayer are distributed fairly. I remember when I was a little boy, one friend's mother used always to say, 'Share and share alike,' which was always a prelude to interfering with, or taking away whatever someone else was enjoying.

God isn't like that. He blesses us, indeed there is rather a lot in the Gospels to suggest that blessings increase rather than get shared. The five-talent person gets another five, to him that has more, more shall be given... (Mt 25:14-30)

What's the remedy?

Pray, pray again, pray differently! Assume that God does hear our prayers. We have the evidence of Scripture, we have the evidence of the lives of the great saints, we have the evidence of those around us. Consult a spiritual director, local clergyman, or trusted Christian friend. We need to approach prayer differently – use meditation, adoration, praise and thanksgiving, pray for others rather than for yourself and your concerns, and remember that God is a generous Father. He will meet us. If we earnestly seek him, he will find us. Our *Seek and you will find* experiences will all be different. For many, Jesus' final words to Thomas will be crucial: 'Blessed are those who have not seen, and yet have believed.'

In faith, rather than by sight,[22] we shall be met. Nevertheless, we may begin to expect real encounters. I close this chapter with several very different prayer experiences, told to me by friends whose testimony I can vouch for.

A lady in waiting

Here is her testimony:

'Some time ago (18/5/79) I picked up a book, quite by chance, in church – *When the Spirit comes* by Colin Urquhart, and later, as I read it, I knew that I too wanted the "Spirit to come". The following Sunday, with no clear idea of what this meant and not sure whether such a desirable Christian thing could actually happen, as I knelt at the Communion rail I told God exactly what I wanted. Not surprisingly nothing happened and I forgot the whole incident.

'Then, some weeks later, as I sat at home seeking to pray for five minutes, I became aware of an odd feeling of happiness, in my body rather than in my mind, as if it had been poured through the top of my head. it increased and deepened, became more alive and I began frantically to wonder what was wrong with me. And then suddenly *I knew it was God.* I don't know how I knew, but I knew with a certainty of both body and mind, with a knowledge that had somehow come from deep within me, released in amoment which lives forever, outside time, eternal in itself. And it was as if I had always known.

'And happiness became joy and joy became a love such as I could never have imagined possible, a love which filled my body from deep in my soul to the tips of my fingers – a living love that moved and filled me. I tried to capture it in words, the depth of one's soul, the essence of life, the ground of one's being, but who can describe God? Not I. I knew I didn't understand, but that I didn't have to – just to accept. And as I sat there life and death came together and I felt myself in God's world, at one with him and creation. And I felt his power within me, and I knew the greatness of God.

'All this time this feeling of love was in me and all around me – it was as if God from without had come into me and released a God from deep within my soul and the two had come together in an explosion of divine love, and the overwhelming feeling was of this love pouring out from me, a living stream, complete yet endless. Again I knew I did not understand, but that one day I would, even if I had to die first. And I knew that God had done all that he intended and that even though I could sit there all afternoon and he would stay with me, I got up and walked away.

'And so the Spirit came, so gentle, yet so devastating, asking nothing, yet irresistible – divine love which captures the soul and holds it fast in invisible bonds, yet gives it a divine freedom to explore the eternal boundary of its own existence.'

Later, she experienced many other touches of God's love. She writes of a deep moment, when after a painful rejection by the local church, she felt that she should walk out of the church. They were singing 'Dear Lord and Father of Mankind, forgive our foolish ways.' She looked round, out through the new porch, on to the snow. Somehow she couldn't leave. Walking up to take Communion, she felt completely helpless. Kneeling, she told God that she didn't want to feel like that, but there was nothing that she could do, except to ask for his forgiveness.

'Later that afternoon, inwardly, I heard a voice call my name.

There was a quality which seemed to say, "Didn't you know that I've been with you all the time?" For her it was 'the still small voice of calm.'

Prayer for her family has been a priority. Two experiences stand out. Her youngest daughter was suffering from eczema so badly that it was totally affecting her early grown-up years. She went, reluctantly, for prayer at the local church – and the eczema disappeared gradually day by day. Her life was greatly transformed.

Even more wonderful was her experience with the rowan tree in the front garden.

Another daughter was unable to have children. She and her husband had been through all the tests and were considering adoption. She asked her mother to pray – not in so many words, but the request was clear.

The rowan tree had been bought many years earlier, during the week of this daughter's wedding. It had never bloomed, and her husband was threatening to cut it down.

Betty prayed, 'When the rowan tree blossoms, I will take this as a sign that you will bless my daughter's marriage with the baby that they dearly want.' (cf Mk 11:12-14 and 20-25).

She continues: 'I felt quite safe as I believed that the tree would never bloom, but late in the spring, the following year, a solitary blossom appeared. My first thought was that there was a prayer gone to waste. I didn't believe that there was any possibility that my daughter would have a baby, and I discounted the sign.

'Within a few weeks, she rang to say that, without telling the family, they had embarked on IVF treatment, and were expecting twins! Not miracle babies, but statistics show only a 20% success rate for IVF, and I was surprised that she had even tried the expensive and somewhat controversial treatment.

'Some would say just a coincidence, but I don't doubt God's hand. A seemingly impossible event following a totally un-expected sign.'

Prayer before a service

Many of the quietest people have lovely experiences in prayer that are such a joy to hear about. One of our ladies who often brings her grandchildren to church writes:

God can speak to you!

'On arriving in church one Sunday, I knelt down to pray. My prayer was, "I know that you are near to me, help me to be near to you." I had never prayed these words before, so was more than amazed when the visiting preacher began his sermon with, "God will come close to you, if you will come close to God."

'Was this coincidence? I don't think so – according to Psalm 139 – God knows our thoughts and the words we say, even before we say them. The prayer was, I believe, put into my mind by the Holy Spirit.'

A visiting Bishop

At theological college, some time in the spring of 1971, we had a quiet day led by Bishop Frank Houghton. He was an old man of seventy-seven, with just one more year to live, but I shall never forget either his presence or his message.

It was easy to sense that we were in the presence of one of God's saints. His talks revolved around, what has become for me, a key verse of Scripture: 'For God did not give us a spirit of timidity, but a spirit of power, of love and of self-discipline' (2 Tim 1:7).

I had a brief talk with him in his quiet room. I don't really remember what he said, but I do remember the godly love that emanated from him. He had the fragrance of Christ (2 Cor 2:14,15). He had lived through years of difficult, yet exciting missionary experience in China. Eventually, he had become Director General of the China Inland Mission just before the war, experienced God's blessing in wartime China, only to see everything apparently shattered by the Communist takeover.

Two poems from that period speak eloquently of his self-discipline:[23]

God is very close in our deepest disappointments

WHEN GOD IS SILENT
When God is silent for a space,
And when thick darkness veils his face,
Until I hear his voice once more,
Until I see him as of yore,

On this firm ground my feet are set –
His promise, 'I WILL NOT FORGET'.

THE THICK DARKNESS
I thought I was walking all alone
Into the darkness immense and drear.
But where it was densest a Hand touched my own,
And a Voice spoke, gentle and clear:
'Do you not think you might have known
That I should be here?
Your need is met, your way will be shown,
Be of good cheer!'

These poems, written in 1951, came to him in the most difficult year of his life. The Mission had withdrawn from China, some missionaries were in prison, and the future of the church seemed uncertain. But God spoke to him with the clarity of a vision. Thick darkness was darkness 'where God was' (Ex 20:21; 1 Kings 8:12, Is 50:10).

Out of the darkness, came an extraordinary vision. Withdrawal from China didn't mean the end, but a new beginning. This cable came from a directors' conference in 1950: 'Lengthen cords! Strengthen stakes! While emphasising priority prayer for China Conference unanimously convinced Mission should explore unmet need preparatory to entering new fields from Thailand to Japan. Haggai 2:5: "My spirit abides among you; fear not."'

For Frank, it meant the shattering experience of giving up the leadership of C.I.M. and seeing it become O.M.F. (Overseas Missionary Fellowship). But the power of the Lord was greatly seen as revival came to many Eastern churches –notably in Singapore and Hong Kong. But God is often to be experienced in these situations. All he requires is that we keep trusting – and praying.

We cannot really know what is happening in China, yet there are many stories of great faith. The indigenous church survives, and flourishes, under intense persecution, as it never could in the days of the missionaries.

I left Bishop Houghton's old and frail presence, just beginning to understand something of the amazing power of prayer. His

One man's faith influences another quiet, measured words, and radiant face, live on in my memory. Another testimony to the gracious Father whose living presence is our greatest hope and joy, and where love is felt most when we hear the words of his Son: 'Come with me by yourselves to a quiet place and get some rest' (Mk 6:31).

When God feels very distant, when prayer seems at best difficult and at worst a waste of time, these are the times when the generous Father becomes strangely present. 'God is faithful, he will not let you be tempted beyond what you can bear.' (1 Cor 10:13).

We will have many deep intimate experiences of the loving Father, but he will never become so familiar as to allow us to forget his awesome majesty and overwhelming glory.

Notes

1. See Jeremiah 31:31-34.
2. Oscar Cullmann, *Prayer in the New Testament* (SCM 1995) p 18.
3. Cullmann, *ibid* p 41 for a very useful discussion of the precise meaning of 'Abba Father' (Mark 14:36).
4. *Mission Praise* (Marshall Pickering, 1990), No. 1, by Roy Crabtree.
5. *Hymns Ancient & Modern Revised* (William Clowes & Sons), No. 372, by W. Chalmers Smith.
6. Julian of Norwich, 'Revelation of Divine Love' – quoted from *Enfolded in Love – daily readings with Julian of Norwich*, p 3, (DLT, 1980).
7. Chaos theory has produced a new mathematical constant that appears in many apparently unrelated situations. It is a very beautiful theory suggesting that there is deep order even in the midst of uncertainty – a pointer to the Creator?
8. Cullman, *ibid* p 3 and elsewhere.
9. David Prior, *The Message of 1 Corinthians* (IVP, 1985), pp 83, 84.
10. See any art book with Max Escher drawings.

11. The basis of perspective drawing – Desargue's theorem on perspective triangles is breathtakingly simple! Draw three lines VAX, VBY, VCZ. The $\triangle$'s ABC and XYZ are said to be in perspective. If you join AB and XY at R; AC and XZ at Q; BC and YZ at P, you will find that PQR is a straight line (the vanishing line!). Curiously, it can be proved in three dimensions very quickly as follows: ABC and XYZ are 2 planes. Planes intersect in a line. That line contains P, Q and R! To prove the theorem in two dimensions is quite tricky!

12. Ruth Gledhill, religious correspondent of *The Times*, Saturday July 27th 1996.

13. Fr Francis SSF, *Life of Brother Douglas* (Mowbray, 1961), p 48.

14. Cullmann, *ibid* p 9. The quotation is from F. Nietzsche 'Also sprach Zarathustra' (Harmondsworth, 1961).

15. I wrote this just the day after the massacre of many infant school children, and their teacher at Dunblane in Scotland in March 1996. For a deeply understanding comment see W. H. Vanstone *Love's endeavour, Love's expense'* (DLT, 1977) p 65, on the Aberfan tragedy.

16. Cullmann, *ibid* p 5 and elsewhere.

17. Jackie Pullinger, *Chasing the Dragon* (Hodder & Stoughton, 1980).

18. Patricia St John, Autobiography *op cit* p 106, and *Would you believe it?* p111.

19. Cullmann, *ibid* p 141.

20. Charles Wesley, *And can it be.*

21. *Mission Praise* (Marshall, Morgan & Scott, 1990), No 313, by Max Dyer.

22. 2 Corinthians 5:7

23. Frank Houghton, *Faith Triumphant* (OMF Books, 1973), pp 131-132.

5

Thanksgiving, Praise and Adoration

(Does God really need our praise?)

This chapter takes us on a journey beginning with the simple, but important prayer of thanksgiving and continues by exploring the ways in which we praise God, and why we find this difficult. Finally, we climb the mountain to start to adore God. We see that thanksgiving, praise, and adoration are a necessary response to God's love.

Thanksgiving, Praise and Adoration

In this chapter, we look at some of the basic principles of prayer. We shall consider the importance of the simple thank you, move on to the question of praise, and finally, look at the more difficult and profound prayer of adoration.

> Set me as a seal upon your heart,
>   as a seal upon your arm;
> for love is strong as death,
>   passion fierce as the grave.
> Its flashes are flashes of fire,
>   a raging flame.
> Many waters cannot quench love,
>   neither can the floods drown it.
> If all the wealth of our house
>   were offered for love
> it would be utterly scorned.   (Song 8:6-7[1] – RSV)

These majestic words are somewhere near the summit of the journey which we must make. They are words of adoration, expressing the almost inexpressible, describing the almost indescribable.

The other day, I climbed the Tour du Pin, near where I'm staying. Most of the journey was hot, and not particularly beautiful. But all the way there was that sense of anticipation, the delight at finding the small essential track, perfumed with broom, the pleasure of the shaded trees towards the foot of the tower, the growing sense of anticipation, and the view beginning to open out along the ridge to the east and to the west. Then the steep scramble to the top. There is one nasty overhang – dare I attempt it with my damaged hip? A couple are already on the top, and for once I'm pleased to see other people who will surely help me down. The view is breathtaking, it's like a sweet scented garden at the top where wild thyme and other flowers proliferate.

I did need help on the way down, the German residents were very friendly. I enjoyed the journey down with them. At the village of Estraussan we parted. I took another lower path and was rewarded when first one, and then another of my favourite butterflies, glorious maroon-coloured Camberwell Beauties, leapt up off the warm path, circling me, telling me I was intruding in their territory. I remembered George Herbert's words in his poem *The Pulley*[2]:

> He would adore my gifts instead of Me
> And rest in Nature, not the God of Nature,
> So both should losers be.

Words that remind us that the object of the purest prayer is God himself, and not his works, his favour, his experience. But, if we are to climb the hill of adoration, we must first dwell in the valley of thanksgiving, and use the highway of praise.

The prayer of thanksgiving

'Thank me no thankings,' says Capulet, Juliet's father, to her at a very tense moment in the middle act of the play.[3] We do find it hard to say thank you, and even harder to accept thanks! Yet we rightly teach our children, or at least we used to, to say thank you, to write thank you letters, and to make thank you prayers. The Tablespoon Prayer (TSP = Thank you, Sorry, Please) is taught in many Sunday Schools.

Giving thanks, a natural way to pray

Giving thanks springs from a grateful heart. The more we are in tune with God's Spirit, the more naturally we will give thanks. It is an important part of prayer, and unlike most prayer, relatively easy. It is certainly the easiest way to learn to pray aloud.

My first experience of impromptu prayer was when attending a beginners' group (a distant forerunner of Alpha) at university. Run by the Rector, Keith de Berry, the great incumbent of St Aldate's, Oxford, the evening ended with a brief time of prayer. The choice was bleak – either you prayed aloud, or you touched the knee of the person next to you, as a sign that you weren't praying! It wasn't too difficult to offer a simple prayer of thanksgiving in these circumstances.

It can be deeply moving to hear someone else pray aloud. I feel a great surge in my own spirit; particularly when someone, unused to praying aloud, starts to give thanks. There is a real sense of the Holy Spirit's presence and leading (Rom 8:26).

Biblical examples of the prayer of thanksgiving

It isn't difficult to find things to give thanks for. The Bible gives many examples:

Give thanks to the Lord, for He is good. *His love endures for ever.*
Give thanks to the God of gods. *His love endures for ever.*
Give thanks to the Lord of lords: *His love endures for ever.*
to Him who alone does great wonders, *His love endures for ever.*
(Ps 136:1-4)

That is the beginning of a classic psalm of thanksgiving – the joyful response of a grateful people for part of their salvation history. The book of Nehemiah is a stirring account of the prayer and care that went into rebuilding the walls of the city. The great celebration, near the end of the book, gives a wonderful picture of colour, music, and thanksgiving as the people celebrated round the walls of the city.

At the dedication of the wall of Jerusalem, the Levites were sought out from where they lived and were brought to Jerusalem to celebrate joyfully the dedication with songs of thanksgiving and with the music of cymbals, harps and lyres. (Neh 12:27)

St Paul is full of thanksgiving:

> Do not be anxious about anything, but in everything, by prayer and petition, with thanksgiving, present your requests to God. (Phil 4:6)
>
> We always thank God, the Father of our Lord Jesus Christ, when we pray for you, because we have heard of your faith in Christ Jesus and of the love you have for all the saints. (Col 1:3 & 4)

Beautiful prayers – the first of joy, mingled with thanksgiving and intercession; the second rejoicing in the spiritual progress of a church not known personally to the prayer. Through the ages, Christians have written many such prayers. Johann Kepler[4] (1571-1630), the great astronomer, who deduced many revolutionary ideas about the motion of the planets prayed:

> O Thou who through the light of nature has aroused in us a longing for the light of grace, so that we may be raised in the light of Thy Majesty, to Thee I give thanks, Creator and Lord, that Thou allowest me to rejoice in Thy works. Praise the Lord ye heavenly harmonics, and ye who know the revealed harmonies. For from Him, through Him, and in *Formal examples of prayers of thanksgiving* Him, all is, which is perceptible as well as spiritual; that which we know and that which we do not know, for there is still much to learn.

A deeply moving prayer of thanksgiving from a great scientist. As an example of a fine liturgical prayer,[5] enjoy these words:

> Father of all, we give you thanks and praise that when we were still far off, you met us in your Son and brought us home. Dying and living, he declared your love, gave us grace, and opened the gate of glory. May we who share Christ's body live his risen life; we who drink his cup bring life to others; we whom the Spirit lights give light to the world. Keep us firm in the hope you have set before us, so we and all your children shall be free, and the whole earth live to praise your name; through Christ our Lord. Amen.

Informal prayers of thanksgiving

Using the four biblical, and two liturgical, prayers above, here are some very simple examples of the prayer of thanksgiving. They are designed to help us get started – somehow the more people who pray aloud, the greater the sense of fellowship at any prayer meeting. (The Chinese solve the problem both of time, and potential embarrassment, by getting everyone to pray simultaneously!): 'Lord, thank you for your wonderful love'; 'Lord, thank you for helping us complete...'; 'Lord, thank you for the joy of knowing you'; 'Lord, thank you for the wonderful faith of our unseen friends, especially...'; 'Lord, thank you for the wonder of the universe, the mystery of the stars, and the faith of many scientists (and the beauty of your butterflies!)'; 'Lord, thank you for the gift of Holy Communion. Thank you for all that it means to Christians in so many different traditions.'

Prayers of thanksgiving can be very simple

Thus, the prayer of thanksgiving is just a simple thank you to our great and gracious God. For those too frightened or unfamiliar with prayer groups, try writing down such a prayer before the meeting. Bring it with you, and use it when it seems appropriate. Extempore prayers don't have a monopoly of inspiration!

Two gentle warnings!

We must beware allowing prayers of thanksgiving to become a none too subtle means of blowing our own spiritual trumpet. The Pharisee in Jesus' parable is the prime example: 'The Pharisee stood up and prayed about himself: "God, I thank you that I am not like other men – robbers, evildoers, adulterers – or even like this tax collector. I fast twice a week and give a tenth of all I get."' (Lk 18:11 & 12)

A wrong sort of thanksgiving

The give away is the sequence of 'I', 'I', 'I', followed by the judgemental put-down of the tax collector. Just as it is usually a sign that someone is beginning to emerge from depression when they talk less about 'I' and more about others, so it is a sign of spiritual progress when prayers and thanksgiving don't have too many 'I's dotted around.

We must also beware of allowing the prayer of thanksgiving to become a sort of spiritual talisman.

Be thankful for everything?

On a number of occasions, I have heard preachers quote 1 Thessalonians 5:18: 'Give thanks in all circumstances, for this is God's will for you in Christ Jesus' in a mechanical way. Once in Nairobi, I heard a visiting preacher say, 'If you go out of the church and find you've got a flat tyre, praise God for all the brothers and sisters whose tyres aren't flat.' Such an approach is patently absurd! Did St Paul really expect this verse to become a spiritual talisman to be used in all circumstances – however adverse?

He didn't give thanks when Satan prevented his earlier arrival in Thessalonica (1 Thess 2:18). He certainly didn't give thanks for the errors in the Galatian church (Gal 1:6; 3:1, etc). Indeed, unlike his other letters, there isn't a word of thanks anywhere in the whole letter!

Jesus didn't give thanks when he approached Jerusalem on the first Palm Sunday. He wept! When faced with the sacrilege in his Father's house, he ejected the traders, and denounced the whole corrupt system (Lk 19:35-46).

I have laboured the point, precisely because being thankful is such an important part of our prayer life – and, indeed, of our whole life. If it becomes a spiritual recipe for dealing with adversity, then the whole teaching becomes absurd, and this whole aspect of prayer is devalued.

St Paul's troubles with the Galatian church were like the grit in a spiritual oyster – they produced the pearl of the 'fruit of the Spirit' (Gal 5:18ff). Jesus' sorrow and anger in Jerusalem produced the wonderful praises of the children (Matt 21:14-16) – those who condemn family services beware!

How we meet adverse circumstances is what matters

Adverse circumstances can, and often will, produce things worthy of praise. If we are prone to grumbling, if we feel like W. S. Gilbert's king,[6]

> Oh don't the days seem lank and long
> When all goes right and nothing goes wrong.
> And isn't your life extremely flat
> With nothing whatever to grumble at.

then we certainly need to learn, and apply wisely, 1 Thessalonians 5:18!

Prayers of praise

Having learnt a little about thanksgiving, we must now start to climb. I don't know if it's a particularly British problem, but we don't seem to know how to handle praise. Before we look at it in connection with prayer, just a couple of illustrations.

A few years ago, after a hip operation, I was in hospital. I couldn't sleep. I found prayer pretty difficult! This seems to be a common problem. My salvation lay in the pithy comments of the writer of Proverbs. The book of Proverbs was so simple to read, easy to apply, and often made me smile. For many nights I survived by listening, on headphones, to cricket commentaries from Australia. I immediately noticed the enthusiasm of the Australian commentators. They liked praising their team. They were positive, encouraging. Very different from the spirit of criticism which seems to pervade English sports commentators.

More seriously, if you have American or Canadian visitors in church they will always come and introduce themselves, make some enthusiastic comment, and go on their way – leaving you rejoicing. By contrast, we seem to delight in criticising (and blaming). That is one reason why evangelicals find it hard to worship with catholics and both with charismatics. Critical faculties are immediately engaged. If we would try and appreciate other people's approach (Why is that chorus so important to him? Why is the liturgy used in that way so moving for them? What can I learn from that lengthy sermon?), we would find our lives greatly enriched.

Criticism – a peculiarly British problem?

If we find it hard to give praise to our fellow humans, we find it excruciatingly embarrassing to receive it! Of course, the praise we are concerned with is rather different. It is the praise and worship of our heavenly Father. But it still presents problems. We shall be guided by one great writer.

C. S. Lewis on praising[7]

C. S. Lewis, one of our greatest spiritual writers, had great difficulty with the idea of praise in prayer. These are some of his most lovely thoughts:

When I first began to draw near to believe in God, and even for some time after it had been given to me, I found a stumbling block in the demand so clamorously made by all religious people that we should 'praise' God; still more in the suggestion that God himself demanded it. We all despise the man who demands continued assurance of his own virtue, intelligence or delightfulness; we despise still more the crowd of people round every dictator, every millionaire, every celebrity, who gratify that demand. Thus a picture, at once ludicrous and horrible, both of God and of his worshippers, threatened to appear in my mind. The Psalms were especially troublesome in this way – 'Praise the Lord', 'O praise the Lord with me', 'Praise Him'.

At first, Lewis felt that God was demanding praise as a gateway to spiritual success! Then gradually, he comes to appreciate the real reasons for praise and adoration:

But the most obvious fact about praise – whether of God or anything – strangely escaped me. I thought of it in terms of compliment, approval, or the giving of honour. I had never noticed that all enjoyment spontaneously overflows into praise unless (sometimes even if) shyness or the fear of boring others is deliberately brought in to check it. The world rings with praise – lovers praising their mistresses, readers their favourite poet, walkers praising the countryside, players praising their favourite game – praise of weather, wines, dishes, actors, motors, horses, colleges, countries, historical personages, children, flowers, mountains, rare stamps, rare beetles, even sometimes politicians or scholars. I had not noticed *Praise brings* how the humbler, and at the same time most balanced and *completion* capacious, minds, praised most, while the cranks and misfits, and malcontents praised least. The good critics found something to praise in many imperfect works; the bad ones continually narrowed the list of books we might be allowed to read. The healthy and unaffected man, even if luxuriously brought up and widely experienced in good cookery, could praise a very modest meal: the dyspeptic and the snob found fault with all.

He is making the wonderful point that praise not only expresses, but completes, the enjoyment.

Lewis again says:

It is not out of compliment that lovers keep on telling one another how beautiful they are; the delight is incomplete till it is expressed. It is frustrating to have discovered a new author and not to be able to tell anyone how good he is; to come suddenly, at the turn of the road, upon some mountain valley of unexpected grandeur and then to have to keep silent because the people with you care for it no more than for a tin can in the ditch. If it were possible for a created soul fully (I mean, up to the full measure conceivable in a finite being) to 'appreciate', that is to love and delight in, the worthiest object of all, and simultaneously at every moment to give this delight perfect expression, then that soul would be in supreme beatitude. It is along these lines that I find it easiest to understand the Christian doctrine that 'Heaven' is a state in which angels now, and men hereafter, are perpetually employed in praising God.

C. S. Lewis on the need to praise

All that is beautifully put. But how, in practice, do we manage it?

Praise in prayer and worship

We have very few actual prayers prayed by Jesus. Here is one: 'At that time Jesus, full of joy through the Holy Spirit, said, "I praise you, Father, Lord of heaven and earth, because you have hidden these things from the wise and learned, and revealed them to little children. Yes, Father, for this was your good pleasure' (Lk 10:21).

Jesus, full of joy, through the Holy Spirit. Full of joy! Wasn't he always full of joy? Apparently not! Certainly not when condemning Korazin and Bethsaida a few verses earlier. Praising is not automatic. It springs from deep spiritual joy – in this case a powerful mission conducted by seventy disciples who proclaimed the kingdom, healed the sick, cast out demons, and whose names were written in the book of life.

It should be easy to praise God when wonderful things happen – and, not surprisingly, wonderful things tend to happen when individuals and churches are taking 'praise' seriously.

It is wonderful to praise God when a new believer professes faith. I well remember a sedate schoolboy almost dancing down the passageway beside the chapel where, to our amazement, many had responded after a mission talk.

It is wonderfully easy to praise God when someone is healed. I shall never forget the look of astonished wonder shared by myself, a somewhat bemused missionary, and a previously largely deaf Zambian, whom we all discovered could hear perfectly. (His parish priest, subsequently, wrote a beautiful letter confirming the radical change in the man's hearing, and saying that he was now singing in the choir.)

Praise in response to God's love and power

It is awesome to praise God when we are preserved in some life-threatening situation. Recently, walking in the Welsh mountains with my youngest children, Tim and Katy, the dog, and Tim's godfather, we met a slight hailstorm. Quite unexpectedly, unique that day, there was a flash of lightning. In a split second I saw a bright light just above my head – I've seen an angel at last(!) – then the arc of lightning struck my head and bounced off on to Tim. My hair stood on end, and I can still feel the spot where the lightning touched my head. Tim felt the current pass through him. We were both unharmed. I didn't have time to be frightened, only time to be grateful that none of us had been hurt. Psalm 148 sprang to mind! 'Lightning and hail, snow and clouds, stormy winds that do his bidding' (v8).

It is very necessary to praise the Lord in worship. A discussion of worship is really outside the scope of this book, but so much of our private and corporate prayer life springs from our experience of worship, that we must briefly look at it. Worship is a delicate subject. One man's praise service is another's cringe. If only we would learn to appreciate what helps others to praise, we would then benefit from different insights and experiences.

Variety of worship

I've already mentioned the liturgical rhythm, and deep quiet of prayer at the Friary at Hilfield. In total contrast, I sometimes go to the evening service at St John's Glastonbury for a 'Toronto' style[8] service of praise. There too, I can rejoice, and enjoy the sense of the Spirit's presence. Many people are deeply touched; contrary to popular myth it is all very unemotional, and often they are healed physically and emotionally.

At the New Wine Festival,[9] held on the showground at the very edge of my parish, morning worship usually begins with a glorious catena of choruses. The French worship group, Flamme,

Different styles of worship are important

have an extraordinary gift for combining Scripture, prophecy, and music. A fine exposition of Scripture follows. In 1995, it was deeply moving to listen to John Wimber,[10] obviously very unwell, wrestling with the deep truths of Ephesians as they applied to his life, and the contemporary Christian scene.

But best of all (for me!) is a normal Anglican communion service. The fine liturgical structure provides the framework for both freedom and order. The music can include great hymns from the past, choruses, and the choir may add the music of Bach, Taizé, or Iona. There will be a challenging, but reasonably brief, exposition of Scripture, prayers intelligently led by a member of the congregation, some silence at appropriate points, and the sharing of the peace – not a new-fangled idea, but an integral part of first-century worship.

I always smile when I think of the retired colonel reported to have shared the peace with the words, 'It's all a lot of nonsense, but the peace of the Lord be with you anyway.'

Then there is the sharing of the bread and wine, with no particular theological interpretation thrust upon me,[11] and the possibility of giving or receiving personal prayer during a brief time of ministry.

Unlike Robert Louis Stevenson, who is said to have recorded in his diary, as though surprised, 'Went to church – didn't feel depressed', I can go home (or in my case, on to one of my lovely village churches), after a shared cup of coffee, much conversation, and a few more prayers, rejoicing in the Lord.

'One thing I ask of the Lord, this is what I seek… to gaze upon the beauty of the Lord and to seek him in his temple' (Ps 27:4). How right the psalmist is when he says, 'Better is one day in your courts than a thousand elsewhere; I would rather be a doorkeeper in the house of my God…' (Ps 84:10).

But this raises another question.

What can I do when I honestly can't praise the Lord?

We live in a time of great stress. A bereaved person will find it more natural to weep in church than to sing praises. People who are ill, physically and mentally, find any prayer surprisingly difficult, praise almost impossible, Jesus wept at Lazarus' tomb.

We need to be sensitive in the use of testimony. An un-employed person would find it hard to rejoice with Brother X who has just received promotion. Mrs Y, whose unmarried daughter has just given birth, will *The need for sensitivity* find it hard to appreciate the testimony of the smart London visitor whose miraculous transformation from promiscuity to pilgrimage ought to give her hope.

A marriage service can be unbearably poignant for the divorced or bereaved. By contrast, a funeral service, particularly for a Christian who has lived a full life, can be a tremendous time of praise – and an important witness to a sceptical world. I remember the joy of a funeral service of one unmarried lady, who had a particularly difficult death. Her witness, made clear by her choice of music and readings for her own service, spoke far beyond her grave.

There is a lovely children's chorus[12] whose first line is 'I walk with you, my children, through valleys filled with gloom'. God understands. His own heart was deeply grieved by Israel's apostasy. His heart was always full of compassion: 'My heart is changed within me; all my compassion is aroused' (Hos 11:8b).

He understands when our hearts are heavy. He doesn't expect us to start praising as though nothing has happened. But, and there is a but!, God has an amazing way of transforming the darkest situations. Returning to Psalm 84, if we can go 'through the vale of misery (and) use it for a well' (Ps 84:6, Prayer Book version), we will find that things begin to change.

As an example, here is the very wonderful testimony of one of our Sunday School teachers. She is writing about her father's illness and death on the Island of Mull. He died in December 1995, aged sixty-two.

'...He bore the illness with incredible courage, humour and hope. He believed he could be physically healed by God and attended a very moving healing service during which he came forward for prayer and the laying on of hands. He felt deeply touched by the experience and felt that he may well have received some physical healing, but certainly an inner healing through a great sense of peace. Many people were praying for his healing all over the country and he said he really knew that, and felt strengthened, comforted, encouraged and upheld in prayer. He said it helped him to experience the love of God more closely, and the love and support he received from family and friends made him rejoice in the love and goodness of God.

'Helped by all this, he recovered remarkably from a major operation for bowel cancer in early July, and although he had advanced cancer, the doctors thought that chemotherapy treatment might help to stop it advancing too rapidly. He started an eight week course of treatment, but before the final week, developed a major blockage and was readmitted to hospital. It was discovered that the treatment had been unsuccessful and there was nothing more they could do. He weakened dramatically after this second operation, and it was thought he would only live a few more days. The local Bishop and his wife came every day to pray with him. I was able to read the Bible to him

Prayer and peace near the point of death
– mostly Psalms, Romans, Ephesians and Philippians. Although he was in considerable pain he showed a wonderful peacefulness, and was able to pray aloud for the first time in his life with little or no previous experience. He must have received a huge inpouring of faith, because he suddenly prayed a prayer that God would bless his home, send him home, and that he would live his life committed to God's service.

'The following day he improved noticeably and asked the doctors if he could go home. This was not received very well, since it had seemed the previous day he had only days to live, and going home meant a two-hour journey (an hour by ferry) back to a remote part of a Scottish island, with community nurses an hour's drive away. Over the next few days he was determined. He recovered his strength by taking tiny morsels of puréed food, and walking a few steps further each day until he returned home six days later.

'On arriving home he then proceeded to live out his prayer. Many people came daily to see him and nurse him, and all were greatly touched by his incredible peacefulness in the face of such a dreadful disease that saw him wither away physically, but grow each day spiritually. He showed great humility and gentleness and patience and goodwill – Christlike qualities. He was a great witness to others, and openly shared his assurance of eternal life and his love of Jesus. He constantly thanked God and clapped his hands for Jesus, and sang hymns. He had always been slightly reserved physically, but now everyone was openly and warmly hugged. He talked of the wonderful peace of God and brought us all closer to the Lord, and strengthened our faith in the midst of so much suffering. He lived at home three weeks and certainly lived those three weeks totally committed to God's service, and the glory and love of God was revealed throughout his short illness. Although he was not healed physically, he received inner healing and grew in faith and love.

This lovely story is a good example of what Paul meant in Philippians 1:6 '...being confident of this, that he who began a good work in you will carry it on to completion until the day of Christ Jesus.'

Prayers of praise

Paul and Silas (Acts 16:25) sang hymns after their unjust and painful imprisonment at Philippi. Peter has some interesting comments on praise and suffering (1 Pet 4:12-19, see also 2:18-25, and 3:17). It is far easier to suffer for Christ's sake, than because of the natural or unnatural failings of the world. Richard Wurmbrand echoes this many times – on one marvellous occasion, he records a Romanian response to a lecture of atheism. A great cry rose up, 'Christ is risen – he is risen indeed!' *Praise in* To which there was no answer – except more physical *prison* punishment.

Praise has great power. George Herbert,[13] whose beautiful hymns and poems are so full of praise, captures it perfectly with a beautiful line in a poem about prayer, 'A kind of tune which all things hear and fear.'

Elsewhere he writes:

Let all the world in every corner sing,
My God and King!
The heav'ns are not too high,
His praise may thither fly;

> The earth is not too low,
> His praises there may grow.

and

> Rise heart, thy Lord is risen.
> Sing his praise
> Without delays.

A wonderful description of prayer and praise. Praise brings great spiritual release. Perhaps that's why choirs and music groups often have more of their share of spiritual difficulties – or is that just fleshly problems caused by the 'prima donna' attitude of a few musicians and ministers?

Certain buildings, particularly places that have enjoyed centuries of prayer and praise, evoke a hallowed feel that touches even casual visitors. In such places, the wounded can find their

Praise in holy places tears transformed by a rainbow 'as the sun of righteousness arises with healing on his wings' (Mal 4:2, as quoted in the hymn 'Hark the Herald Angels Sing'). In such places, the wandering sheep can begin the journey back to their loving Father. How important that they are kept open! A locked church is a sullen witness, an open one a beacon to a wandering pilgrim.

Praise is more difficult than thanksgiving to articulate. It is often helpful to build a prayer around a verse of Scripture – for example, after a service of healing. Here is a prayer of praise based on Psalm 103: 'Praise the Lord, O my soul, who forgives all our sins, and heals all our diseases. Praise you, Lord, that the sun of righteousness has been among us and that we have experienced something of your wonder and healing grace.'

Here is another prayer of praise, suitable for that most sacred of all moments when someone has professed faith (see Chapter 8) for the first time. It is based on Ephesians 1:3,4; 2 Corinthians 5:17; and John 14:17. 'Praise to the God and Father of our Lord Jesus Christ, who has blessed us in the heavenly realms with every spiritual blessing in Christ. For he chose us in him, before the creation of the world, to be holy and blameless in his sight. Praise you, generous Father, that you have called your servant out of darkness into the light. Praise you, Lord Jesus, that you *Prayers* have died to save us, and to make us new creations. Praise *of praise* you, O Holy Spirit, for the Father's promise that you will come to dwell within us.'

If that sounds a bit formal, or stilted, we can enjoy the reaction of the Cornish miner and Methodist preacher, Billy Bray who, on hearing that the 19th-century Rector, William Haslam, had been converted (during his own sermon), danced around and on the Rector's breakfast table – shouting 'Praise the Lord!'

The prayer of adoration

Adoration is a natural part of human experience. The small boy worships his great sporting hero. (How can I ever forget watching Len Hutton going out to open England's second innings at the Oval in 1953, the Ashes almost in his grasp – and the awful disappointment when he needlessly ran himself out towards the end of a great day?) The presence of a great teacher leaves us spellbound (I shall never forget C. V. Durrell, the great maths text book writer of the 1920s and 1930s demonstrating, at over ninety, to the maths staff at Winchester his total grasp of the concepts of modern algebra). The performance of a great piece of music, the execution of some marvellous painting, the drama of the theatre, all these can lift us high above our natural state (I can still hear the immortal Amadeus Quartet playing Mozart in the perfect musical setting of lofty Dorchester Abbey). The natural world, too, offers many moments of exquisite ecstacy. (Join me, and watch the darkened chrysalis of a Swallowtail butterfly start to shake, and crack, and almost imperceptibly, the head of the butterfly appears; moments later the whole body, wings crumpled and quarter size. It looks for somewhere to settle, upside *Adoration, a* down, urgently pumping life into its wings. Before our *spontaneous* wondering eyes they expand, until a few minutes later, *human* the perfect insect waits, very still and inconspicuous, *reaction* until it is strong enough to fly.

Adoration plays an important part in human relationships. Deep friendships, especially perhaps where the friends cannot meet too often, have a transcendent quality. I shall always remember returning to Zambia (see Chapter 3, p 52), and meeting again my great friend Archdeacon Tobias. Recently bereaved, Tobias still radiated spiritual love and power, and we shared that very special friendship which is 'in the Lord'. Adoration is deeply experienced in the purest human love (can I ever forget the first conversation with the young lady that I knew I wanted to marry?). As the Song of Songs makes abundantly clear, it is also experienced in the sacred physical union of two people in love.

In most of these situations, words fail, it is quite enough to 'be' and to 'belong'. You watch the master cricketer, you listen to the great teacher, you appreciate great art, you absorb the wonder of nature, you drink the elixir of love.

Yet there is a certain effort required. You wouldn't appreciate, nearly so much, the view from the Tour du Pin if it was possible to drive there. You need to make the effort to 'be' one of the crowd at the Test Match, the finest TV picture cannot provide the atmosphere. You have to know a great deal of mathematics to appreciate a great instructor. You need to know something of art, theatre, or music to begin to delight in a magical performance. The more you know, the more you appreciate (provided that you

Adoration doesn't just happen

are not like C. S. Lewis' critic who has lost his ability to praise). You will appreciate the wonders of nature more, if you understand the difficulty or the rarity of what you're watching.

Deep friendships retain their spontaneous quality of brotherly love, because at earlier meetings there has been a level of self-giving, and spiritual bonding. Past failures may even make new love seem ever more hopeful and more sweet.

The point that I'm trying to make is that although adoration has to be spontaneous, the spontaneity is far more likely to occur when real effort has been made. If we learn to give thanks, if we learn to praise, then we shall at times discover what it means to adore.

One lady, asking a written question at an evening dialogue sermon, wrote, 'The other morning, I prayed for half-an-hour in complete silence. What was meant and achieved by this?'

She ought to have known – she'd just written this experience for me. The lady in question had become a Christian after bereavement, and quickly got deeply involved in the life of our church.

An experience in prayer

'I became a committed Christian in September 1993. By the following May, I became aware that God wanted me to add my prayers to the thousands who were praying for peace in Northern Ireland. I had no idea why as I have no connections with the Province, but I obeyed and this has been part of my daily prayer life since that time.

'During September 1994 I knew I was being guided to go to Northern Ireland; I couldn't believe it – all the usual excuses came to mind, but needless to say, in January I was on my way. I had no idea what I was supposed to do, so while I waited for an answer to my request for accommodation in a Christian community in west Belfast, I decided to go on retreat to try and discern God's will in all this. I went to Swanage immediatley after Christmas and spent as much time on my own as possible, praying, reading – just being quiet before the Lord.

'One afternoon, when most people had gone out, I settled down in a small room with my Bible and books on prayer. The door to this room was mostly glass, so I chose a chair with its back to the door, so that I would not be disturbed; one or two people looked in, but did not enter. I settled into prayer, meditation and contemplation.

'Some time later, I was aware that the door had opened and closed. I did not open my eyes or speak as I wanted to remain quiet. I sensed someone sitting in a nearby chair and gradually became aware that our Lord Jesus Christ was sitting near me. I found it difficult to accept what was happening, so I kept my eyes closed and waited. *Adoration – Christ's presence in prayer* The atmosphere was electric – so still, so warm, so full of peace; it seemed difficult to breathe! Then I heard a voice say, 'What can I do for you?' I knew I had to reply, but how could I get the words out? Could I really speak to my Lord? Eventually I said I was going to Northern Ireland as directed, but had no idea why or what for. The reply I received was, 'Trust and obey – make no plans – just go'.

'The sound of someone moving came to me and the door gently opened and closed again. The stillness and the peace remained and I stayed quiet for a long time, just soaking in the atmosphere and thanking God for so clear a message.

'The only arrangement made for the trip to Ireland was for accommodation, but during the time there, I was enabled to see, talk and pray with many different people and the whole time was completely occupied.'

Sometimes we experience the inexpressible love of God. To use another of C. S. Lewis' expressions, we are 'surprised by joy'. We feel like the great, but depressive poet and hymn writer, Cowper[14] who wrote,

Sometimes a light surprises the Christian when he sings,
It is the Lord who rises with healing in his wings;
When comforts are declining, he grants the soul again,
A season of clear shining to cheer it after rain.

True adoration may occur spontaneously, or it may occur because we're in the right place at the right time. Singing in tongues can be a strange and mystical experience. At its highest, it seems to

Adoration in church

occur when a great gathering of people have been worshipping and praising. There is a moment of stillness, then a sound as of flutes beginning to play, a sound which gradually rises to a crescendo, and after a few minutes, suddenly stops – as though a heavenly conductor has lowered his baton.

True adoration comes sometimes in church, especially when a congregation and leaders, are expectant and attentive. It occurs when groups are at prayer, it occurs when, as at the Mountain of Transfiguration, or on the road to Emmaus, a few friends encounter Jesus as they meet together.

And, of course, it occurs when we are alone. St Paul wrote 'Hope does not disappoint us, because God has poured out his love into our hearts by the Holy Spirit, whom he has given us' (Rom 5:5). He knew it – especially when caught up to the third heaven (2 Cor 12:1-10).

Jonathan Edwards,[15] the great Puritan writer who so influenced

American theology, is often thought to have been an austere 'hell fire' type of preacher. In fact, he had deep experiences of God which led him to write some beautiful words on adoration and praise. He uses the title Canticles for what we know as the 'Song of Songs':

'The first instance that I remember of that sort of inward, sweet delight in God and divine things that I have lived much in since, was on reading those words (1 Tim 1:17) "Now unto the King eternal, immortal, invisible, the only wise God be honour and glory for ever and ever, Amen." As I read the words there came into my soul, and was as it were diffused through it, a sense of the glory of the divine Being; a new sense, quite different from any thing I ever experienced before. Never any words of *A great saint* Scripture seemed to me as these words did. I thought *experiences* with myself how excellent a Being that was, and how *and adores* happy I should be, if I might enjoy that God, and be *his Lord* rapt up in him in heaven, and be as it were swallowed up in him for ever! I kept saying, and as it were singing over these words of Scripture to myself; and went to pray to God that I might enjoy him, and prayed in a manner quite different from what I used to do; with a new sort of affection. But it never came into my thought that there was anything spiritual, or of a saving nature in this. From about that time, I began to have a new kind of apprehensions and ideas of Christ, and the work of redemption, and the glorious way of salvation by him. An inward, sweet sense of these things, at times, came into my heart; and my soul was led away in pleasant views and contemplations of them. And my mind was greatly engaged to spend my time in reading and meditating on Christ, on the beauty and excellency of his person, and the lovely way of salvation by free grace in him. I found no books so delightful to me, as those that treated of these subjects. Those words Cant.2.1, used to be abundantly with me, "I am the Rose of Sharon, and the Lily of the valleys." The words seemed to me, sweetly to represent the loveliness and beauty of Jesus Christ.

'After this my sense of divine things gradually increased, and became more and more lively, and had more of that inward sweetness. The appearance of everything was altered; there seemed to be, as it were, a calm, sweet cast, or appearance of divine glory, in almost everything. God's excellency, his wisdom, his purity and love, seemed to appear in everything; in the sun, moon, and stars; in the clouds, and blue sky; in the grass, flowers, trees; in the water, and all nature; which used greatly to fix my mind. I often used to sit and view the moon for continuance; and in the day spent much time in viewing the clouds and sky, to behold the sweet glory of God in these things; in the mean time, singing forth, with a low voice my contemplations of the Creator and Redeemer.'

Notice his use of the Song of Songs, his deep appreciation of God in nature, and above all, his delight in Christ. Notice, too, that here there is a meeting point with the Catholic mystics – especially St John of the Cross, whose writings are so steeped in Scripture, especially in the Song of Songs. In their days, neither would have appreciated the traditions of the other, but today the fruit of their adoration is available to help us.

I offer no sample prayers. This steep climb to our own 'Tour du Pin' we must travel in our own way. We will be glad, however, as I was humanly, that others have climbed the path and can help us. We need to travel light, a Bible and a notebook are enough. We go expectantly, we are following St James' 'Come near to God and he will come near to you' (Jas 4:8); we are trusting the psalmist's 'Be still and know that I am God' (Ps 46:10). We are listening to Jesus' 'Abide in me, and I in you' (Jn 15:4, RSV).

It is not a selfish, or spiritually self-indulgent journey, it is important because whatever encounters we are granted will help us in our own intercession, and will transform our prayer life.

Adoration, a response   My mind moves to the deceptively tranquil Zambezi. Giraffes chew the foliage of its island trees, crocodiles lurk in its shadows, hippos wallow, elephants wade across the shallows ... and then, just downstream, the sound is like thunder, waters pour over the Falls, rainbows flicker in the sunlight, and the words of the Song of Songs return, 'Many waters cannot quench love' (Song 8:7).

God, who is love, God whom we try to adore, is far greater than these crashing, cascading waters, and yet he also has a place for each of us. Such love needs a response. Prayers of adoration are the best we can offer. 'How right they are to adore you' (Song 1:4)[16]

Prayers of thanksgiving should be one of the staple diets of our prayer life; praise comes naturally to our lips as we appreciate and remember who God is and what he has done for us; adoration can lift us to the very steps of heaven. We join Paul and Isaiah rejoicing that:

> No eye has seen,
> Nor ear has heard,
> No mind has conceived
> what God has prepared for
> those who love him. (Is 64:4; 1 Cor 2:9)

Notes

1. This version in *Celebrating Common Prayer* (Mowbray, 1994), Pocket Edition, p 237.
2. George Herbert, The Pulley, *The New Oxford Book of Christian Verse,* (OUP, 1981).
3. William Shakespeare, *Romeo and Juliet*, Act III, Scene V.
4. *Oxford Book of Prayer* (OUP, 1985), p 59.
5. *Alternative Service Book* (SPCK, 1980), p 144.
6. W. S. Gilbert, *Princess Ida.*
7. C. S. Lewis, *Reflections on the Psalms* (Collins, 1958), p 77ff.
8. St John's Glastonbury, 2nd & 4th Sundays, in the evening.
9. 'New Wine' Christian Festival held every August on Shepton Mallet showground – details from St Andrew's Chorleywood and Parish Office.
10. Leader of the Vineyard Churches, author of many books.
11. The statement attributed to Queen Elizabeth I puts it perfectly:
    'Twas God the Word that spake it
    He took the bread and brake it
    And what the Word did make it
    That I believe and take it.

The Oxford Dictionary of Quotations (2nd Edition, OUP, 1953), p 197.

12. *Fresh Sounds* (Hodder & Stoughton, 1976), No. 84.

13. From *A choice of George Herbert's verse* (Faber & Faber, 1967), quoting from 'Prayer, the church's banquet', 'Antiophon', and 'Easter'.

14. *Hymns Ancient & Modern Revised,* No. 176, verse 1 (William Clowes).

15. Iain H. Murray, *Jonathan Edwards* (Banner of Faith 1987) p 35.

16. Surprisingly, this appears to be the only use of the word 'adore' in Scripture.

6

Intercession – Faith and Persistence Required

(What on earth am I meant to be praying about?)

This chapter looks at practical answers to prayer, shows that intercession is a very necessary part of our prayer life, and considers the whole question of persistence. We look at some of the 'blocks' to our prayers being answered, and offer some practical help with intercession lists and guidance. We note how praying about something often leads to God showing us what action needs to be taken, and what are to be the priorities in our own prayer life.

Intercession: Faith and Persistence Required

For many people, prayer is just intercession – asking for things. Some people feel guilty about praying for their own needs, some feel disillusioned because their sincere and desperate prayers remain unanswered, others are just bewildered by the vast array of problems and never quite begin.

I begin this chapter with a number of examples with very different outcomes.

A clergyman[1] started to prepare his last sermon. He prayed without great expectation. Tomorrow morning, he would announce his resignation. After all it was pretty absurd to have come as an English missionary in South America, and to have ended up trying to teach a bemused Japanese congregation the ways of high church Anglicanism.

A surprising answer to prayer

Next morning, he started to deliver his message. But different words came, the Holy Spirit took over, and his ministry (and his sermon) were transformed. In addition to the Japanese Anglicans, he found a new vocation among the abandoned street children with the Catholics, and praying for healing and deliverance with the Pentecostals.

For a long time, Joyce and her friends, prayed for her husband Frank to give up smoking. He had a really bad chest, and an unpleasant cough. He became unwell, and struggled to do the work he loved as Verger of our church.

On August 24th, 1995, Frank had a very serious and nasty operation. The surgeon made it clear that smoking *Persistent* would be a great hindrance to his recovery. As he *prayer* started to get over the operation, Frank's desire to *answered* smoke grew. But Joyce and her friends kept battling in prayer. Suddenly, Frank agreed not to smoke. In fact, he hasn't had a cigarette since the operation. For Joyce, it was the answer to a long-awaited prayer, and has helped her greatly through the dark and difficult post-operative days.

On a Sunday morning, Don Latham[2] was preaching in a country parish. He heard the Lord say, 'I want you to give the Vicar a cheque for £63.87p.' Don is a generous *Specific* man, and he's used to these sort of instructions. But he *instructions* queried the curious sum. In the afternoon, he drove over to see the Vicar, and left the cheque on the mantlepiece.

That evening the Vicar rang up to thank him. He said, 'My wife and I were quite desperate. We weren't sure whether we should be doing this job, and we asked the Lord to help – in particular, we asked him to solve the problem of a gas bill that we couldn't afford. Your cheque was for the exact amount.'

The psalmist wrote of a similar experience:

I waited patiently for the LORD; he turned to me and heard my cry.
He lifted me out of the slimy pit, out of the mud and mire; he set my feet on a rock and gave me a firm place to stand.
He put a new song in my mouth, a hymn of praise to our God.
Many will see and fear and put their trust in the Lord. (Ps 40:1-3)

Notice how he writes of his patience, his desperation, and God's answer. The result was a new testimony, a new faith, and a new hope. (Notice, too, that the psalm becomes more difficult as it continues, and although it ends in faith, it passes through quite a struggle after the initial blessing.)

The night of my mother's funeral, I felt quite desolate. I was an only child, and I sensed, all too correctly, that my father wouldn't cope well with the bereavement. She was only fifty- *A word from* seven, and had taken the risky (but I believe correct *the Bible* course) of an early heart operation. Her prospects without it were a slow and certain decay, but with new valves she could live a normal life. Anyway, the result was unsuccessful. I opened the Bible and read:

> Jesus saw that they wanted to ask him about this, so he said to them, 'Are you asking one another what I meant when I said, "In a little while you will see me no more, and then after a little while you will see me"? I tell you the truth, you will weep and mourn while the world rejoices. You will grieve, but your grief will turn to joy.' (Jn 16: 19,20).

It was just the word that I needed. Then I noticed the next verse. A somewhat lonely, unmarried schoolteacher, I had just fallen in love. Very uncharacteristically, I'd taken my new girl friend to meet my mother in hospital. The meeting had made my mother very happy.

> A woman giving birth to a child has pain because her time has come; but when her baby is born she forgets the anguish because of her joy that a child is born into the world.

It seemed like a promise from the Lord, that one day (and because of various circumstances I knew that one day meant about five years' time) we would be married. I fell asleep much happier.

Shortly afterwards, starting at theological college, I received a letter from a close relative. It contained the memorable line, 'I can't think why you're getting ordained. Your prayer didn't do your mother much good.' I laughed. Perhaps, without the experience on the night of her funeral, I would have crumpled.

Now, I know, that many people reading these stories, and hearing other far more dramatic ones, may say something like this: 'It's all very well, I know it works sometimes and for some people, but it didn't work for me.'

This causes great pain, and the temptation is to give up on intercession, and turn to other forms of prayer. But God does meet our prayers, and the desperate prayers of others. When he says 'No' there is a reason. As we saw in the opening chapter, we have to live with the paradox and the promise.

Intercession is for beginners and fools?

There is a rather lofty view expressed sometimes from the high up mountains of contemplative prayer, that intercession is either selfish ('We shouldn't pray for our little concerns'), or pointless ('God knows anyway') or a distraction from the real work of prayer ('God's changing our characters, not giving us presents'). There is a rather lowly view expressed sometimes from the trials and disappointments of the spiritual bog that intercession is a waste of time (God didn't answer me).

Neither view is scriptural, neither view is experiential, neither view is prepared to take the risk of learning in the hard school of intercession. Intercession is certainly for beginners! Jesus said 'Let the little children come to me, and do not hinder them, for the kingdom of *Intercession is a vital part of prayer* God belongs to such as these. I tell you the truth, anyone who will not receive the kingdom of God like a little child will never enter it.' (Mk 10:14,15)

Little children, and older ones (!) often ask for things. It's part of growing up. Parents are often delighted to respond, even if sometimes there has to be a little teaching as to why something is inappropriate, unaffordable, or just 'not on'. God wants us to ask. Listen again to Jesus (to quote just three of many such sayings):

> So I say to you: Ask and it will be given to you; seek and you will find; knock and the door will be opened to you. For everyone who asks receives; he who seeks finds; and to him who knocks, the door will be opened. (Lk 11:9-10)

> Until now you have not asked for anything in my name. Ask and you will receive, and your joy will be complete. (Jn 16:24)

> Give us each day our daily bread. (Lk 11:3)

'Give us each day our daily bread'. Oscar Cullmann[3] discusses the meaning of this petition. Eventually, following the teaching of most of the great Reformers (particularly Luther and Calvin, etc) he decides that this is a practical petition, praying literally for tomorrow's bread. Practical necessities can, and should, be prayed for.

The previous petition, 'Your kingdom come', by contrast, is a direct spiritual prayer. It opens the gateway to all sorts of ministry. We shall discuss this more fully in Chapters 9 and 10.

Such prayers can sound quite foolish. But as St Paul says, we are called to be fools for Christ's sake. (See 1 Cor 4:10 and 3:18).

Perhaps the most 'foolish' church notice that I ever heard was given, with due solemnity, by a Zambian churchwarden at the end of two days of teaching on the Holy Spirit: 'Tomorrow,

An unusual gentlemen, we will see signs and wonders.'
church notice I was working with my friend, Peter Hancock, on my first SOMA trip. We had arrived, with some difficulty, after travelling through a dangerous corridor in Zaire, at the Chipili Mission Station in North Zambia. We shared a house with vast spiders, a scorpion, and the ceiling had gaping holes in which we suspected, quite correctly, that snakes could live.

Was the notice presumptuous, or a word of prophetic faith? The next day we knew. Hundreds of people flocked into the old mission church. They surged forward for prayer. We split into four teams led by Peter, Archdeacon Tobias (see Chapter 3, p 52), and the local priest, Isaiah Chabala, and myself. What really surprised us all was the extraordinary reaction when we began to pray. Many crashed to the floor – shaking, screaming, even hissing, or moving like a snake. With four teams praying in quite a small area, there was pandemonium. Yet, beneath it all, there

Kingdom was great calm. People went away smiling, feeling
experience physically better, and spiritually free. Many seemed to be healed, many released from evil spirits, others were filled with the Holy Spirit in a new way, and some professed conversion.

I survived four hours of prayer, standing, despite a bad hip in urgent need of replacement. Our prayers were simple and direct. Mine must have been strengthened by the intercessions of my home parish for my own suspect health and physical strength.

Towards the end of the exhausting morning, the locals said, 'There's a man in the gallery who needs prayer'. I declined to climb the rickety stairway, and asked him to be brought down. I was feeling very tired, and as he approached, he seemed to get larger and larger. He looked pretty fierce.

Something within me said, 'Ask if his father or grandfather has been a witchdoctor.' I felt pretty foolish. There was a sort of snarled 'Yes'. I made the sign of the cross, and prayed aloud to cut off the power of his ancestors from him. As he was advancing close to me, he crashed to the ground. A few minutes later, he got up quite well. We all felt that we had experienced an answer to the petition 'Your kingdom come'.

The work continued to several days. The Sunday morning service began twenty minutes early (in Africa!!) because the church was full. It began at 9.40 and we didn't finish praying with people until nearly 3 p.m. Even then the work wasn't finished. One of the local leaders, Jason Mfula, a former Zambian diplomatic head in Australia, who had returned to retire in his home village, said, 'You have taught us about the water of the Spirit – now we need practical running water.' We spent the rest of the day discussing Chipili's run down water system. Over the next few years we were *Practical matters as well as spiritual* involved in many improvements. Not exactly 'daily bread', but something even more basic and practical for the mission station.

Perhaps the most important part of the whole experience was that it helped to raise everyone's level of faith. The local leaders were greatly encouraged, they were involved in the prayer, they could continue to pray for others long after we had left.

Watchman Nee[5] tells an even more dramatic story. He was trying to evangelise a Chinese offshore island. The locals were quite uninterested. 'We worship Ta Wang and it is his festival in a week's time on January 11th.' A young member of the team, Brother Wu said, 'I promise you that it will certainly rain on the 11th'. Everyone laughed. The Christians retreated. Had the young man spoken out of turn? Had they been presumptuous? Or had they spoken as 'fools'?

As they prayed, they received the word, 'Where is the God of Elijah?' (see James 5:17, 18, and also the discussion in Chapter 2 p 33). They felt they shouldn't pray any more, but continue to preach. The weather remained very fine. 'No stir in the air, no stir

A miracle leads to many conversions
in the sea'.[6] Ta Wang's diviners knew about the weather! On the morning of the festival, Watchman Nee and his team got up very early to pray. They felt that they could now remind the Lord of his promise. Very quickly it started to rain, then it poured. They found the luckless statue of Ta Wang and his followers floating down the street. Many were converted. Ta Wang's power was broken.

Many years later, Watchman Nee was in an aeroplane. He recognised the pilot, Brother Wu, the young evangelist who had made the 'foolish' remarks about the weather. He asked him if he still followed the Lord. 'Mr Nee!' he said, 'do you mean to say that after all we went through I could ever forsake him?'

And that is the beauty of foolish prayers; when God answers them we, like Brother Wu, should never forget.

A similar example of direct divine intervention is provided by the Victorian missionary to the New Hebrides, John Paton.[7] In 1862, after a few years of dangerous ministry amidst the cannibals on the Island of Tanna, he, and two other missionaries, Mr and Mrs Mathieson, were under attack. A group of natives, armed with clubs, had set fire to the fence surrounding the mission house. John went out, taking an unloaded revolver, to confront them and to beat out the flames. He was surrounded by a group of natives, none of whom dared to strike the first blow. His friends remained inside, deep in prayer.

He said, 'Dare to strike me, and my Jehovah God will punish you! He protects us, and will punish you for burning his church, for hatred to his worship and people, and for all your bad conduct. We love you; and for doing you good you want to kill us. But our God is here now to protect us and punish you.'

In the midst of all this, there was a mighty roar. Every head turned, and they all knew a tornado was coming. First wind, which drove the flames away from the mission house, and then torrential rain which put them out.

The natives fled in terror, John Paton returned to the mission hut, and his companions said, 'If ever in time of need God sent help and protection to his servants in answer to prayer, he has done so tonight!'

The next morning, they were still in great danger. Friends

warned them that an attack was about to be mounted. Then a second providential event occurred. A sail was spotted, a rare event indeed, and a ship came to rescue them. John and his friends left Tanna. Soon afterwards he returned to the nearby island of Aneityum, where his ministry bore much fruit for the next twenty-five years.

If we are presumptuous, and sometimes we are, God will let us know. We shall have no peace, and we shall have no answers. But if you've made that mistake (and all of us who take risks in our praying have), take heart – God will teach you through the experience. Long ago I didn't learn to ride a bicycle by reading books, or by polishing it in the garage, I learnt by falling off and getting up!

Once I felt I deserved a sabbatical. I filled in the form, and produced a wonderful sophisticated scheme for comparing the effectiveness of evangelism and social action by the Anglican Church in Zambia and Kenya. It sounded wonderful, but the Bishop thought otherwise. The next year I repeated the application, and again the Bishop said 'No'. I gave up and tried instead to change jobs. Two years later, as part of showing me that he didn't want me to move, the Lord suggested a very different, less spectacular, more restful sabbatical – and the Bishop agreed! None of us is very good at submitting to authority, yet I've had to admit that on this occasion authority was completely right! The first plan would have been a complicated disaster, the second seemed to be a real learning and refreshing experience!

'No' can be the right answer

Persistent prayers

Thus far, we have considered the relatively easy side of intercession – desperate circumstances requiring urgent prayer. But the far more normal situation is that we find ourselves praying about the same situation time and time again – a husband praying for his unbelieving wife, a mother for her son, a friend who constantly relapses into depression, a couple consistently on the edge of marital breakup, warring partners within a small church, an unemployed man who needs a job … the list is endless.

One question that I am asked regularly is, 'Do I go on and on praying about this particular situation?'

Jesus had one of his hilarious stories about this (see Lk 18:1-8). The judge comes out as a ridiculous figure, the widow as a little old lady who, as such people often do, gets her own way. But the punch line of the story is quite a surprise. It is not only about persistence, but also about faith: 'However, when the Son of Man comes, will he find faith on the earth?' The widow needed faith that her case would be heard; Jesus is challenging our faith.

Persistence and faith are linked

Do we believe that the person or the situation about which we are praying will change? What is God's will in the situation? Is there any particular biblical teaching to give us hope or encouragement?

Although each situation is unique, there seem to be a number of general guidelines which are worth considering, not least because we have only a limited amount of time for prayer. If we waste this precious time praying for the wrong things, we shall be discouraged and have less time to pray for what God really wants us to pray about.

Road blocked

In Chapter 4, we considered how the powers of evil attempt to block God's purpose (see also 1 Thess 2:18). In the next chapter we shall consider how our unwillingness to forgive can block our prayers. Here we consider a different problem – are there situations where it is improper for us to pray?

I think there are; let me illustrate. A Christian leader, in the midst of what he perceives as a difficult and unsympathetic marriage, leaves home, taking with him a member of his congregation. Sadly, an all too familiar tale in today's church. How should the church pray? In one sense, it is already too late. It is difficult enough to pray for a crumbling marriage; it is hard to pray for forgiveness after an adulterous relationship has been established; it seems impossible once the new couple have set up home together. The couple, hurt by their previous marriages, and what they see as the rejection of their former friends in their church, are defiantly hardened in their

A time not to pray?

new relationship, which is all they have left to cling to.

Can we pray? Jesus, when sending out the seventy, had some tough things to say, including:

'He who listens to you listens to me; he who rejects you rejects me; but he who rejects me rejects him who sent me' (Lk 10:16), and earlier, in Luke 10:10,11: 'But when you enter a town and are not welcomed, go into its streets and say, "Even the dust of your town that sticks to our feet we will wipe off against you. Yet be sure of this: The kingdom of God is near."'

Obviously, this is in the context of evangelism, but the same principle applies to prayer. There are some situations which we should leave alone. They are God's business, not ours. Other people may eventually be able to help the couple, we cannot say what is unforgivable, but we can recognise that they have excluded themselves from their original church, and our prayers must be elsewhere – not least with the families and children left behind. Under God's sovereign grace everything may change, but the basic situation seems totally blocked as far as our prayers are concerned.

Of course, there are other sorts of block. A young man in our church feels called to ordination. He has had this 'call' for many years. He is proving himself as a church leader and in a difficult secular job. Many people support his application in prayer. They are all disappointed and hurt when a church selection conference rejects him.

With hindsight (or even foresight), it becomes obvious that God's timing was different from ours. The man was not yet ready, there was too much to be learnt, not least from the pain of rejection. Two years later, and much more spiritually *A time to* matured, he goes forward and is accepted. On this occasion, *accept a* the original prayers of his church and friends were blocked *difficult* when the wider church discerned, almost certainly *decision* correctly, what was perceived to be the will of God.

Five Christian candidates are shortlisted for an important job. They all have good track records, all feel a measure of 'call' to the job, all have prayed about it; yet, obviously, only one can be chosen. (Many are called, but few are chosen – Mt 22:14). The other four have to pick up the pieces and try to discern what next.

God cannot answer, positively, the prayers of all five. Four are going to have to learn from God's No!

Eventual joy

Persistent prayers do get answered. A couple left a church. It was a great sorrow to the minister – they had been, humanly, one of the many reasons why he had accepted the job. They joined another Christian group, and although they were happy, one member of their former church was sure they had taken a wrong decision. This faithful member prayed for and befriended the couple. After many years, the group they had joined lost their direction, and they rejoined their original flock, curiously strengthened by their circuitous spiritual journey. Without the prayers and friendship of the one, it is highly unlikely that this could have happened.

Persistent prayer brings fruit

A young man, living in our town, is suddenly converted. He had a church allegiance in childhood, now he is brought to a real point of faith and commitment. He has great gifts, and many people prayed for his conversion. But there are two problems – his wife is not a Christian, indeed she is increasingly hostile to his conversion. Also, they are childless, struggling with adoption procedures. His faith progresses. Eventually, they adopt their first child. Even the wife sees some higher hand in that. Reluctantly, she goes with her husband to a Christian residential conference called Spring Harvest. For her it's a holiday. To her surprise, she is drawn to some of the main meetings. To her astonishment, she, faced with the awesome choice of continuing to reject Christ, or seeking change, is converted. A very short time afterwards, she finds that she is pregnant. A colleague, of a very New Age outlook, hearing of this asks, 'Has anything strange happened to you recently?' 'Yes,' she replies, 'I became a Christian.' (Obviously, things don't always work out like that. I have a number of very committed Christians who have been unable to have children. It is one of the hardest 'No's' to receive – even worse in Africa where the 'disgrace' can lead to a wife being divorced.)

What made the wall fall down?

Persistence is particularly required in more weighty matters.

Patricia St John[8] tells the story of Lilias Trotter, who could have been a brilliant artist, but who felt called (much to the great art critic John Ruskin's disappointment) to give up painting as a career and become a missionary in Algeria.

A parable about persistent prayer

It was very hard work and she, who had loved beauty so much, started her life abroad in the slums and alleys of a large town. But she travelled too, and loved the great spaces of the Sahara and often painted desert scenes. Over her bed hung a map of North Africa and she would spend many hours kneeling in front of it praying for the scattered towns and villages of Algeria.

Only a very few people listened to her message of the gospel and sometimes she was tempted to ask, 'What is the good of praying? God does not seem to be answering and so few are coming to believe in Christ!' But one day something happened that taught her to keep on praying, because prayer is never wasted.

She was sleeping very early one morning in the house in the crowded alley when suddenly, without the slightest warning, the wall between her house and the next fell in with a crash. Mercifully, she was not hit, but her room was littered with dust and lath and plaster and she found herself staring into the narrow passage that divided her home from the baker's shop next door. She could not understand it for she had seen no crack in the wall. But she sent for the local builder and asked him to rebuild the wall and also to try and discover the cause of the collapse.

The builder, who was also something of an architect, took a good look at the damage and then went for a stroll outside; he came back quite excited. 'I have found the cause,' he said, 'I will tell you truly why your wall fell.' He explained that under the baker's shop was a sort of stone cellar with an oven and a see-saw like machine for kneading the bread. Every night the baker set this machine in motion and for over twenty years the nightly vibrations had shaken and weakened her wall, until that fateful early morning when the last vibration had done its work and the wall collapsed.

So the wall was rebuilt and the neighbourhood was most sympathetic and, no doubt, urged her to sue the baker, but Lilias did not regret the incident for it had taught her something important. She realised that her prayers had not been wasted. She was working in a stronghold of sin and suffering, but great wars are not won in a day. They are won inch by inch and blow by blow. Just as every vibration had weakened her wall, so every prayer prayed in the name of Jesus was weakening the stronghold, and she and others with her went on praying daily. For they knew that one day, if they persevered and believed and endured, the fortress would fall.

I remember visiting St Michael le Belfry, York, in 1975 for one of their Renewal Conferences for church leaders. It was a wonderful experience, and great to meet David Watson, his family, and the other leaders. The most surprising evening for me was when one of them announced to a gathering of about 500 – 'We're going to intercede tonight – for the Soviet Union.'

Persistent praying for political situations   For over half an hour, a large congregation, probably expecting a 'bless up' and manifestations of 'gifts of the Spirit', prayed for Russia. It was deeply moving. I don't suppose many of us really expected that within twenty years the mighty Soviet Empire would have fallen, and that Christians would be free to worship in the streets of Moscow. Obviously, the overall results of the collapse of the Soviet Union have been very mixed. But at least there is a spritual freedom and real elections take place.

I am not suggesting that half an hour's prayer caused this. What I am suggesting is that the persistent prayers of many millions of people over many years made the wall (the Iron Curtain) fall down. The fact that there were many faithful Christians, suffering for their faith within the Soviet Empire, must have made an incalculable difference. How much harder, say, to pray for all those who suffer under Iraq's brutal dictatorship.

Once again, we may not understand, we may not even have great faith, but Scripture calls us to pray: 'I urge, then, first of all, that requests, prayers, intercession and thanksgiving be made for everyone – for kings and all those in authority, that we may live peaceful and quiet lives in all godliness and holiness' (1 Tim 2:1,2). The emphasis here is for rulers to enable people to live quiet and peaceful lives. If that is not possible, and sadly it isn't in many countries, then the words of Revelation 13 may be more appropriate. Here the godless state (contrast Rom 13:1-7) is seen as demonic, and Christians need patient endurance and faithfulness (Rev 13:10) under extreme circumstances. The tremendous sacrifice of prayer offered for South Africa (see Chapter 2) bears witness to the importance of praying about national matters.

A question of faith

As we have seen, particularly in the parable of the unjust judge, Jesus valued faith greatly. Indeed we might say without exaggeration that faith is to prayer what love is to service. We shall examine this question of faith under a number of headings – intercession lists, guidance, faith that leads to action. The issue of faith will be central to Chapters 8 – 10 when we consider 'praying for the kingdom'.

Intercession lists (in churches)

Some people in our parish used to regard being on the Parish Intercession List as a sort of advance death notice. What are the purposes of such lists, and do they serve any useful purposes?

In our church, they form guidelines as to what might be publicly prayed for each week. They will include national and international matters. They will include parish matters, missionary links, the sick, those in old people's homes, and the families recently bereaved. While I'm away, I know that the parish will pray for me and my family, and I'm grateful for that, as I was during my times in Zambia. Provided there is a certain amount of spontaneity – ensured by having enough people to lead the prayers that each one only does it a few times a year; provided there are praying people available for *Intercession in public* more personal needs and intercessions; provided there is some openness to the Holy Spirit leading us in a completely different direction (for instance in response to a sermon on the Holy Spirit – it might be appropriate to scrap the intercessions and to wait in silence), the (dreaded) intercession list can become an aid to better prayer and help the congregation to remember, and to continue to pray for, certain key issues and people.

Intercession lists (for private prayer)

Most of us find it hard to intercede for any length of time. There are some notable exceptions. A friend of mine was greatly influenced at school by the preaching of a well-known evangelical clergyman, a busy man with a worldwide ministry and author of many books. After my friend's conversion some years later at university, he wrote to thank the clergyman for the human part he had played. He was pleasantly surprised to get a reply, and even more by its contents: 'I have been praying for you ever since I visited your school, I remember you well.' Such faithful praying care puts most of us, much less busy people, to shame.

Intercession in private

I believe we'd all intercede a great deal more if we organised our intercessions. I find a sort of 6 x 4 matrix helpful – in other words, different people on each of the weekdays under, perhaps, four different headings (e.g. Monday – wife, wherever I am staying and/or have stayed recently, writing, children's godparents; Tuesday – eldest daughter, principal church that I'm involved with, godchildren, pastoral contacts; Wednesday – second daughter, my second church, marriages (especially those in trouble), Zambia and other overseas links; Thursday – my son, my third church, the sick, Kenya (especially mother-in-law's project); Friday – my youngest daughter, missionaries, evangelism (especially Alpha courses), preparation; Saturday – the family and their friends, the Diocese, Training in the parish, the local town. There's nothing very special, or exhaustive, about this list. It needs constant change, but it does ensure that a large number of people should be prayed for in the course of a week.

A very interesting idea for intercessory prayer was sent to me by Caroline, a long-standing friend who suffers from multiple sclerosis, and seems to use much of her time and energy in prayer. She wrote, 'My friend Tom was dying; I was sure he had not been much of a praying man. Praying was something I could do for him. I prayed the Lord's Prayer for Tom:

Father in Heaven, hallowed be your name for Tom.
Your kingdom come for Tom. Your will (not mine) for Tom be done,
on earth as it is in heaven. Give Tom today his daily bread, and forgive
him his sins as he forgives those who sin against him. Save Tom from
this time of trial and deliver him from evil.

Faithful prayer will often lead to action. If I pray for someone, I
may need to visit them, I may need to write to them, I might need
to send someone a gift ('missionaries' reminded me of a promise
made to my eldest daughter to send a small gift to one of her
Youth With A Mission friends overseas).

Faith that leads to action

What good is it, my brothers, if a man claims to have faith but has no
deeds? Can such faith save him? Suppose a brother or sister is without
clothes and daily food. If one of you says to him, 'Go, I wish you well,
keep warm and well fed', but does nothing about his physical needs,
what good is it? In the same way, faith by itself, if it is not
accompanied by action, is dead. (Jas 2:14-17)

The Revd Geoffrey Raymond and his wife, Kathleen, bought a
small house in Shepton Mallet. It was, they thought, to be a
'bargaining counter' for a retirement house elsewhere. They liked
Shepton and felt called to retire there. For a long time we had
been praying about the problem of the young homeless. Even in a
small rural town in the late 1980's, teenagers were sleeping
rough. Inevitably, a committee was formed. (I have a poster that a
parishioner gave me for Christmas. 'God so loved the world that
he didn't send a committee'.) After many years of patient
preparation, Geoffrey became its chairman in the autumn of
1991. A critical stage had been reached. A suitable *God inspires*
house had been found, but the partnership with English *action*
Churches' Housing Group was not yet cemented.
There was little money, and even less certainty of more to come.
In faith, Geoffrey prayed and acted. He authorised the putting
down of the deposit on what was to be Grace Harris House.[9] The
project took off, a partnership was formed, financial support
(much from the oft-maligned official sources of government and
local councils) came in.

Soon after, in February 1992, Geoffrey died quite suddenly. Kathleen has stayed in Shepton, remaining a much-valued Reader and member of our congregation. Geoffrey's faith made his sudden death very hard to understand. But we cannot legislate for these matters; what we do know is that God greatly blessed his decision to settle in Shepton and his great act of faith on behalf of the homeless young people of the surrounding area.

Preservation, or otherwise, from death and serious accident is an awesome mystery. The early church faced the paradox of the untimely death of James (Acts 12:2), and miraculous preservation of Peter. They presumably prayed for both leaders.

A few years ago TEAR Fund faced the great blow of the death of George Hoffmann, their former leader. Such tragedies are not uncommon in the dangerous and hectic lives that those in front line mission work lead.

A year before Geoffrey died, we lost another valued retired clergyman, Gordon. Gordon had for a number of years done an amazing amount of work, particularly amongst the elderly, the mentally handicapped, and the dying. He had been amazingly preserved in a terrible motor cycle accident years earlier; but even so, we all felt his relatively early death very deeply.

The courage to do nothing and to do it well

The House of Peers throughout the war
did nothing in particular, and did it very well.[10]

This little couplet, apparently, so infuriated Queen Victoria that it cost W. S. Gilbert his knighthood until after she had died. But there are times when we pray and God says 'do nothing'.

Some time ago, a great friend rang up in some distress. There had been a spiritual spat in his church. It was all very trivial, but it could have led to a serious breakdown of relationships. I listened, and asked him to do something quite difficult: to go and apologise (it really didn't seem to be his fault – but it seemed to be the best way forward). We prayed over the phone. I was tempted to race up the hill and sort the matter out. God said, 'do nothing – wait'. A few minutes later, my friend rang up. The other party had already rung up, apologised, and the matter was sorted out.

It is very hard to do nothing, but there are times when we just have to leave people to sort themselves out with the Lord. If people storm out of church, it doesn't usually help to follow them. (Obviously, if they are tearful, they may need a compassionate ear). If people have wronged you, it seldom is right to go and confront them. In due course, maybe, but not as soon as it has happened.

Guidance: faith or wishful thinking?

Guidance is a key subject for our prayers. Many wonderful stories can be told of God's gracious directing. Before we look at a few of these, two preliminary thoughts.

There are, I believe, many situations where God leaves us to choose. We have the mind of Christ (1 Cor 2:16), and we need to believe that! An important text illustrates this:

> O people of Zion, who live in Jerusalem, you will weep no more. How gracious he will be when you cry for help! As soon as he hears, he will answer you. Although the LORD gives you the bread of adversity and the water of affliction, your teachers will be hidden no more; with your own eyes you will see them. Whether you turn to the right or to the left, your ears will hear a voice behind you, saying, 'This is the way; walk in it.' (Is 30:19-21)

Whether we turn to the right or to the left, we will hear God's voice. In other words, even if God doesn't make a particular path clear, we may walk down it trusting that if it is not God's will, he will block it. This takes the sting out of many situations: it allows us to use our spiritual common sense (Rom 12:1,2); it allows us to listen to our friends; and it helps us mature spiritually – it is a matter of faith.

Guidance – God says you choose!

If we are spending a reasonable time in quiet contemplative prayer, we are likely to make the right decisions by spiritual instinct. If we are rushing about without stopping to pray, then we shouldn't be surprised if we take a lot of wrong turnings and make a lot of mistakes.

Wishful thinking?

It is all too easy to try and manipulate guidance. David Prior[11] has a good example of that. He describes how he decided if a certain run of traffic lights were all green, that he would propose to a certain young lady. They were! As he writes, 'Probably, unconsciously, I drove at a convenient speed. The end result was near disaster. But, mercifully, a mistaken engagement didn't last long.'

A potential church organist was very hurt when I didn't offer her the job. She wrote an aggrieved letter saying, 'The Lord has told me to come.' It was the old problem – the Lord hadn't told me! As each journey to the church would have involved a forty mile round trip, common sense seemed to indicate that the answer was no!

Sometimes seemingly unsuitable people put themselves forward for work in the church – part of a prayer team, reader, churchwarden, ordained… It requires great courage to say a gentle, but firm No (never without consulting other leaders). It also requires great courage to support an unlikely candidate and to admit that your first judgement has been wrong.

The apostolic church was reduced to drawing lots on one occasion (Acts 1:23ff). I hope that with sufficient prayer and charity, we may be able to come to the right decisions. it is a great measure of grace when people accept an initial No. I've known a number of outstanding leaders who have overcome this initial rejection.

A very difficult area, which we shall discuss in Chapter 9, is the matter of guidance when faced with terminal illness. Wishful thinking, expecting a miracle, can destroy a lot of peace of mind; yet we, of all people, must realise that God does change even the most pessimistic prognosis.

Learn from each situation and don't give up

A clergyman I knew well was convinced that a young priest and a certain young lady ought to marry. He had pushed his case rather hard, but the potential couple had split up. He preached a sermon on Romans 4, especially verse 18. 'Against all hope, Abraham in hope believed.' The young priest was present and was not pleased when the elderly clergyman told him that this text applied to his broken relationship. He was just getting over it, and it was the last thing that he wished to hear. It sounded like a typical piece of wishful thinking.

The safest means of guidance are the principles of Scripture, and sometimes particular texts, the searchings of the heart in prayer, the advice of praying friends (especially those *disinterested* in your decision), and occasionally signs from nature, special revelations of one sort or another.

As I look back over a very ordinary twenty-five years as a priest, and rather longer as a Christian, I am amazed by God's kindness in his guidance. My first 'issue' was whether to try, the following term, to start a small Bible study group in the school where I was teaching. I had been rather influenced by David Wilkerson's first book,[12] and was looking for a 'sign'. I prayed that if God wanted me to begin this (risky) venture, he would show me whom to ask. He seemed to say that there was one key pupil, and that I'd meet him at the early Communion in the Chantry Chapel at 7.30 a.m. on Thursday.

When I woke up at 7.25 a.m. I remember saying, 'Sorry, Lord, that's blown it!' Somehow a whirlwind ejected me from bed, and got me to church, somewhat unkempt, a few minutes late. You can imagine my surprise when I noticed amid a small congregation of about fifteen people, about six members of staff, eight boys who were about to leave, and the boy I'd been told would be there.

We did begin a small group, and it proved the way for something much larger in the future.

The next great 'issue' was ordination. I'd prayed (under pressure from my chief spiritual director, the late Canon Keith de Berry, then Rector of St Aldate's Oxford) for a year – with singularly little response. At the end of the summer term in 1967, I said to the Lord as I closed my Bible, 'You'd better make it clear – if you want me to be ordained.' A few weeks later, on holiday, I spent a grim Saturday night. I had got into a romantic tangle, and the Lord seemed to speak very clearly: (1) Wrong girl – wait! (2) Wrong career – change! (3) 'I will show you *A personal* my loving kindness in the morning' (Ps 143:8 *testimony* approximately). I could have easily talked my way out of all that as sheer emotionalism; the trouble was the next morning three things happened. First, we sang Psalm 143; secondly, the preacher (it was August 6th, the Feast of the Transfiguration) challenged us with the somewhat untheological words, 'When Jesus came down the mountain, humanly he had a choice. He could go back to Galilee as a fairly successful minor prophet, or he could do what he was called to do – go on to Jerusalem. Some of you have to make that choice. You can stay where you are, fairly successfully, or you can go on to what God is calling you to do, which will be much harder!' Thirdly, I felt overwhelmed by the Holy Spirit. I knew that this was it. I'd asked for guidance, and I'd been given it.

I mentioned earlier the help received on the night of my mother's funeral. The next 'crisis' was the matter of the gifts of the Spirit. One evening, the night before my 31st birthday, I entertained Canon Tom Smail[13] to supper. He had spoken to the slowly burgeoning Christian group on charismatic matters. I asked him to pray for me. Nothing outward happened. Tom was very kind and sensible. He asked me about one very personal, and rather painful relationship. We prayed, and he left.

The next day I received an unexpected birthday present, and an even more unexpected letter – the most surprising and important letter that I've ever received. It seemed quite a confirmation of Tom's ministry the night before. The broken relationship could be repaired. Once again 'Sorrow was turning to joy!' And the old clergyman's interpretation of Romans 4:18 proved to be correct!

I could go on, but I think it would be inappropriate. Suffice to say that at key times God has greatly guided me in the matters of healing, deliverance ministry, choice of job, overseas missions, being turned down for jobs, and not least from a friend who gave us a wonderful prophecy over the telephone which confirmed our call to Shepton Mallet in 1982. When I consulted him later about a possible move, he came back a few days later and said, 'I haven't got anything to say.' Like the dog that did nothing in the nightime,[14] this was probably the most significant piece of guidance throughout a disappointing experience.

Frequently, God has used other people, and their gifts, to help me. Similarly, from time to time God has given me insights which hopefully have helped other people. The biggest block to giving guidance is to assume an air of infallibility. All guidance needs testing.

Who should I be praying for?

'All the world's a stage, and all the men and women merely players'.[15] We can't pray for everyone and everything. God will put certain people on your heart, and certain causes. One member of our congregation (see Chapter 5) has a great burden of prayer for Northern Ireland. It has led her already to make two difficult visits. At the end of 1995, she became quite ill. Eventually, I rather shocked her by telling her to release, for a while, the burden of intercession for Northern Ireland. Temporarily, the battle had been too much. Others in the parish, and elsewhere (!) could carry the prayer baton.

One lady, who lives nearby, had a great concern because a particular organisation was holding a service in her parish church. She stood outside the church with a friend praying against this group. For several days, she felt very ill. It was a battle that the Lord had not commanded her to take on! Later, she felt very concerned at some disastrous goings on at her influential place of work. Rightly, in my judgement, this has become a major matter for her prayer life.

Share the burden of prayer

Intercession is never easy. If it has become boring, then you are going about it the wrong way. Like many things in life, we have to ring the changes; but above all, we need to 'approach the throne of grace with confidence, so that we may receive mercy and find grace to help us in our time of need' (Heb 4:16) and to learn, with Paul, what it means to 'pray in the Spirit on all occasions with all kinds of prayers and requests. With this in mind, be alert and always keep on praying for all the saints' (Eph 6:18). That is a sound basis for intercession that is scriptural, effective, and imaginative.

The beauty and wonder of intercessory prayer is that we often don't know when it is proving most effective. Two years after the Chipili visit, I returned to Zambia leading another SOMA team. Friends, particularly in Glastonbury, covered our visit with prayer. One day, they felt a great darkness and a great need to pray for our protection. It turned out to be the first day we were preaching at Mutwe Wa Nkoko (see Chapter 3). The next day, the Zambian lady saw the angel, and everything changed.

Intercession is, I believe, the staple food of prayer. We shall see so many encouragements as we persist in this form of prayer; like Lilias Trotter and her fallen wall, we shall participate in many spiritual battles whose importance may well remain hidden during our earthly life.

Notes

1. A leading USPG missionary told this story, of himself, at a Shepton Mallet missionary evening in November 1990.
2. Don Latham, then Chairman of West Wiltshire District Council, is a frequent speaker at Full Gospel Businessmen's International meetings, and in churches.
3. Oscar Cullmann, *Prayer in the New Testament* (SCM 1995) p 51.
4. Peter Hancock, at that time Diocesan Healing Advisor for Bath & Wells Diocese.
5. Watchman Nee, *Sit, Walk, Stand* (Kingsway, 1962), p 57ff.
6. Robert Southey, *The Inchcape Rock.*
7. John Paton, *Missionary to the New Hebrides* (Hodder & Stoughton, 1893), Part 1, p 347.
8. Patricia St John, *Would you believe it?* (Pickering & Inglis 1983), p 100.
9. Grace Harris House (see also Chapter 9).
10. W. S. Gilbert, *Iolanthe.*
11. David Prior, *Living by Faith (Abraham)* (Hodder & Stoughton, 1986), p 36.
12. David Wilkerson, *The Cross & The Switchblade* (Lakeland Publishers, 1964).
13. Canon Tom Smail, one time leader of the Fountain Trust, author of many books.
14. Conan Doyle, *The Silver Blaze* from *Memoirs of Sherlock Holmes.*
15. William Shakespeare *As You Like It.*

7

Forgiveness – to be Received
and to be Given

(How do I forgive the man who stole my wife?)

In this chapter, we look at the real difficulty that we experience when trying to forgive those who have hurt us. We look at Jesus' teaching on prayer and forgiveness. We discover that receiving forgiveness is the gateway to forgiving others and accepting oneself. We look at the deep inward work of the Holy Spirit who enables us, like Jesus, to pray 'Abba, Father'.

Forgiveness – to be Received and to be Given

We find the whole question of forgiveness incredibly difficult. Despite much teaching from Jesus, we find it desperately hard to forgive others, and we find it hard to ask to receive God's forgiveness. When we are forgiven, we find it hard to believe, and frequently need reassurance that it has really happened.

The unforgiving civil servant[1]

Lord Egremont, one time private secretary to Prime Minister Harold Macmillan, noticed a fellow civil servant looking unusually anxious. He asked him what the trouble was. The man explained that at school, in Winchester, he had been very badly bullied. Known to suffer from claustrophobia, his chief tormentor had even shut him up in a trunk. His old enemy, now a clergyman, had written to him. The cleric was dying of cancer, and wished to put his earthly affairs right. He wrote to Hancock, the civil servant, asking for forgiveness. The civil servant, a fearfully upright and honest man, went through agonies. Eventually he sent his old adversary a brief telegram. 'Sorry – cannot forgive. Hancock.'

The unforgiving martyr[2]

Sulpicius, a Presbyter of Antioch, was arrested and brought before the Imperial Legate, who asked him, 'Of what family art thou?'

Forgiveness can seem too hard

   'I am a Christian.'

   'Know that all who call themselves Christians will be put to the torture unless they sacrifice to the immortal gods.'

   'We Christians,' answered Sulpicius, 'have for our King Christ, who is also God.'

   He was then tortured and led away to be beheaded. As he was on his way to execution, a Christian called Nicephorus rushed forward, and fell at his feet. Between him and Sulpicius there had been a bitter quarrel, and Nicephorus felt that he must win his forgiveness while there was yet time.

   'Martyr of Christ,' he cried, 'forgive me for I have wronged thee.'

   Sulpicius did not reply, and even at the place of execution maintained the same silence. Then followed a scene which struck the beholders with astonishment and the Christians with awe.

   Sulpicius, who had not flinched under torture, was seen to be growing paler as he was told to kneel down under the sword of the executioner. 'Do not strike me!' he cried. 'I will obey the Emperor, I *will* sacrifice to the gods.'

   Once more Nicephorus rushed forward, but this time it was to implore Sulpicius not to forfeit the martyr's crown which he had well nigh won. But it was in vain.

   'Then,' said Nicephorus, 'tell the Legate I will take his place, I am a Christian,' and he was forthwith taken at his word.

   The fall of Sulpicius was quoted by the early Church to show that the sacrifice of life itself is not accepted on high when offered by those who have not learnt from their Saviour to pardon injuries.

The forgiveness of St Chrysostom[3]

More than fifteen hundred years ago, St Chrysostom, the 'golden-mouthed', by his eloquent preaching was attracting great congregations to the church of the Holy Wisdom in Constantinople. He was striving hard by his sermons and his life to make Constantinople more Christian, but his work and influence were being constantly undermined by the Emperor's favourite, Eutropius. Eutropius was a base-born slave who had risen until his power was such that he was able to hinder much that the good Bishop tried to do. There came a day, however, when his power declined, he fell from the Emperor's favour, was discovered to be the villain he was, and was condemned to die. He had to flee for his life, and the sanctuary he sought was none other than Chrysostom's cathedral. Entering the building, he ran, pushed aside the great curtain that divided the sanctuary from the rest of the church, and flung himself down by the altar, clinging to it for safety. No one might touch a criminal who had thus sought sanctuary unless the church gave him up.

A powerful Christian witness   On Chrysostom lay the responsibility. The enemy of the church was in his power; but mercy counted with him more than justice. The Bishop came and stood between Eutropius and the band of armed men who had pursued him into the church.

'None shall enter this sanctuary except across my dead body,' he cried to the soldiers, and between two rows of spearmen, Chrysostom went to ask the Emperor's mercy for the very man who had done his best to injure himself and the church.

Worshippers had been in the cathedral while all this happened, and when, the next day, St Chrysostom celebrated the Holy Mysteries and repeated the Lord's Prayer, the congregation realised, as perhaps never before, those words 'Forgive us our trespasses as we forgive them that trespass against us.'

Forgiving the man who stole my wife[4]

Watchman Nee tells a powerful story from twentieth-century China. After a service a businessman came to him with a tale of woe. He had returned from a long trip away to find that his 'best friend' had set up house with his wife and children. As a Christian, he knew that he ought to forgive them, but he couldn't; he asked Watchman Nee for help and prayer.

'How can I forgive my wife?'

'You can't' came the surprising answer.

Forgiveness needs God's grace

The businessman was about to turn away downcast, when Watchman Nee added, 'You can't – but God can enable you to. The epistle to the Romans (6:11) says, "Count yourselves dead to sin, but alive to God in Christ Jesus." Tell Jesus you can't forgive. Tell Jesus that in him you are dead; and ask him, alive in you, to enable you to forgive your wife.'

The man smiled. He understood, and went away happily.

Forgiving the man who helped to kill my sister[5]

Corrie Ten Boom tells how, after the war, she was called to preach a message of forgiveness and reconciliation. Most of her family, including her father and her beloved sister Betsie, had been killed by the Germans. They had been discovered hiding Jewish people. She and Betsie had been imprisoned in the notorious Ravensbruck concentration camp. Before Betsie died, she had extraordinary visions of the future; visions which helped to establish Corrie, who lived before the war as a quiet, unmarried, clockmaker's daughter, as an international speaker, writer and evangelist. She told the Lord that she would go anywhere – except Germany. Almost inevitably, she had little peace until she went on a speaking tour in Germany.

One evening, after she had been preaching about forgiveness, a German walked forward to speak to her. She recognised him as a particularly brutal SS officer from Ravensbruck. He, of course, didn't recognise her. He held out his hand. He explained that, after the end of the war, he had become a Christian. Now he would like to receive forgiveness from someone who had suffered at his hands.

Corrie shrank back. It was impossible! Yet wasn't this the basis of her preaching and her praying? Didn't God love the unlovable and forgive the unforgivable? She prayed – quite desperately. A current of warmth passed down through her shoulders to her hands, she embraced him. Forgiveness and reconciliation, for both, were complete.

Working with, and forgiving a former torturer.

Another story from the South African elections, told by my friend Brian Blancharde[6] illustrates the double-edged nature of forgiveness – given and received!

In November 1993, the cities and townships east of Johannesburg were known as 'South Africa's No. 1 killing ground.' Desperate meetings were held between most unlikely groups of people in efforts to calm the situation.

One such was a meeting between the local white police brigadier and his staff on one side, and church representatives led by two black ministers on the other.

They were talking together, planning peace moves in the East Rand. Nothing too unusual as the new South Africa approached! But there was something very unusual. One of the ministers had a permanent limp. Years earlier, when they had been theological students, they had both been arrested and tortured after a demonstration against the apartheid state. A young white lieutenant had led the punishment. Now the old adversaries were meeting as equal human beings, with a common prayerful purpose to help avert further tragedy.

Forgiveness can lead to future co-operation

The black ministers had the grace to forgive, the brigadier had the grace to accept their forgiveness!

Forgiveness – a spiritual battleground

A final story illustrates even more clearly the tremendous spiritual battle surrounding the whole question of forgiveness. Martin Cavender,[7] and his wife Cesca, travelled to Kigali, Rwanda, in July 1995. It was just a year after the terrible genocide which had swept the nation in 1994.

The Anglican church was reconvening its Synod. Martin, with his legal experience, was sent by Archbishop George Carey to try and sort out some of the legal problems caused by absentee bishops, and other grave problems. There was much bitterness, much grief, and considerable distrust. One senior church leader who had lost many members of his family, was so bitter that people found it difficult to stand close to him. As with the Holocaust, the level of trauma in Rwanda was so great that it caused the spiritual death of the people who carried it. Everyone, out of sympathy, made room for him to speak. But his presence, quite demonic in its hatred, especially of one other leader who was present, made progress almost impossible.

Cesca, watching from the edge, walked around the hall praying. They had only two days, and there was no progress. Lunch with the very gracious American ambassador seemed like an intrusion on the spiritual battle. After lunch she went into the cathedral, pouring herself out before the Lord. 'How can you leave this church, and these people to perish? Haven't they suffered enough already?' *A major part of the spiritual battle*

She lay on the floor, weeping. After a time a stillness came over her: there was a certainty that God had answered. A young black face came beside her. 'You pray beautiful! You pray for me, please.'

In the hall, Mme Gasane Venontie, aged about forty-five, was a great antidote to bitterness. She spoke seldom, but her few words, accompanied by a photograph of all the dead members of her family, have amazing power. In April/May 1994, she lost her husband, brother-in-law, and all five children to the killer squads. Her two older children, aged about sixteen, were on the telephone when the vigilantes came. 'They are coming through the door now, Mummy – don't worry, we love you very much!'

Martin says he could hardly bear to hear her testimony – her face was so serene. Only this sort of testimony could bring healing to a situation of unbelievable ferocity. And suddenly it started to happen. As Cesca finished praying, decisions began to be taken. She could sense God's right arm reaching down into the building. Elections took place. There was much cheering and singing. Everything was finished by candlelight – the electricity having characteristically failed at 11 p.m.

For both Martin and Cesca, with their different rôles, it was a deeply moving experience.

Seven stories with very different outcomes. But notice the spiritual battle in each case. Hancock, an honest man (we aren't told, but he sounds like a good Prayer Book Anglican), couldn't.

Sulpicius refused, and so lost both his martyr's crown and the respect of the early church. Chrysostom, by God's grace, knew what Christ commands and did it. Watchman Nee showed his friend how impossible it was, 'But all things are possible with God' (Mk 10:27). And Corrie Ten Boom, under direct orders from God, received supernatural grace to overcome her very understandable feelings. The final stories illustrate how the grace of forgiveness opens the way for future co-operation.

Jesus' teaching on forgiving others

Many times, Jesus taught of the absolute necessity for his followers to forgive their fellow humans. His words are invariably in the context of teaching about prayer: 'Forgive us our debts, as we also have forgiven our debtors' (Mt 6:12). 'If you forgive men when they sin against you, your heavenly Father will also forgive you. But if you do not forgive men their sins, your Father will not forgive your sins' (Matthew 6:14,15).

That is the entire message of the long parable of the unmerciful servant (Mt 18:21-35) which concludes with the awesome words, 'This is how my heavenly Father will treat each of you unless you forgive your brother from your heart' (Mt 18:35).

After the strange incident of the withered fig tree, Jesus teaches the disciples about the importance of faith in prayer, and then concludes with these surprising words about forgiveness. Faith and forgiveness go hand in hand.

> Therefore I tell you, whatever you ask for in prayer, believe that you have received it, and it will be yours. And when you stand praying, if you hold anything against anyone, forgive him, so that your Father in heaven may forgive you your sins. (Mk 11:24,25)

Jesus, as we would expect, put his own teaching into practice. The first word from the cross is a prayer of forgiveness: 'Father, forgive them, for they do not know what they are doing' (Lk 23:34), and, a little earlier, Luke records: 'The Lord turned and looked straight at Peter. Then Peter remembered the word the Lord had spoken to him: "Before the cock crows today, you will disown me three times." And he went outside and wept bitterly (Lk 22: 61-62). Jesus' look, surely a look of wondering forgiveness, began Peter's healing and restoration. He knew his Lord's forgiveness. If only Judas could have felt the same, perhaps his suicide could have been averted.

Forgiveness and justice

Forgiveness offered doesn't mean that justice is ruled out. Some years ago, one of my parishioners, a young bride, found burglars in her house. They asked her to let them go. She refused. They attacked her and left her for dead. She made an incredible recovery. The skill of the doctors, supported by the fervent prayers of the healing prayer group and my curate, who anointed her with oil, brought about a wonderful outcome.

A few weeks later, she was home. I said, 'We must pray that you can forgive your attackers – and that they will be caught and punished.' Soon afterwards they used her credit card in a public place, and with the help of Crimewatch, were arrested and convicted. She and her husband grew spiritually. Forgiveness is not a soft option.

The need to offer forgiveness

All this teaching about forgiving others is desperately unfashionable. We live in a world that cries for vengeance:

> Abel's blood for vengeance, pleaded to the skies,
> But the blood of Jesus, for our pardon cries.[8]

Everywhere scapegoats are called for. Tragedies happen, and lawyers arrive with briefcases, inciting relatives to sue for the highest possible damages. Gordon Wilson, whose much-loved daughter was killed by the IRA bomb at Eniskillen, was a remarkable exception, calling for forgiveness and reconciliation. More normally, grief-stricken parents look for vengeance and damages, against drunken drivers, incompetent leaders of school expeditions, anyone who causes the death and injury of their children. It's very understandable – let's be quite clear about that. It is an entirely natural reaction – and completely futile. The awful tragedy is that the cry for

A spiritual problem

vengeance seldom affects the guilty party, but it continues to affect the unforgiving person for the rest of their lives. It is a poison that infects the soul, often causing physical illness and psychological breakdown.

There is only one simple spiritual law. We cannot truly pray forgiveness for others unless we have received forgiveness ourselves. Gordon Wilson, as a Christian, found it possible to react in the way that he did. We shall return to the question of forgiving others, but first we must look at the beam in our own eye (Mt 7:5).

A prayer of self-examination

Another of Patricia St John's stories[9] tells of the five finger prayer. Like many of the best prayer exercises, it is beautifully simple. She tells how a visiting preacher, presumably around the turn of the century, stayed in a small family hotel in a forest in Northern Canada. He held prayers for the family and their guests; as he did so, he couldn't help noticing a sorry, unkempt Red Indian girl who was a worker in the hotel. The family told him that she was a very sad girl, with no family, and seemingly no will to work, or to care for herself.

As Andrew, the preacher, talked with her, she asked him to
The need to teach her a very simple prayer: 'It must be short, sir,
know oneself I'm no scholar.'
'It is very short,' Andrew replied. 'Five words, one for each finger. O Lord, show me myself.'

'And how long shall I pray it for?' she asked.

'Until I return, next week.'

When Andrew came back, he asked how she was, and was told that she was even worse, morose, and often crying. Andrew sought her out, and listened to her tale of a 'heart growing heavier'.

'What shall I do?' she whispered.

'I will read you another short prayer – O Lord, show me yourself.'

'And how long shall I pray it for?' she asked.

'For the rest of your life!'

Some years later, Andrew opened a new church near the hotel in the forest. He heard about some wonderful youth work led by a young Red Indian woman, who had recently married. *Knowing God* After the service, a dark haired woman, attractively *transforms us* dressed, stepped forward. She smiled and clasped his hand. 'Do you remember me, sir?' Andrew looked doubtful. Then she pointed to her five fingers. 'I've prayed that prayer every day. I am learning to love him more and more!'

In this case, the prayer of self-examination led to the Red Indian woman's remarkable conversion. For all of us, it should be an integral part of our prayer life. St Paul stresses the need, placing it in the context of preparation before receiving communion: 'A man ought to examine himself before he eats of the bread and drinks of the cup' (1 Cor 11:28). Such examination can usually be done on one's own. Sometimes we will need the help, and prayers, of a friend, pastor, or spiritual director.

For Anglicans, the Alternative Service book provides a good challenging base. In the appendix to the Rite A *Prayer of self-* Communion service, paragraph, 78, page 161, there *examination* is a list of the Ten Commandments – with a positive New Testament command alongside. For instance, 'You shall not steal' to which, perhaps, many of us might plead not guilty, is followed by the searching positive command, 'Be honest in all that you do and care for those in need' (cf Eph 4:28). This is deeply challenging. How are we managing our finances? What are we giving to God's work? What are we doing to help, materially and in other ways, those in need? These questions spring quite naturally out of the text!

There is just one problem. Some people, on reading an elementary book on psychiatry, will decide they have all the different personality disorders – so it can be with spiritual self-examination. St Paul tells us to take a *sober estimate* (cf Rom 12:3). It does not help to be either too hard to too soft with ourselves – that is why we will need others' help.

Once again, in order to pray we need to understand something of God's nature and his promises.

God's offer of forgiveness

God is unbelievably generous! Listen to a verse near the end of Micah,

> You will again have compassion on us;
> you will tread our sins underfoot
> and hurl all our iniquities into the depths of the sea. (Mic 7:19)

Corrie Ten Boom (see earlier in the chapter), characteristically, adds 'and we should put up a notice saying "NO FISHING ALLOWED!"'

But he does require three things of us – first, that we want and ask for forgiveness, as did the servant in the parable (Mt 18:26). Secondly, that we receive not only his forgiveness, but also receive Jesus into our hearts by faith (see Jn 1:14 and Eph 3:17). Thirdly, that unlike the servant in the parable, we forgive other people.

To receive the true benefits of his forgiveness, we need to go through a clear process which leads from darkness to light, from the tangled undergrowth of our sin, at least back on to a woodland path, and hopefully out of the wood into a sunlit meadow.

How to receive forgiveness

I would like to suggest that there are six stages – they won't all be appropriate on every occasion, and often they are accomplished subconsciously, but it may be helpful to spell them out.

Admit our sin (and don't try blaming someone else). *Believe* that God is serious in his desire to forgive. *Confess*, privately, or with a friend, or to a counsellor or priest. *Discern,* with the help of others, if appropriate, what needs to be done. *Experience* God's cleansing. Know his *Freedom*.

Admit our sin

A good beginning is the African school girl's prayer:[10] 'O thou great Chief, light a candle in my heart, that I may see what is therein, and sweep the rubbish from thy dwelling place.'

God's candle, the Holy spirit, convicts us of sin (Jn 16:8), and helps us to make a sober estimate of the problem (Rom 12:1-4). We must beware of false guilt. Satan, the accuser of the brethren, (Rev 12:10) delights to plague us with unnecessary accusations. We speak a firm word to someone and feel guilty, we preach a robust sermon and want to retract it. Often these very actions have been required of God. They have required faith and we must not spoil it all by allowing false guilt to fester.

Nevertheless, often God's Spirit will convict us – 'John, you were less than Christlike on the phone. John, you shouldn't have called the noisy choir a bunch of monkeys. John, you shouldn't have shouted at your daughter. John, you should have been kinder to that wayfarer, to whom you gave a grudging sandwich. John, you weren't listening to her problem. John…'

Admitting our problem

Of course, some sin is mucher deeper and more serious than that. We shall look at that later in the chapter. But the first step is to admit that we have a problem: 'If we claim to be without sin, we deceive ourselves and the truth is not in us' (1 Jn 1:8), and then to believe God's promises.

Believe that God wants to forgive

Basically, it is a matter of trusting God. Read again, Luke 11:11-13. God doesn't give us scorpions and snakes. He wants to give us eggs and fish. In others words, he is not concerned (usually) with punishing us, with making us feel miserable. His nature is to set us free. If he does hide his face from us, it is to help us realise that we're wandering from his path and his standards: 'Jesus replied, "I tell you the truth, everyone who sins is a slave to sin. Now a slave has no permanent place in the family, but a son belongs to it for ever. So if the Son sets you free, you will be free indeed"' (Jn 8:34-36).

Believing God's word

But we need to make a clear confession.

Confess our sins

The next step is to make a prayer of confession. It needs to be quite simple, and unconditional (not hedged about with 'ifs' and 'buts' and 'other people's faults'). We need the radical prayer of a John Baillie.[11]

Confessing our sin – alone or with others

> Almighty God, spirit of purity and grace, in asking thy forgiveness, I cannot claim a right to be forgiven, but only cast myself upon Thy unbounded love.
> I can plead no merit or desert.
> I can plead no extenuating circumstances.
> I cannot plead the frailty of my nature.
> I cannot plead the force of the temptations I encounter.
> I cannot plead the persuasions of others who led me astray.
> I can only say, for the sake of Jesus Christ, Thy Son, my Lord.
> Amen.

Or we may feel the need to be even more specific: 'Lord, I am sorry that I hurt X. I shouldn't have treated anyone in that way. I believe you want to forgive me. I confess my sin to you, and pray for your cleansing through the blood of Jesus. Please show me what I can do to help put the situation right, through Jesus Christ our Lord.'

Such prayers are usually made alone. If you lack confidence in God's forgiveness, read and learn 1 John 1:8-10!; if you don't know how to handle the situation with X, or if you believe that God is calling you to, then it would be wise to pray with a friend, a counsellor, or a priest (or church leader).

Occasionally, such prayers are made in a group (see Jas 5:16). There are difficulties in such a practice – confidentiality (you don't want anyone else to know you have a problem with X), or inappropriateness (I've occasionally heard prayers containing the line 'Lord, please forgive my family for being angry with Mr Y who has grievously hurt Jemima'). On some occasions, such confession is very effective. I remember doing a Bible study with a housegroup who were going away the following weekend. The group was very tense, and I knew something had to be said. Taking my life in my hands, I said 'I think if you're going away together, you'd better first confess all the things that are holding you back – especially with one another.' There was a short silence, someone in the group said that she had a verse of Scripture, but had felt too nervous to share it, which confirmed this. Then the floodgates opened. Everyone confessed – even some who, to the best of my knowledge, had never prayed aloud before. Not surprisingly, the weekend was deemed a great success.

After confession, we have to discern what God requires us to do.

Discerning the way forward

St Paul, as so often, sorts out the men from the boys. Listen, carefully, to this key verse: 'Godly sorrow brings repentance that leads to salvation and leaves no regret, but worldly sorrow brings death' (2 Cor 7:10). It is so easy to 'repent' and to 'regret', and to change nothing. Perhaps we need to destroy some unhelpful literature (Oh dear, I couldn't do that, Emily gave it to me as a gift). Perhaps we need to write a letter (Oh, I couldn't do that, Sue would be so embarrassed…). Perhaps we need to give a long-promised gift to some individual or mission (Oh dear, my bank balance is in such a mess…). Perhaps we need to ask someone round, and show that we've accepted their apology (Oh dear, I'd much rather leave sleeping dogs lying…).

Discerning the way forward

Of course, sometimes, we must do nothing! If a pastor falls in love with someone he's counselling (an all too common problem, it seems, best avoided by not counselling the opposite sex on one's own – or certainly not alone in a house), the least helpful thing he can do is to 'confess' – thereby neatly unloading his guilt on to her and greatly increasing the probability of disaster.

More usually, if someone profoundly irritates me, I need to learn patience, not to tick him off! But if his manner, or assertiveness in a group, or way of praying (Lord just please… we *just* need… just…) is annoying a lot of people, then very gently someone will need to talk to him (Mt 18:15).

There are two big problems that can remain. We need to realise that forgiveness doesn't wipe out the consequences of our wrongdoing. King David is the classic biblical illustration of this truth. His most notorious sin – the adultery with Bathsheba, followed by the 'military' murder of the unfortunate Uriah – was exposed, very bravely, by Nathan the prophet. After much pain felt, tangibly, by the death of the first child of the union, and spiritually in the agony of Psalm 51, David received forgiveness. So much so, that the second child, Solomon, was said to be 'loved by the Lord' (see 2 Sam 11 and 12, in particular 12:25). This remarkable verse might encourage those seeking God's forgiveness after sexual transgression.

Sin is forgiven, but its stain remains

Nevertheless, although David was forgiven, the chaos in his family – which began when his first wife despised him for dancing nearly naked before the Ark of the Lord (2 Sam 6:16) – grew dramatically. David's reign went from bad to worse, and the rebellion and death of his favourite son, Absalom, hurt him grievously.

It is a strange fact that David's adultery nearly brought down the Israeli Government some 3,000 years later in 1995! (One of the government party made a flippant allusion to the event and this almost caused the minority strict religious party to leave the coalition!)

God's forgiveness is very wonderful – but he cannot turn the clock back – and we all feel, to some extent, the consequences of our past sins.

What we are obviously required to do is, prayerfully, to try and mitigate the consequences of our sin. Zacchaeus (Lk 19:1ff), offered fourfold restitution to those he had cheated. To re-emphasise what I've said, we may need to write a letter, make a personal visit, replace an object, publicly undo false witness. God will direct.

Our attempts may be refused. In the famous parable of the lost son (Luke 15:11-32) the wretched, self-righteous, elder brother refused to forgive the returning prodigal, and then brushed aside his father's efforts at mediation. We may genuinely try to apologise, but we must realise that our efforts may not be accepted. If that happens, we have to trust God's forgiveness and to await further instructions from him.

Reconciliation may be refused

We need to be patient. For instance, after a marriage failure, it may take years before one partner can forgive the other. People often think they've forgiven people – but haven't! A good test of the meaning of forgiveness is if we catch ourselves thinking about the person when we should be praying, or worshipping, or even when we're driving, doing the washing, or in bed. Dreams, too, are often significant.

Sometimes it takes both time and good fortune to achieve reconciliation. I once led a disastrous house party. Everything went wrong! We started facing a financial penalty for not bringing enough people, a needy family we had paid for brought mumps with them, and, far worse, a young man who suffered from epilepsy, not one of our congregation, got over-excited watching the Rector and the Chairman of the PCC giving a fencing display, and had a *grand mal* in the night – and died.

In the chaos that followed, I cancelled one expedition to some nearby gardens, but I failed to get a message to an old friend who was in charge of the gardens. He didn't reply to any of my subsequent apologies. A friendship seemed severed. It still bothered me and I prayed for a number of years. About eight years later, I was packing up my Aunt's pictures – she had moved into a nursing home. On the back of one were instructions that it was to be given to my friend. I organised this, wrote again, contact was re-established and forgiveness received.

One last word on discerning the way forward – don't be too literal! Zacchaeus (Lk 19:1ff) took very radical action, offering to repay fourfold those whom he had swindled, and surrendering half of his largely illgotten gains to the poor. Fine! We would do well to do likewise. But one great early church leader, Origen, took the warnings of Matthew 18:7-9 literally and emasculated himself. Not a course to be recommended!

Now we need to experience God's cleansing love.

Experiencing God's cleansing

> I will sprinkle clean water on you, and you will be clean; I will cleanse you from all your impurities and from all your idols. I will give you a new heart and put a new spirit in you; I will remove from you your heart of stone and give you a heart of flesh. (Ezek 36:25,26)

We need to experience that sense of cleansing and wellbeing that Mother Julian of Norwich[12] writes about, 'Sin is behoveable (it behoved that sin should be suffered to appear) but all shall be well, and all

Experiencing God's cleansing

shall be well, and all manner of things shall be well.'

What Mother Julian is considering is why sin was allowed by God. Like St Irenaeus' 'O felix culpa', she accepts that sin plays a necessary part so that we may experience the wonder of redemption. And often it is! Forgiveness, given or received, is wonderfully cleansing. Tears flow, expensive ointment is used, Pharisees grumble (see Lk 7:36ff). It is deeply moving when God's healing grace brings reconciliation.

My old friend, Fred Smith,[13] used to tell a lovely story. Before he was a preacher, or involved in his great ministry of healing, he was on holiday and he heard the Lord say (and Fred *did* hear) 'Fred, you're to preach tomorrow.' He was a bit shocked. In the morning he, and Stella, went off to the Pentecostal church. Nothing happened. As he was leaving, someone came up to him

Sin exposed proves to be a blessing

– 'You're the man we need. You'll preach this evening!' Somewhat shocked, Fred spent the afternoon preparing God's message for this unknown church. Nothing came! They arrived in church. Fred didn't join in the lengthy worship. He prayed for guidance. Nothing came! Reluctantly he walked up to the pulpit and began to speak... Words flowed from Ephesians 2 on the need for reconciliation.

The result was astonishing. Tears, handshakes, embraces... The congregation had previously been split into two, and was likely to have divided. God used Fred's first sermon so that many could experience forgiveness.

Demos Shakarian's[14] grandfather experienced this in Armenia in 1900. The Amenian Church had a visit from a group of Russian Pentecostals. The grandfather had to entertain them. The best cow, which would most easily feed the whole group, had a defective eye. He knew (see Lev 22:20) that he shouldn't use it for the Lord's feast. But he did, and slaughtered it, and burned the skin and the defective eye. At the beginning of the feast, disaster struck. The Russian leader refused to say grace, and moved the embarrassed grandfather out and showed him where he had hidden the corpse!

The grandfather was so impressed that he listened to all their teaching. He believed in the possibility of God speaking directly to his family. As a result, he took seriously the prophecy given some years earlier by an illiterate villager. He had drawn a map – quite recognisable as far away America – and told the villagers that there would be a terrible persecution, and they must flee to where the map indicated. About fifty years later, the now-elderly prophet said that his words were about to be fulfilled. 'We must flee to America, all who remain will perish.' The instructions were heeded by many of the villagers, including Demos' grandfather. They escaped, fled to America in 1905, and eventually founded the Full Gospel Businessmen's International – a very successful organisation in evangelism.

Most of those who remained were killed in an appalling massacre in 1914. The Turks ethnically cleansed the Armenians. Under cover of the First World War, little was said or done. The awful pogrom is said to have impressed Hitler; and, of course, has continued in another guise in former Jugoslavia.

But for Demos' grandfather the consequences of one exposed and forgiven sin were momentous. For him it was certainly true that 'Those who sow in tears will reap with songs of joy (Ps 126:5).

However, for many it's not quite so simple. The ivy of sin clings and there seems to be no freedom.

Freedom – deferred or received?

In Kakamega Forest, in Kenya, and elsewhere, birds eject the seeds of figs. Sometimes they fall in the soft crown of a growing forest tree. The 'strangler' fig takes root, and grows downwards, quietly killing the host tree. When it reaches the ground and puts down its own roots, the host tree is ready to die.

Some aspects of sin are like that. We never seem to get free, and the consequences are dire. Prayer needs to be strong and firm! I like the prayer of a Nigerian:[15] 'God in heaven, you have helped my life grow like a tree. Now something has happened. Satan, like a bird, has carried one twig of his own choosing after another. Before I knew it he had built a dwelling place and was living in it. Tonight, my Father, I am throwing out both the bird and the nest.'

A long time ago, a young man came to discuss a problem that

he had with a 'habit' he couldn't get rid of. Before we got down to the details, I asked him if he'd been involved in any occult practices. He looked surprised at what he considered was an irrelevant question. I explained that such things can be a sort of spiritual ivy, blocking growth, which (as in the Nigerian's prayer above) enables other unwelcome birds to lodge there. He admitted some minor involvement. I prayed to cut him free from any occult influence. He prayed a simple prayer of repentance. We agreed to discuss the 'habit' next time. When he returned a fortnight later, he felt free and able to cope. Past occult experience is often the seed base for the spiritual 'strangler fig'.

Sins that cling from the past

My curate gave a surprisingly similar testimony during a recent sermon. At theological college, some six years after his conversion, he was suffering terrible dreams. Each night, Satan would appear and claim him. A discerning counsellor traced the problem back to his use of ouija boards at school. After prayers, the problem completely disappeared.

Such ministry need not be prolonged or complicated. Very often, a simple retaking of one's vows of baptism is quite sufficient to bring freedom. Occasionally, people are in deep trouble, and weird things happen. Such ministry needs to be handled by those with experience. The effects can be wonderful. A real danger, however, is the pursuit of non-existent demons. This does immense harm and often leaves the person seeking help very vulnerable and over dependent on the 'guru' who has been 'helping' them.

Some of us can be badly affected by the sins of our ancestors[16] (see Ex 20:4-6). While this never excuses our sin, it may help to explain it. I have known a number of people (including myself) who have been greatly freed by prayer to release the negative spiritual influences of past generations, particularly relating to suicide, murder, white magic, 'occult' gifts, freemasonry, depression, migraine, etc.

It is not possible in a short book like this to cover this area, but it is usually quite simple to deal with – if (and it's a big if) the diagnosis is accurate!

Where Satan treads destructively, he is only distorting

something divine. Psalm 103, read at the graveside in Anglican funeral services, has a wonderfully positive statement: 'But from everlasting to everlasting the LORD's love is with those who fear him and his righteousness with their children's children' (Ps 103:17).

Newly married Christian couples should be praying not only for their unborn children, but also their grandchildren! I am convinced that God wants to raise up righteous families – especially today to counter the chaos in so much family life.

Of course, such grace is not automatic, but it is helpful to pray in this way. I do know of many families with a remarkable number of Christians in many generations.

A more subtle strangler fig, comes with the problem of self-rejection. Many people have a deep, deep sense of rejection, echoing the psalmist: 'Surely I have been a sinner from birth, sinful from the time my mother conceived me.' (Ps 51:5) They feel alienated from God and their fellow human beings. This is often caused by trauma in the early years – unloving parents, angry and violent parents, divorced parents, no parents, sexual abuse... The list is endless. Such people need deep and gentle help. My wife battles with ground elder in the garden. This tiresome weed with its pretty white flowers, causes endless problems, returning year after year. It needs great ***The problem of*** persistence to clear a patch. Self-rejection is like ***self-rejection*** that, it so easily reappears, and like a weed, it stifles beautiful flowers from growing.

I would not dream, in this short book, of trying to offer a trite and simple remedy. The best one is to be found in the knowledge of God's love. Read Psalm 139:1-18. Discover that, as Reg East puts it,[17] God knows all our thoughts – good, bad, and useless!

As we understand that, as we learn to love ourselves – which is the third part of the great commandment – Love the Lord your God... Love your neighbour as *yourself* (Lk 10:27), so we will begin to be able to receive God's love and to forgive ourselves – and other people.

This last point is important. People who have a self-rejection problem have a dual difficulty. They don't feel God's love, and they are easily hurt by other people. Like the mesembryanthemum flower on a cold day, they need the warmth of God's sun to open up, and look beautiful.

Jesus has some lovely words: '...you will know the truth, and the truth will set you free' (Jn 8:32). He wants us to be free! Free to receive his love. Free to forgive others. Free to feel forgiven. Free to serve his needy world. Complicated prayer ministry to help people with problems of self-rejection, past generations, or previous occult activity, must have only one end. To leave them free, like the Gadarene demoniac whom Jesus told: *Jesus wants to set us free* 'Go home to your family and tell them how much the Lord has done for you, and how he has had mercy on you' (Mk 5:19). Many a time after deep prayer we've wanted to sing:

> Long my imprisoned spirit lay[18]
> fast bound in sin and nature's night;
> Thine eye diffused a quickening ray –
> I woke, the dungeon flamed with light;
> my chains fell off, my heart was free,
> I rose, went forth, and followed Thee

from Charles Wesley's great hymn 'And can it be?' And when we're truly free, we're free to forgive our brother! Then we experience the generosity of God.

The generous Father

Because those who are led by the Spirit of God are sons of God. For you did not receive a spirit that makes you a slave again to fear, but you received the Spirit of sonship. And by him we cry, 'Abba, Father'. The Spirit himself testifies with our spirit that we are God's children. Now if we are children, then we are heirs – heirs of God and co-heirs with Christ, if indeed we share in his sufferings in order that we may also share in his glory. (Rom 8:14-17)

This great passage, which Martyn Lloyd Jones[19] sees as a hallmark of evangelical faith, is concerned with at least three deep levels of spiritual experience. The first is in some form normative for all Christians, the second is something which all

Christians need, and the third is a very touchstone to the deepest ways of God.

The AV translates verse 15a as 'For you have not received the spirit of bondage again to fear.' When we become a Christian (and we shall say more of this in the next chapter when we consider prayer and evangelism) we will have had some sense of our sin, and the holiness of God. For some, conversion will have been gradual, for some sudden; for some there is a deep and appalling sense of sin.

Conviction of sin usually precedes understanding God's grace

John Bunyan,[20] in *Grace Abounding*, tells us that he was in this condition for eighteen months. On one occasion, this spirit of bondage and fear was so terrible that he could have sworn that he smelt brimstone in the air. This was the Holy Spirit convicting Bunyan of sin. In his earlier, pre-Christian days, he had felt very free, very careless, and apparently happy.

For others, the sense of deep conviction of sin comes much later. We may read a book like the Lamentations of Jeremiah:

> Is it nothing to you, all you who pass by?
> Look around and see.
> Is any suffering like my suffering
> that was inflicted on me,
> that the LORD brought on me
> in the day of his fierce anger? (Lam 1:12)

We may be moved by the sufferings of Jeremiah, and Jerusalem and Judah. We may go deeper, and see in it a prophecy of the sufferings of Christ. We may be moved by his suffering for the world. Then quite suddenly, an arrow from heaven pierces our complacent soul, and we begin to see our part in the whole matter. My sin helped to inflict that suffering, my sin brought on God's anger.

If we are already Christians, we are deeply moved, we begin to understand what Isaac Watts meant with the phrase, 'When I survey the wondrous cross.' If we are not yet Christians, we may cry out for God to release us from our sin.

Trees survive great storms if they have deep roots. Christians survive (and even prosper) in great spiritual turmoil if they have a deep conviction of their sin.

Jonathan Edwards,[21] just before the Great Awakening, resolved 'to set apart days to meditate upon particular subjects; and sometimes, to set apart a day for the consideration of the greatness of my sins.' I could quote many examples where he is deeply affected by 'his own sinfulness and vileness' and yet at the same time he could have this sort of experience:

> Sometimes, only mentioning a single word caused my heart to burn within me; or only seeing the name of Christ, or the name of some attribute of God. And God has appeared glorious to me on account of the Trinity. It has made me have exalting thoughts of God, that he subsists in three persons; the Father, Son and Holy Ghost. The sweetest joys and delights I have experienced, have not been those that have arisen from a hope of my own good estate, but in a direct view of the glorious things of the gospel. Once as I rode out into the woods for my health, in 1737, having alighted from my horse in a retired place, as my manner commonly has been, to walk for divine contemplation and prayer, I had a view that for me was extraordinary, of the glory of the Son of God, as Mediator between God and man, and his wonderful, great, full, pure and sweet grace and love and meek and gentle condescension. This grace that appeared so calm and sweet, appeared also great above the heavens. The person of Christ appeared ineffably excellent with an excellency great enough to swallow up all thought and conception – which continued, as near as I can judge, about an hour; which kept me the greater part of the time in a flood of tears and weeping aloud. I felt an ardency of soul to be, what I know not otherwise how to express, emptied and annihilated; to lie in the dust, and to be full of Christ alone; to love him with a holy and pure love; to trust in him; to live upon him; to serve and follow him; and to be perfectly sanctified and made pure, with a divine and heavenly purity. I have, several others times, had views very much of the same nature, and which have had the same effects.

The wonder of experiencing God's generous love

The spirit of bondage gives way to the spirit of sonship. We cry 'Abba, Father', because we can echo the words of St Paul, 'I know whom I have believed' (2 Tim 1:12).

This is so important, because when we have this confidence,

we can ask for forgiveness of our day to day sins (which, as with Edwards above, will grow in importance and seriousness as we approach the throne of grace), and we will be able to forgive others – and ourselves.

How do we pray about this?

This is a great question! The Holy Spirit is sovereign, and we must beware of any sort of 'recipe' for spiritual experiences. Nevertheless, if we quietly meditate on the sufferings of our Lord, we are going to be hard hearted if we don't feel some new strong conviction of sin.

There is a story, which one of my spiritual teachers used to tell, of some youths who mocked a Catholic confessor by confessing all sorts of invented sins. The confessor set them to kneel before a crucifix and say, 'I hate you Jesus' a hundred times. One of the boys couldn't do this. He was convicted of his careless, blasphemous sin. A former Archbishop of Paris used to tell the story, adding, 'I know that it is true – I was the boy.'

As to praying to receive 'the spirit of sonship', we may properly ask God to give this understanding of himself. Galatians 4:1-7 has the same theme, and Paul includes the powerful words: 'But when the time had fully come, God sent His Son, born of a woman, born under law, to redeem those under law, that we might receive the *full rights of sons*. Because you are sons, God sent the Spirit of his Son into our hearts, the Spirit who calls out, "Abba, Father!"'

'Abba Father'
a deep
experience in
prayer

If we can receive Christ into our hearts by faith (see again Jn 1:12 and Ephesians 3:17), we can pray to receive 'the full rights of sons.' Not through any merit (less still right) of ours, but because of the grace of God and the implanted righteousness we receive when we become Christians.

It is a deep mystical experience to know that we are part of God's family. We may not feel this always – we may lose this assurance through sin. Just as on a dark, rainy day, we know that the sun is still shining in the sky, we shall know by faith, that we are 'sons', even though our experience may suggest otherwise. At times, God seems to withdraw, and we have to walk through the valley of the shadow, through the vale of misery. All around us, others may be experiencing deep blessing, and we have to walk a darker, less outwardly fruitful, path. At such times, the memory of previous experiences, perhaps noted in our prayer diary, will be very important.

If we are Christians, and if we have never felt that we have received the deep assurance of God's presence in 'the spirit of sonship', then we might read, quietly, (and learn!) these two key passages from Romans and Galatians. We might pray along these lines: 'Sovereign Lord, your word encourages me to believe that I should be able to cry 'Abba, Father' and to receive 'the spirit of sonship'. By your grace, will you visit my soul and assure me of your presence?'

This assurance is a very important part of Christian experience. Without it, we feel uncertain of God's forgiveness and have great difficulty in forgiving others. With it, we feel confident enough of our calling to be able to pray for and to minister to others.

Yet there remains a deeper experience, the most sublime of all, when the Spirit himself testifies with our spirit that we are God's children (Rom 8:16). This experience Martyn Lloyd Jones[22] calls 'one of the most glorious statements containing Christian experience found anywhere in the Bible from beginning to end'. Evangelicals, and the old Puritan writers, often talk of 'the sealing of the Spirit'. Those of a more Catholic persuasion refer to it as 'union with Christ'. Charismatics and Pentecostals write of 'the Baptism of the Holy Spirit'. Truly understood, each will be experiencing one of God's greatest gifts.

We shall look at this in detail in Chapter 10. Meanwhile, remember where we began. Unless we truly know God's forgiveness, and through his grace are able to forgive others, we shall seek such experiences in vain.

Notes

1. Lord Egremont, *Wyndham and children first.*
2. Higham, *Torches for Teachers* (SPCK, 1937), p 141.
3. *Ibid,* p 140.
4. Watchman Nee, *Sit, Walk, Stand,* (Kingsway, 1962), p 18.
5. Corrie Ten Boom, *Tramp for the Lord* (Hodder & Stoughton, 1974), p 55.
6. See also Chapter 2, note 4.
7. See also Chapter 3, p 52.
8. *Hymns Ancient & Modern Revised,* No. 107.
9. Patricia St John, *Would you believe it?* (Pickering & Inglis), p 154.
10. *The Oxford Book of Prayer,* (OUP, 1985), p 108.
11. *The Oxford Book of Prayer, ibid,* p 108.
12. Julian of Norwich, *Revelation of Divine Love* (DLT 1980), p 57 (Thirteen Revelation).
13. See Chapter 1, p 20.
14. Demos Shakarian, *The happiest people on earth* (Hodder & Stoughton, 1975), Chapter 1.
15. *The Oxford Book of Prayer, ibid,* p 107.
16. Dr Kenneth McAll, *The Healing of the Family Tree* (Sheldon Press, 1986).
17. Reg East, *Relaxing into Prayer*, a meditation tape on inner healing. Available via Reg East, Shepherd's Cottage, Whatcombe, Nr Blandford Forum, Dorset.
18. From Charles Wesley's hymn, *And can it be.*
19. M. Lloyd Jones, *Romans: Exposition of Chapter 8:5-17* (Banner of Truth, 1974), throughout.
20. Quoted by M. Lloyd Jones, *ibid,* p 202.
21. Selected works of Jonathan Edwards (Banner of Truth, 1974), p 32.
22. M. Lloyd Jones, *Ibid,* p 285, also pp 242-3 where, as a staunch evangelical, he mentions the experiences of some well known Catholics, and p 316 where he describes the three stages in Howell Harris' life. The great 18th-century evangelist was convicted of sin on Palm Sunday, March 30th, 1735, received assurance of salvation on Whitsunday, May

25th, and three weeks later, in secret prayer in the church tower of Llangasty, received an experience of God which caused him to write (later): 'Were it not for that love I had experienced, I would have drawn back, I would have given up. I could never have struggled against the flood. Love fell in showers upon my soul, so that I could scarce contain and control myself. I knew no fear and had no doubt of my salvation.

Interestingly, in view of today's 'Toronto' experience, Lloyd Jones also writes (p 328), 'Sometimes it has been such an overwhelming experience that Christians have literally fallen down in a dead faint. But to others, this has not happened.' He adds, wisely, 'We must be very careful not to limit the experience in terms of certain possible accompaniments.'

8

Your Kingdom Come – Prayer and Evangelism

(If God has chosen, why pray?)

This chapter sees evangelism as a primary sign of God's Kingdom. We explore both the need to pray for our families and those outside. We ask 'What is our story?' and see that faithful prayer is a key part of many conversions. We consider the problem of unbelief and how the 'veil' can be lifted (2 Corinthians 3:12ff). We give examples of praying for enquirers – for repentance and the new birth.

Your Kingdom Come –
Prayer and Evangelism

Every day, many Christians pray 'Your kingdom come'. If asked, they would probably have only a vague idea what they were praying for. Some would assume that they were praying for the Second Coming, others that they were praying and working for social justice here on earth.

At one extreme, Adventist groups spend much time preaching about, and even waiting for Jesus' return. Occasionally, the results are ludicrous, people stop working (a problem hinted at in *Different views of the kingdom* 2 Thess 3:6), fail to educate their children, fit their cars with sunshine roofs[1] so as to be ready to meet the Lord in the air, and, more destructively, welcome any new tension in the Middle East as a hopeful sign that Armageddon is about to take place.

At the other extreme, liberal theologians dismiss the whole idea of the Second Coming as absurd (citing texts like Lk 9:27 as examples of Jesus' fallible expectation of his own imminent return). As a result, social justice and the creation of the kingdom of God are emphasised, sometimes to the exclusion of evangelism and other things commanded and taught by Jesus.

The biblical view, I believe, is another paradox. The kingdom of God is growing, but has not yet been accomplished.

Jesus, in a rather neglected parable, sees the kingdom of God as like a seed growing secretly:

> He also said, 'This is what the kingdom of God is like. A man scatters seed on the ground. Night and day, whether he sleeps or gets up, the seed sprouts and grows, though he does not know how. All by itself the soil produces corn – first the stalk, then the ear, then the full kernel in the ear. As soon as the grain is ripe, he puts the sickle to it, because the harvest has come.' (Mk 4:26-29)

He responds to John the Baptist's spiritual crisis with quotations from Isaiah[2] to the effect that the signs of the kingdom are very present in his ministry: 'The blind receive sight, the lame walk, those who have leprosy are cured, the deaf hear, the dead are raised, and the good news is preached to the poor' (Mt 11:5).

The signs of the kingdom

After the mission of the seventy, Jesus comments, 'I saw Satan fall like lightning from heaven' (Lk 10:18). Nevertheless, the battle is far from won. That is the teaching of the great final discourses (see Mk 13:4ff; Mt 24), and the book of Revelation.

In 1944, Cullmann[3] used, what was then, a daring analogy. The decisive battle of the war had been fought when the Allies landed in Normandy in France; their victory was certain. Once the Allies had regained a foothold in France, they would inevitably win, but a fierce fight remained. But how long would it take?

For Christians, of course, Calvary is the decisive battle, the place of defeat for the dark powers: 'And having disarmed the powers and authorities, he made a public spectacle of them, triumphing over them by the cross' (Col 2:15). The Second Coming, whatever, whenever, will be the final victory. So when we pray 'Your kingdom come', we are praying with Jesus for the completion of a kingdom whose coming began with his earthly ministry. When we feel that there are few signs of it, we feel guilty and pray with greater urgency. Jesus taught (Mt 24:14) that the gospel had to be preached throughout the whole world, a daunting task for the first Christians! There are many gospel signs of the kingdom. In this chapter and the next, I shall concentrate on three – evangelism, healing, the healing of society. All feature in Jesus' reply to the imprisoned John. All are necessary for a balanced proclamation of the gospel.

Evangelism – the church's supreme task

Evangelism must spring out of our love for Christ. Without this love, given and received, evangelism can become a technique.

We must retain our love for Christ Without love, disaster beckons. Listen to Jesus speaking solemn words to the once great church at Ephesus: 'Yet I hold this against you: You have forsaken your first love. Remember the height from which you have fallen! Repent and do the things you did at first. If you do not repent, I will come to you and remove your lampstand from its place (Rev 2:4-5).

Without this love, without evangelism, churches must die. There are two sorts of evangelism, both need our prayer, for those 'within' and for those 'without'.

Evangelism within the Christian family

> But from everlasting to everlasting the LORD's love is with those who fear him, and his righteousness with their children's children. (Ps 103:17).

This is one of the most encouraging promises in the Bible for worried Christian parents. I often surprise engaged Christian couples at wedding preparation by telling them to pray for their grandchildren. Happily, there are many examples of Christian families with distinctive discipleship running through many generations.

An old lady was converted, in Chile, at the age of eighty. She felt sad that she had wasted so much of her life. 'What shall I do now?' she asked the evangelist. He told her to concentrate on prayer – for her family. She prayed, particularly for her grandchildren. One, already a Christian,[4] told me the rest of the story.

One grandson was travelling in Spain, near Avila. He was a typical student dropout. Quite suddenly, he was aware of Jesus' presence. His conversion was as sudden and as unexpected as St Paul's! He soon studied to become a pastor. He led many of his grandmother's large family to faith. The last thing that the old lady did at the age of ninety, just before her death, was to attend his ordination. Her last ten years had been very fruitful!

Of course, there is nothing automatic in all this. It is a great joy when our children follow the Christian way. Our responsibility is to pray, and to believe, but we cannot presume, therein is part of the mystery of evangelism. *Praying for Christian families*

One friend has had the great joy of seeing two grandsons come to faith despite extreme scepticism in the middle generation. Personally, I take Dr Kenneth MacAll's[5] teaching on the Family Tree very seriously. If negative problems, due to such things as occult activity, suicide, abortion, can affect future generations, *how much more* should we believe that God wishes to produce Christian families descending through many generations.

I believe that we shall increasingly see this as God's answer to the secular world with its ever growing divorce rate and all the associated problems.

However, before we set out on some great programme of prayer and evangelism, we need to prepare ourselves. Every Christian should learn: 'But in your hearts set apart Christ as Lord. Always be prepared to give an answer to everyone who asks you to give the reason for the hope that you have. But do this with gentleness and respect' (1 Pet 3:15). *A key text*

We are not required to leap on unsuspecting victims and overwhelm them with our unwanted witness. Such action is usually counterproductive and can help harden the other person's heart. We are required to reverence Christ as our Lord. If we do this, we will want to obey him, and we will be serious about talking to other people, when they give us an opportunity, 'in season and out of season'. (2 Tim 4:2)

My friend Randy Vickers[6] has a good account of evangelism and healing at the local golf club! He noticed, on the first tee, the very short swing of one of his opponents. This, Randy was told, was caused by an incredible injury to his right shoulder. By the tenth tee, Randy had plucked up courage to say, 'Martin, your shoulder can be healed!' This led to an immediate prayer, and a dramatic healing, on the tenth tee. The result of this was that a long weekend spent with 'The Hairdressing Manufacturers and Wholesalers Asssocation', as well as being devoted to golf and a dinner dance, became a *Evangelism at play* weekend of healing and evangelism. Five other people were dramatically healed, onlookers amazed, and several appear to have become disciples.

What is your story?

Following 1 Peter 3:15, each of us should have our 'story'. Our testimony ought to include a mixture of intellectual reasons for our faith, especially the Resurrection, and some experiential evidence of God's grace in our own lives and the lives of others. Don't be put off by the standard objections. 'Vicar, I'm not coming to your church, it's full of hypocrites.' 'Come and make one more', was my effective reply.

We are required to do this with 'gentleness and respect'. Gentleness is a very strong word – literally meaning the quality of a well-broken-in horse. Gentleness is being Christlike. We do no one any favours by trying to bludgeon them into the kingdom of God.

When I was being appointed to my present living, the Patron's representative said, 'Are you a Bible basher? My employer doesn't like Bible bashers.' I replied that I took the Bible very seriously, but that didn't mean that I was a Bible basher!

Evangelism at work   One of my friends works at putting fireplaces in people's houses. This leads to lots of conversations. He's an effective evangelist, sharing with many surprised customers his surprising discovery of faith. His evangelism is much helped by the fact that he's an excellent workman. Nothing would be worse for the kingdom than leaking gas fires fitted by an over enthusiastic fitter!

A good prayer for us would be, 'Lord, I'm not much good at sharing my faith – but please give me an opportunity to talk to someone. Please give me the right words, the right manner, and your Holy Spirit.'

Evangelism as a priority

It is very easy for Christians to spend most of their time involved in good works, meeting and ministering with Christian friends, worshipping and praying. We must be prepared to leave these safe havens, go out and look for those who want to hear, and not waste time with those who don't (see Lk 10:10ff).

St Bonaventure makes the point rather well:[7] 'In prayer, we talk to God and listen him, and we walk with the angels. But in preaching, we have to descend to the human level and live among others as one of them, thinking and seeing and hearing and speaking on the human level.

But in favour of preaching, there is one argument which seems to count more than all the rest in God's eyes and it is this: the only begotten Son of God, who is Infinite Wisdom, descended from the Father's embrace to save souls – he renewed the world by his own example, bringing the word of salvation to human beings. The price of this salvation was his precious blood, which washes us clean and is a fortifying drink. He kept nothing for himself, but generously gave all for our salvation. We, then, are bound to act according to the model which we see shining in him as on a high mountain. Thus it seems more in accordance with God's will that I leave the repose of contemplation and go out into the world...'

We need to prepare ourselves, in prayer, and go (or wait) as God directs.

Praying for God's grace to be outpoured

Occasionally evangelism seems easy, God's grace is so obviously outpoured. We can only watch and marvel. In September 1995 a young man visited our church. He was bowled over by a clever, but not particularly deep, children's talk for Harvest Festival. He came to see me in the afternoon. It was obvious that I didn't have to do anything – except to pray with him. That night, he rang his girlfriend in Canada. It must have been an expensive call! He was overwhelmed by the Spirit when he tried to explain what was happening. The next day, he asked me about a good church in Cheltenham, where he was studying. He was thrilled to find a flourishing church, with an Alpha course. A little while later, he was confirmed. His family were impressed. I wonder when God will touch them. Behind it all lies the mystery of God's grace and our prayer. His Christian girlfriend and her father, an Anglican clergyman, must have been involved. But in the end, God's call was so powerful that his conversion seemed inevitable.

By contrast, Iain, a young member of our congregation,

experienced conversion through the sovereignty of God, greatly helped by the gift of a Bible, and the prayer of a faithful young Christian. For him, conversion was a lengthy spiritual battle.

He described his life up to the age of twenty-five as 'running away from God, whom I'd experienced as a young child. I'd felt his presence and peace at the age of twelve. I'd asked my surprised parents for a crucifix as a birthday present. I even joined the local church choir for a short time. Most significant was the gift of a New Testament from a Gideon visit to my school. I was very struck by the words which seemed to have been part of my life already. The clearest challenge came from Matthew 7:13-14;

> Enter ye in at the strait gate: for wide is the gate, and broad is the way, that leadeth to destruction, and many there be which go in thereat: Because strait is the gate, and narrow is the way, which leadeth unto life, and few there be that find it (AV).

'I knew that I was being offered a choice – life eternal, or death. But then I started to turn away from God. I reached a point of no return, by the age of twenty-five I'd lost my girlfriend, my car, my job, my pride… I was in debt, and struggling with drink, fights, sex, and worst of all, a deep depression which led to bouts of great anger.

'My long-suffering mother, and I put my parents through hell, said "Iain, get out of Shepton before it kills you." I went away for a year, working at Butlin's in Skegness. I started to pray – but to whom was I praying? I remember watching an ambulance race by with lights flashing. I said, "Lord, please give my blessing to that person, they need it, I don't deserve it."

'Soon afterwards I returned from Butlin's and started to return to my old habits. Then God brought a committed Christian friend, Kim, to help me. Eventually, I told her that I wanted to follow the narrow way. She smiled, a smile of thanksgiving to God!

'The battle was fierce. I fell and lost my way. Eventually, I joined the parish church, received a warm welcome, and got involved with helping some of the youth. But my past was pulling at me.

'One Sunday, with great difficulty because it seemed that the devil was trying to stop me, I stood up at Parish Praise and said:

"Be careful with your lives, and the love of God, or he will be gone." A few days later, I fell asleep. I had a vision. I was in a bar with my footballing friends. Suddenly, I was surrounded by a beam of light, coming from above. My friends couldn't see it, but they were still laughing and talking. Then I saw myself, arms outstretched and raised, in the light. I was still in the bar, but separated – no better than anyone else, but with a different heart.

'This experience seemed to seal my conversion. Although the battle remains, from that moment I felt that I was certainly walking in the narrow way.'

By contrast, David,[8] an unusually talented organist, was brought up in a strongly Christian home. But at the age of eighteen, he describes his spiritual journey as follows:

'I began, as a lapsed Christian, to re-investigate Christianity. I was shown the need for a clear choice for or against Christ. My decision was triggered, rather unexpectedly, by an account of various modern-day healing miracles.[9] This brought an absolute conviction of the truth of the Resurrection, and a personal encounter with the Risen Lord.

'This was confirmed a week later at a church meeting when the speaker invited people forward to make a public commitment, which I did. The speaker laid hands upon me, encouraging me to speak in tongues – which I did, briefly. The result of this anointing was an immediate energisation and enthusiasm to work for the gospel.

'Although about a year later, my commitment was broken (for a while) in quite a deliberate and sustained way, I don't think that invalidates the experience. The sovereign act of the Spirit made me a believer – but not yet a mature one.'

For David, the faithful prayers of his family, the evidence of modern signs of the kingdom, and a deep encounter, combined to make the path of discipleship clear.

As I wrote in Chapter 3, at Mutwe,[10] many responded to an evangelistic address after the sign of the angel. The supernatural occurrence made preaching much simpler! I have never known an occasion when it was so easy to preach and to expect a response to an evangelistic message.

No one knows why revivals take place. After I was made a

school chaplain,[11] I persuaded the headmaster, in October 1974, to invite Canon Keith de Berry, then Rector of St Aldate's, to visit the school. Two of us prayed a great deal for his visit. God had encouraged me with a rare visionary experience. In August, Jane and I were on holiday in Austria; one morning, as I was praying outside our tent, the Lord seemed to point out a field of corn stooks. There were about thirty at the near end of the field, and then a thin line stretching up the right hand side of the field over the horizon. God seemed to say, 'Those nearest will be converted next term, and the work will continue...'

A promise of evangelism

Keith's visit began inauspiciously. A compulsory talk to the Upper School was resented. After a few minutes he told a really terrible joke: 'There was this man who went to the lunatic asylum. He asked, "Why are you lot all here?"'

"Because we're not all there!" came the reply.'

I didn't know where to look – but the school, perhaps the most intellectual in England, fell about with laughter. After that, he could do no wrong. Nearly two hundred came to each of his talks – a miracle in itself; the previous distinguished speaker, a diocesan missioner, had managed less than twenty! At the end, about sixty responded. About thirty made a real profession of faith, and the work continued for many years, until a strange combination of opposition, and Christian failing, brought it to a sudden end. There are a number of Christian leaders whose discipleship began in that mission, or in the years that followed.

A time of reaping

On a much larger scale, who would have predicted a hundred years ago that South Korea would become a world centre for Christianity? Who would have predicted the Pentecostal revival in South America? Who, in the eighteenth century would have predicted the evangelical revival in England and America? Truly, 'The wind blows wherever it pleases. You hear its sound, but you cannot tell where it comes from, or where it is going. So it is with everyone born of the Spirit' (Jn 3:8). Our task is to pray and to be bold.

I love the story at the end of Acts 4 (vv23-31). After threats and persecution, the believers prayed in these great words: 'Now,

Lord, consider their threats and enable your servants to speak
your word with great boldness. Stretch out your hand
to heal and perform miraculous signs and wonders   *God's*
through the name of your holy servant Jesus (vv29-   *sovereignty*
30). And the result was dramatic: 'After they prayed,   *and our need*
the place where they were meeting was shaken. And   *to pray*
they were all filled with the Holy Spirit and spoke the word of
God boldly' (v31).

Effective evangelism is costly. Opposition can be aroused.
New disciples disturb and ask hard questions. They expect high
standards. A comfortable church all too easily dispenses with
fervent prayer and then is, secretly, quite glad that it can continue
at its normal safe level.

By contrast, where the church is growing, for example in many
parts of Africa and Asia, there is much prayer, much expectation,
and somehow more space for God's sovereign will to convert. We
must accept this paradox – God's electing choice and our need to
pray for a response. Jesus sums it up: 'All that the Father gives me
will come to me, and whoever comes to me I will never drive
away' (Jn 6:37). Our prayers and our witness are our privileged
part in the second half of that process.

Praying for people to see their need of God

A major problem is that most people don't see any need of God.
A close relative of one of the men mentioned in the previous
section said to me, 'I'm so glad for him. He needed something to
give his life a purpose.' He needed! So did his relative, but as yet
she is moved, but unresponsive. Basically, most of think we are
decent people; we think that our good works and occasional
religious observances are 'doing our duty by God' and we are
very offended if anyone suggests anything to the contrary. The
18th-century Duchess of Buckingham was more than offended by
the evangelical Countess of Huntingdon. She wrote, tren-
chantly,[12] 'I thank your ladywhip for the information concerning
the Methodist preachers: their doctrines are most repulsive,
strong tinctured with impertinence and disrespect towards their
superiors, in perpetually endeavouring to level all ranks and do

Evangelism is not always popular

away with all distinctions. It is quite monstrous to be told that you have a heart as sinful as the common wretches that crawl on the earth. This is highly offensive and insulting and I cannot but wonder that your ladyship would relish any sentiment so much at variance with high rank and good breeding.'

The Countess of Huntingdon, a particular friend of the evangelist George Whitefield, was a courageous lady. She annoyed the Archbishop of Canterbury by complaining of the balls and parties that he held in Lambeth Palace – thereby earning the praise of the king! Her theological efforts were more successful with the Duchess of Marlborough, who wrote, 'Your concern for my improvement is very obliging, God knows we all need mending, none more than myself, women of wit, beauty and quality cannot bear too many humiliating truths – they shock our pride. But we must die; we must converse with earth and worms!' She, at least, was beginning to understand Romans 3:23: '...for all have sinned and fall short of the glory of God.' The Holy Spirit was beginning his great work: 'Where he comes, he will convict the world of guilt in regard to sin and righteousness and judgment' (Jn 16:8).

When someone says to me, 'I'm not a Christian', unless they are the diffident sort who need encouragement, my usual response is 'Alleluiah!' When they've realised that, the veil of spiritual blindness is being removed: 'Whenever anyone turns to the Lord, the veil is taken away' (2 Cor 3:16). It is important to study the whole passage (2 Corinthians 3:12 - 4:6).

The veil of unbelief

Evangelism is a strange business. Sometimes so simple, yet at other times – despite God's apparent leading – we come up against a seemingly inpenetrable barrier.

I remember praying hard for a businessman. His wife, despite a serious progressive illness, was a recent and radiant believer. Her husband was delighted to discuss theological matters; he would take me out to lunch, and be good company until the moment when I felt he was ready to make a Christian commitment. Then, quite suddenly the shutters would close, he would laugh, and change the subject.

I was very frustrated, and prayed hard to know the reason. The answer came! No word of knowledge, no inspired line of questioning. Some months later, he was found to be defrauding the small business that he managed. He was dismissed, and very fortunate not to be prosecuted. Suddenly he was able to repent, and rebuild his life – as a Christian! For him the 'veil' had been drawn tightly closed by dishonesty.

Occult involvement, sexual sin, bitterness, refusal to forgive others (and God and oneself), and intellectual pride, are other problems which keep the 'veil' firmly over people's spiritual eyes. Sometimes God will reveal a problem to an evangelist. He never does this to embarrass the person, but rather to help them repent.

Fred Smith[13] tells a nice story which illustrates this, and which links evangelism and healing. A lady came up for prayer in Oxford Town Hall, accompanied by her very tall husband. Fred was about to pray for her, when he felt that the Lord was saying, 'Don't pray for her. Tell her she must forgive her husband.' Fred, a tall man, looked apprehensively at her companion and gave her God's message.

'You're quite right!' she replied, 'I haven't forgiven my first husband'. Healing and discipleship followed her repentance.

In England and Western Europe, most people's lives are too comfortable. They don't want to be bothered with God – their 'veil' is a pleasant round of work, family activity, and a few good works. Then disaster strikes – redundancies, divorce, accident, bereavement – and they have a difficult choice. Do they swallow their pride, and turn to God because they are in trouble? Or do they soldier on as their comfortable lives disintegrate? Our prayers and presence can make a decisive difference! We might pray along these lines: 'Lord, your word encourages me to believe that you want all to be saved (1 Tim 2:4). Please open my friend's eyes. Please show what is blocking him (her) from hearing the gospel. Please help me to know when to speak and when to keep quiet.'

Another great privilege is to pray with people at their point of commitment to Jesus.

Praying for enquirers

It is exciting to see a butterfly emerge from a chrysalis. With most species, the wing patterns appear, the chrysalis darkens and cracks, and the butterfly emerges. Wings, small and crumpled, expand before our wondering eyes; and the butterfly hangs helpless, waiting for them to harden so that it can fly.

It is thrilling to see a child born. 'A woman giving birth to a child has pain because her time has come; but when her baby is born she forgets the anguish because of her joy that a child is born into the world' (Jn 16:21). Usually the birth, however difficult, is not dangerous. Recently, however, a friend of mine's baby tried to strangle itself with its umbilical cord. Prompt action by midwife and doctors prevented a tragedy.

It is an enormous privilege to be with someone when they make their first halting prayer of faith. If we are to be spiritual midwives, we need to know what to do.

'I planted the seed. Apollos watered it, but God made it grow' (1 Cor 3:6), says St Paul. People need to make a prayer of repentance and a prayer to receive. It is vital that we don't force or hurry anyone – if God is at work, he will bring them through. The butterfly seldom needs any help – a little heat is sometimes useful, other interference is usually fatal. The midwife is there to encourage, the doctor perhaps to perform an emergency operation. Usually nature knows best

When someone is really seeking God, I give them several choices. 'Would you like to go away and think it all through – you may not be ready yet?' 'Would you like to take this book (booklet) and pray by yourself?' 'Would you like to come back next week, and we will pray together?' 'Would you like to pray now?'

If they choose the last option, I like to go somewhere very quiet. In my case, the church is the obvious place. We prepare the ground by discussing repentance. A seed needs to be planted in good, clean soil!

Praying for repentance   Sometimes people believe that they are too bad to be forgiven. Occasionally, they convince themselves that they have committed the unforgivable sin (see, for instance, Mk 3:22-30). Jesus makes it clear that what is unforgivable is to attribute his work to the powers of darkness. What is unforgivable is to call black white, or vice versa. While a few revisionist historians may occasionally argue that Hitler didn't kill Jewish people in the war, no serious seeker after faith is remotely likely to have committed the blasphemy against the Holy Spirit.

Occasionally, in desperation, I've asked people who cannot accept that God will forgive them, 'What is so special about *your* sins that Almighty God cannot release them?' They usually laugh and admit that it is a subtle form of pride to believe that they are unforgivable.

Radical repentance involves turning. It is a U turn – death to self, alive to God. A former British Prime Minister, Margaret Thatcher, once famously said, 'The lady's not for turning.' But that is exactly what a true prayer of repentance means.

I often illustrate this in my study by turning away from the person I'm talking to, looking out of the window, and talking for a while about the garden and the church. Then I ask them what I need to do to communicate with them properly.

'Turn and face me,' is the invariable reply.

I explain that that's what repentance means. Up until now they've run their own lives, now they must turn and go God's way. Repentance is not about confessing our individual sins. That follows when we've realised that our major sin is leaving God out of our lives. 'When he (the Holy Spirit) comes, he will convict the world of guilt in regard to sin...' (Jn 16:8). We may encourage them to pray – or lead them in prayer – along the line, 'Lord, please forgive me for my sin, particularly for ignoring you. Thank you that through the cross, Jesus bore my sin, and help me to believe that.' Then they may wish to confess particular sins – usually that can wait, but some sins, especially occult involvement, are a major block to receiving the Holy Spirit.

I remember myself as a twenty-year-old undergraduate. Fairly self confident, with a church background and a belief in the Resurrection, a regular church attender, I offered myself for a month's work in the South London Industrial Mission. When I returned to Oxford, I expected a pat on the back from the Vicar of St Aldate's, Keith de Berry. Instead, he asked me if I'd given my life to Jesus. That conversation, and a friend with whom I shared digs, prodded away at me for nearly a year. Eventually I was ready to repent. As far as life style, at that time the only serious issue was the game of bridge! (There have been many more over the years since.) Several of my friends, admittedly rather better players, became international players. One writes the daily column in *The Times* newspaper. But God released the hold of this game. Soon afterwards, there came a crunch moment. My parents played every Sunday with a local couple. They liked me to join in. One fateful Sunday, I refused (I continued to play on other days). I felt that the Lord wanted me to spend Sunday afternoon in prayer and Bible study. Looking back, it was a vital decision, and curiously, after much mockery, it helped my parents' faith – they suddenly knew that I was serious!

Repentance alone is not enough, indeed it drives us deeper into the spiritual mire. The other side of the spiritual coin is receiving. 'Yet to all who received him, to those who believed in his name, he gave the right to become children of God' (Jn 1:12).

Praying to receive

There are many metaphors for the new birth experience – receiving Christ, putting on the Lord Jesus (Rom 13:14), receiving the gift of the Holy Spirit (Lk 11:13; Acts 2:38), Christ dwelling in our hearts by faith (Eph 3:17). Many metaphors – one experience.

And so comes the great moment, we pray for the spiritual butterfly to leave its chrysalis. A butterfly needs faith to fly! I once witnessed a Large Tortoiseshell, just emerged from its chrysalis, sitting high up on the trunk of an elm tree. A hornet descended on it, and four pierced wings fluttered to the ground. The hornet enjoyed its meal. Another butterfly appeared, sitting within centimetres of the hornet, flapping its wings uncertainly. Jane and I threw stones into the tree. Eventually, Jane hit the trunk just below both insects. Hornet and butterfly flew off in opposite directions. That evening a Red Admiral, resident in our camp site, was sitting on our roof rack – its normal evening position. A hornet zoomed past, the butterfly took off, flapped its wings around the hornet, and shooed it away. The Red Admiral then calmly returned to its evening roost. I reckoned that I had seen

1 Peter 5:8b, Jude 23, and 1 Peter 5:9 illustrated by the hornets and the butterflies!

We need faith to pray with someone, and they need faith: 'If you confess with your mouth, "Jesus is Lord", and believe in your heart that God raised him from the dead, you will be saved' (Rom 10:9). So they may pray for example: 'Lord Jesus, I believe that you rose from the dead, I believe that your Father promised the gift of the Holy Spirit to those who ask, and now in committing my life to you, I ask you to fill me with your Holy Spirit.'

If appropriate, we may lay hands on them and pray that they may feel the presence of the Spirit. Each situation is different, each experience is different, but it is important that we know what to do when God gives us a real opportunity. It is pastorally helpful sometimes to share this sort of prayer – occasionally it can be done in semi-public at a confirmation class, or an Alpha course. This wonderfully helps the faith of others, especially those who have brought the new disciples along, and been important links in the spiritual chain. Which leads to our next great prayer task.

Praying for disciples to grow

Apollos watered! Paul prayed. Jesus, at the end of Matthew's Gospel (Mt 28:16-20), called us to make obedient disciples. Paul, in particular, prayed:

> I keep asking that the God of our Lord Jesus Christ, the glorious Father, may give you the Spirit of wisdom and revelation, so that you may know him better. I pray also that the eyes of your heart may be enlightened in order that you may know the hope to which he has called you, the riches of his glorious inheritance in the saints, and his incomparably great power for us who believe. That power is like the working of his mighty strength, which he exerted in Christk *Praying* when he raised him from the dead and seated him at his right *for growth* hand in the heavenly realms, far above all rule and authority, power and dominion, and every title that can be given, not only in the present age but also in the one to come. And God placed all things under his feet and appointed him to be head over everything for the church, which is his body, the fulness of him who fills everything in every way (Eph 1:17-23)

A breathtaking prayer. Each church should have Alpha courses, instruction courses, adult confirmation courses, to help enquirers and new believers. Our task is to cover them in prayer, to befriend, and to teach.

Each 'profession of faith' is different. Some people are very emotional, some very happy, some quite detached. Some are over enthusiastic, some too laid back, all need help. A young plant needs protection and watering. Often such people are immediate evangelists. They have two advantages – they are full of new enthusiasm, and they have plenty of non-Christian friends!

Cuthbert Bardsley, former Bishop of Coventry, used to say that you cannot ooze into the kingdom of God. He illustrated from his own life. Converted as an undergraduate, he tried to hide it from his rowing eight. God convicted him of this, and he had to witness to other sportsmen. Immediately, he discovered that he was an evangelist.

A lovely saying attributed to St John of the Cross:[14] 'And such is the fervour and power of God's charity that those of whom he takes possession can never again be limited by their own souls or be contented with them. Rather it seems to them a small thing to go to heaven alone. Wherefore they may strive to take many to heaven with them. This arises from the great love which they have for their God and it is the true fruit and effect of perfect love and contemplation.'

Evangelism, our prime task

When we have that sort of understanding, we must be praying for the extension of God's kingdom, and we must be praying to be part of that great work ourselves. Nothing else will do!

Notes

1. Based on a literal interpretation of 1 Thessalonians 4:17.
2. Isaiah 61:1.
3. Oscar Cullmann, *Prayers in the New Testament*, (SCN 1995), p 47.
4. Rosemary Prior, David's wife, see above Chapter 6, note 11.
5. See Chapter 7, note 16.

6. See *Renewal Magazine,* May 1996. The Revd Randolph Vickers is a non-stipendiary minister. He and his wife Dorothy run the Northumberland Christian Healing Centre.
7. See Franciscan cycle of daily readings, April 3.
8. David Goode is now assistant organist at Christchurch Cathedral, Oxford.
9. Fred Smith, *God's Gift of Healing* (New Wine Press, 1986).
10. See Chapter 3, p 52ff.
11. At Winchester College, where I taught 1962-1975.
12. See Garth Lean, *John Wesley Anglican* (Blandford Paperbacks 1964) p 72.
13. See Chapter 1, note 9.
14. Sister Eileen Lyddon, *Door through Darkness* (New City 1994), p 96.

9

Your Kingdom Come – Prayer for Healing of the Individual and Society

(The wounds are so deep – can anything be done?)

To pray for healing is a great privilege. We look at the possible results of such prayer. The ministry of the local church, how to pray, and the vexed question of deliverance. We also look at the important question of praying with the dying.

The second part considers various projects which are bringing healing to a part of society, and the importance of the prayer which undergirds them.

Your Kingdom Come – Prayer for Healing of the Individual and Society

Healing and evangelism are inextricably linked. They present similar theological problems. God's sovereignty is just as apparent in healing as in evangelism. Praying for someone's healing, whether it involves physical illness, emotional needs, forgiveness, deliverance, or any combination of these, is a great privilege, and a wonderful experience of God's grace.

As with evangelism, there is a mystery. Some people receive extraordinary miracles, others struggle on without any obvious improvement. There can be a real measure of frustration. As in the Gospels, people are healed, but apparently unchanged spiritually; at other times, like Randy Vickers' golfing opponent on the tenth tee (see Chapter 8), there is a dramatic change.

Prayer for healing was, and I believe is, an essential part of Jesus' message (Lk 10:9; Mk 6:13, etc). Prayer for healing raises the spiritual atmosphere of a church. People, sometimes complete outsiders, sense God in a new way. Let me give a few examples.

One old lady, who seldom came but often seemed critical of the modern church, came to one of our healing services. Some months later, I met her. She fixed me with a beady eye and said, 'Vicar, I came to one of your healing services.' I waited for the inevitable criticism! Her next words astonished me.

'Vicar, I felt a presence that I'd never felt before.' It was a transforming experience. She wasn't healed of her illness, but she knew God's love for the first time. When she faced a terminal illness a few years later, she faced it with great bravery, humour, and faith. One brief moment at a village church healing service seemed to give her spiritual hope and comfort.

Karen, who comes from time to time to our church (her family commitments lead her to worship elsewhere) came to our recent mission services. At the end the evangelist, Jon Peters from St Paul's Onslow Square, called people forward. A number responded. *Experience God's love in a new way* He prayed, quite simply, for the Holy Spirit to touch them. Karen felt a great power, fell to the ground, and experienced a deep sensation in her head. She had asked for prayer for her persistent migraines. When she went home she looked in the mirror and gasped. Her eye, which had endured many unsuccessful operations to cure a childhood squint, was normal! Her husband and her optician were most impressed. Other relatives, and some medical people with whom she works, found it rather less impressive. This wonderful experience has given her and her husband confidence to testify to Christ in magazines, on local radio, and in their everyday life.

Physical healing, particularly when it can't be explained away as 'psychosomatic', is very baffling to the unbeliever – a clear sign of God's kingdom on earth. I believe that it is one that God is increasingly using as a sign in our unbelieving society.

Who should pray?

The Bible doesn't give a great deal of instruction. James 5:14 implies that it is the job of the elders of the church (whoever they are!). 1 Corinthians 12:9 lists gifts of healing as one of the gifts of the Holy Spirit. The Gospels and Acts imply that healing was exercised by the disciples, the seventy, and the leaders of the church.

Current experience suggests three levels of ministry. A few are called to make healing their priority ministry. Fred Smith[1] was one such. Early in his public ministry, he described how he was having a flask of tea overlooking the city of Bath, and he asked for 'the gift of faith' (1 Cor 12:9) for that night. Everyone was healed! Fred, henceforth, had an extraordinary expectation which led to miracles of healing being recorded on Radio Oxford, the *Oxford Journal*, etc. Of course, people weren't always healed (any more than everyone who goes to hear Billy Graham is converted), but even those who weren't healed were blessed. Many were converted, as Fred always preached the need for commitment to Christ before he prayed for their healing.

The healing ministry today – leaders

On one occasion I took Fred to pray with my neighbour. He had serious lung cancer and was facing a long, painful illness. A very committed Christian, he felt God's presence as Fred prayed – that night he died very peacefully and far sooner than might have been expected.

Obviously, in recent years, God has called countless individuals to such ministries, and it would be impossible to name them. Some specialise in inner healing, some in deliverance, some in physical healing. All expect God to be glorified, all are deeply humble people, all hope and pray that their healing ministry will be a sign that helps people into the kingdom.

A second level of ministry is within the local church. A few people will feel called, or reluctantly respond when asked to be part of a ministry team. Such a group will need to spend time in prayer, waiting upon God and sharing experiences. I was very impressed to visit Holy Trinity Leicester recently and to be asked to attend their time of 'listening prayer'. About twelve people prayed for about half-an-hour. They shared themes and particular 'words'. On this particular Sunday, the theme of rejection seemed important, and various particular words were given – one of the team had an unexpected pain in the left arm. These were mentioned half-way through the service. After Communion, about twenty people came for prayer, many responding to the particular topics or illnesses mentioned in the service. I felt that this church had an effective ministry which God was blessing. Of the few people that I was privileged to pray for, in one case both my prayer partner and I felt there was need for deep, future ministry.

The healing ministry today – the local church

Independently, we sensed that we were only touching the surface of a deep spiritual iceberg. I shall be interested to hear how it works out.

There are obvious dangers in such teams! If the wrong people arrive in them, it is very hard to ease them out without deep hurt. Also, the existence of a team may give the impression that everyone else can forget about healing and leave the 'experts' to get on with it.

Which brings me to the third and most important level of ministry – the body of Christ! If our church is functioning at all, then it will be an every-member-ministry church.

> It was he who gave some to be apostles, some to be prophets, some to be evangelists, and some to be pastors and teachers, to prepare God's people for works of service, so that the body of Christ may be built up until we all reach unity in the faith and in the knowledge of the Son of God and become mature, attaining to the whole measure of the fulness of Christ. (Eph 4:11-13)

and

> Now you are the body of Christ, and each one of you is a part of it. And in the church God has appointed first of all apostles, second prophets, third teachers, then workers of miracles, also those having gifts of healing, those able to help others, those with gifts of administration, and those speaking in different kinds of tongues. (1 Cor 12:27,28)

The healing ministry today – you and me

That means that we can all pray for other people – in the house group, over a cup of coffee, after the church service. There are just a few conditions – we need a measure of faith, and ideally we shouldn't be on our own. (Jesus always sent people out in pairs! It releases us from both the spiritual burden of 'failure' and the awful spiritual pride of 'success'!) We should be right with the Lord, and we shouldn't rush in blindly. As with evangelism, ill thought-out, unasked-for prayer for healing can do a lot of harm. We would be wise to pray along these lines, 'Lord, if you want me to pray with my neighbour, please give me some clear indication. May she ask me to pray, and will you please show me how to pray and what to pray for?'

Here is a lovely testimony of a mother praying with her daughter, and one of her own experiences in prayer:

'In early 1993, at the end of a difficult weekend when, it seemed, our eldest daughter, Jasmine, had been particularly demanding and impossible to please, we discovered that she was developing some very worrying physical symptoms and was having difficulty in walking. The doctor arrived and was concerned enough to send us off to hospital immediately. On arrival at the hospital, doctors seemed perplexed for quite a while, and we were placed in a side room on our own. Jasmine was in great pain and we were distressed to see this, especially as there was nothing anyone could do for her and her symptoms were worsening. Eventually, late that night, a diagnosis was made and we realised that we would just have to let the rare disease run its course. Nick went home,and I settled down for an uncomfortable night on the camp bed close to Jasmine's. As soon as I was on my own, I began to pray in the darkness of the little room.

Jesus' presence   Immediately I saw the shining outline of Jesus at the end of Jasmine's bed. I thought, simply, "Jesus is here". I looked back to the place and saw him again. At that point I fell asleep peacefully, only waking from time to time as the staff came in to check on Jasmine.

'I awoke in the morning to see Jasmine's smiling and peaceful face looking across at me. We spent a wonderful day together in the hospital and returned home that evening. Two days later she had made a complete recovery. I didn't mention my meeting with Jesus to Nick for a few days. It had seemed such a natural part of my prayer that night, not just a sign and wonder to marvel over. Jesus came to me simply and gently and was there to comfort at exactly the right moment. It has never happened since, but the gift I received at that moment was not just for that moment, it was for ever. It is still there for me to draw strength from and nothing can take it from me.

'I would also like to mention another example of Christ's gentle touch of healing in my life which, again, came unexpectedly; a fleeting moment revealing a great truth about God's love for me. You, John, have often preached about the difficulties of recognising God's qualities as a loving Father for those who have not experienced a loving father themselves. I believe my father did love me in his way, but as he himself had lost his father at the age of three, and was at boarding school from the age of seven, he had very little experience of loving fathers to pass on to his four children.

'One evening, during the time I had set aside for prayer, I saw a picture of myself as a tiny child of about three years old. Jesus was walking ahead of me as climbed a craggy hillside. Every so often he would lift me in his *God as loving Father* arms and hold me up high to see the view. He lifted me gently and lovingly, just as Nick lifts our two daughters, Jasmine and Tansy, when each touch is full of warmth and affection, to be enjoyed and welcomed by both father and child. I couldn't understand God's love for me through my childhood experience, but I have been shown another way.'

How should we pray?

There are, not surprisingly, many different approaches. The more 'Catholic' way is to lay hands upon people, silently, and leave what happens between God and the person. This is quite similar to the 'Toronto' approach when the Holy Spirit is invoked with some prayer like, 'Come, Holy Spirit', and the results are left between the person and God. The difference is, perhaps, one of expectation!

Many people find it helpful to ask why someone has come for prayer (most people, in my experience, expect this and are helped by this sort of enquiry) and then to pray as seems appropriate. But how should we actually pray with those who come for help?

It is important that each person prayed for is given time, and enabled to relax. A long queue of people in a prayer line, waiting to receive brief prayer from a visiting expert, needs very careful handling. They need to be talked to, given some idea of how long they will have to wait, and receive proper follow-up afterwards. Obviously, a visiting speaker can have only a short time with individuals; back-up teams to follow up, and if necessary continue in prayer, are important.

More normally, prayer will take place in a quiet corner of the church, a study, or a home. The person asking for prayer often ***How to pray*** brings a friend, and usually there will be a pair of prayers. I find that one person usually leads the prayer time, the other mainly listens – for a word of knowledge from the Lord, a key question, or just observing what seems to be happening as a result of the prayer.

There is often a marked physical improvement, that is an encouragement to pray more. If there is no improvement, it is usually best to cease, and enquire later how they are. Occasionally the person feels physically worse, which is usually a sign of some quite deep spiritual disturbance. Following James 5, I sometimes anoint with oil. This can be done formally, following liturgy provided by the Church of England,[2] or more informally. It seems appropriate for persistent illnesses, depression, migraines... and also as a follow-up to any sort of deliverance prayer.

Sometimes healing prayer takes place without any physical contact, or even the knowledge of the person prayed for (Lk 7:1-10). When recovering from a hip operation in the Spring of 1991, someone gave me an article written in the *Evening Standard* by Archbishop George just before his enthronement. He described his belief in the efficacy of prayer and recalled how he was struck down by a migraine at a particularly busy time, just before Pentecost 1988, when he was hosting a very special day in Wells Cathedral. He remembered that the Rector of Shepton Mallet, hearing about his problem, rang up and prayed down the phone. Apparently, the migraine left.

My memory, also being quite involved in the Pentecost celebration, is of ringing up and offering 'to come over and pray. If the Chairman of the Diocesan Healing Group can't do that...' Bishop George politely, but firmly, said he was too busy! In desperation, and to be honest, with a tinge of annoyance, I offered an immediate prayer over the phone. I had no idea it was efficacious, until I read the article nearly three years later!

Do the words matter, and what about those strange phenomena? What we say, provided it is prayed in faith and love and in the name of Jesus, is relatively unimportant. Some people curse cancers (like the fig tree in Mk 11:14), some rebuke illnesses (like

Jesus with Peter's mother-in-law in Lk 4:39), some see much illness as demonic (as Jesus did occasionally, see Lk 13:16), some pray in tongues (I remember once consciously not praying in tongues because I thought it would embarrass. Only to be told 'please pray in tongues – it's much more effective when you do'), most have different approaches in different situations.

Phenomena are not of primary importance

Some people do receive strange phenomena – a strong sensation of heat, a transference of pain, a gentle power which causes the prayed-for person to fall over... None of these are essential, or even important, but they do happen! Jesus had some strange experiences (power left him, see Lk 8:46), and he did see strange things (see especially Mk 7:33 and 8:23)! The best thing we can do about such happenings is to relax – neither to seek them, nor to try to quench them.

Usually coming to receive prayer is just the tip of a spiritual iceberg. Discerning prayers, led by the Holy Spirit, often uncover unexpected needs – for conversion, for release from the occult, for the ability to forgive others, for deep inner healing. For instance, the old lady whom I mentioned at the beginning of the chapter was, I believe, brought to a real faith and discipleship through her experience at a small village healing service.

The great joy of the 'Toronto experience' is that a few minutes, or several hours, flat out before the Lord often bring effective healing that would otherwise have taken hours of counselling. The danger appears to be an uncritical acceptance of 'phenomena' – many of which certainly cause me, and others, to believe that people are more in need of deliverance rather than encouragement to shake, shout, scream, or whatever.

We need to prepare ourselves in prayer. It is not always practical just before a service, but it is the responsibility of each team member to make sure that they have plenty of time with the Lord before praying for others. Leaders, too, need to receive prayer. I always remember Colin Urquhart saying at a Good News Crusade, 'Leaders, if you want an effective healing ministry in your church, be prepared to be prayed for publicly by your own people!'

Obviously, I can't do justice to healing prayer in a few short pages. We need to read good books.[3] We need to live with the paradox of God's sovereignty and our need to pray in faith. The response will be varied. Much depends on the spiritual climate of the church and the country. In the Third World, where there is little medicine and much faith, healing praying can seem amazing. May 1996 *Renewal* magazine records: 'Over 200,000 Christians gathered from all over Southern India to hear J John, director of the Philo Trust and one of the UK's leading evangelists, address an annual retreat at the Divine Healing Centre in Chalakudy.'

An outpouring of healing grace

J John and his team witnessed many miracles during the meeting: 'I caught a glimpse of what it may have been like during the time of Christ', he said on his return. 'Thousands of people were hungry to hear the gospel and many came to Christian faith. As the gospel was preached, many experienced miraculous physical healing. I felt deeply humbled by the whole experience, and moved by the simple, yet staggering faith of those attending.'

After that, I hope the next heading won't seem faithless. But it's a real issue which I believe deters more ministers and churches from getting involved in the healing ministry than any other.

What happens if they die?

So many people's first experience of praying for healing is death. Just after my conversion, in the uncomfortable prayer circle,[4] I knew I had to pray for a young man from my school. He had just been knocked off his motorbike; a brilliant games player, a charming person, he had everythng to live for – but he didn't.

We all have to face this, we are all human. When we pray for people, as when Fred Smith prayed for my neighbour, or his much

Death as an important witness to God

loved granddaughter (see Chapter 1), they may die. Many people find faith at such times. Their newborn faith helps their relatives, transforms their funeral, and leaves hope instead of despair.

One parishioner suffered from a terrible bone cancer. Prayer which had helped her through crises like claustrophobia didn't help. Modern medicine could do little to alleviate the pain. Yet, in the darkness, she held on to her faith, and in her death helped others. In such situations, we need to remember God's promises like 'No eye has seen, no ear has heard, no mind has conceived what God has prepared for those who love him' (1 Cor 2:9).

Of course, it is difficult to pray for the terminally ill. I have witnessed a few miraculous cures or remissions, and many deaths. But those who die, who have sought God's healing, seem to die positively and at peace. This is a great gift.

Sometimes we may feel it right, gently and reverently, to pray for God to release a suffering soul from earthly life. This requires as much discernment and faith as praying for a miraculous cure. The constant expectation of physical healing right up to the point of death can be a real hindrance in a situation where everyone should be praying for a holy death.

Nevertheless, we can make spectacular mistakes. I consigned one very dear member of our congregation to the next world, only to find that she made a remarkable recovery, and is still alive and well several years later! She was much amused, and very forgiving, about my mistake.

Long ago, as a very junior member of the Oxford Diocesan Synod, I asked the Bishop a written question to the effect, 'If you are giving out so much blessed oil for healing on Maundy Thursday each year, could we have some teaching about the healing ministry of the church?'

We did on April 1st. It was a disaster! A gloomy hospital chaplain decided we were all extreme Pentecostals and began his talk, 'I deal with the terminally ill. When they come to my hospital, whether they are Christians or not, whether they are prayed for or not, they die!' This gem set the tone for the day. Later he tried to demonstrate that healing was dying out even in the Acts. He said that it disappeared as the book progressed.   *An unhelpful conference*

'What about Paul in Malta?' I asked innocently (Acts 28).

'Oh,' he said, 'What does verse 10 say?'

'They honoured us in many ways...'

'Who did Luke mean by "us"?'

'Paul, Luke, other Christians.'

'Exactly. Luke healed the islanders with his herbal remedies.'

'Weren't they washed overboard in the storm at sea?'

The gloomy hospital chaplain was silenced, but the damage was already done. It took another much more positive conference, some time later, to restore the balance.

What about deliverance?

Such ministry is sometimes necessary. But it should be left to specialists, who should be training others to share the work. Most Anglican dioceses in the UK have competent people who can be called upon. I believe that there is far too much 'deliverance' ministry, and that it should only be embarked on when other gentler approaches have been tried.

Let me illustrate. In Zambia in 1994 I spent a few days in Luansha working with Randy Vickers and his wife Dorothy.[5] They had joined me as part of a SOMA team[6] to Zambia. We were taken to preach and to pray in a nearby church. Nearby, we learnt that a boy was tied up by his parents. Apparently, something had gone wrong at university, and he had become violent and out of control. His parents (and we met this elsewhere) had tied him up.

Love brings freedom Now he had lapsed into a total withdrawn silence. While I spoke, Randy and Dorothy visited the boy. They were taken by a white missionary, who perhaps expected prayers of exorcism.

Randy and Dorothy exercised a ministry of love. Gradually, they won his confidence, got the boy untied, and brought into church. They visited him again, and saw a real improvement. Shortly after returning home, they got a letter from the boy, and a confirmatory letter from the local Zambian priest, saying that he was well. He was healed by the touch of love, not by the shock treatment of deliverance.

In contrast, a few days earlier in a remote village in Northern Zambia, I was preaching on Philip the evangelist and the fireworks that followed his preaching. We'd experienced the fire the previous night when around the campfire, a local evangelist illustrated the destruction of Sodom and Gomorrah by fire eating!

As I spoke, there was a commotion – a turbanned member of

the Mothers' Union crashed out of her pew onto the *Deliverance* ground. She was screaming. I decided that I'd *needed in* finished my address, and we took her outside to pray *Zambia* for her. Quickly she gasped out the name of several spirits; and, on instruction, prayed herself to be free. She was just able to do this, and to call on the name of Jesus. Instantly she was well. Meanwhile the local priest carried on with the Communion service. I didn't realise until lunch time that we had been praying for his wife! Her husband had calmly continued the service as though this was a normal occurrence.

This sort of ministry is not confined to Africa! A parishioner once asked me to exorcise her stables. She said they were full of explicit graffiti which indicated dubious practices by someone who had previously lived in the house. With resigned obedience, I prayed. Something so powerful left the stables that my very solid Yorkshire Reader was nearly knocked over. He's never forgotten the experience.

There was a strange sequel about seven years later. My *And in* friend had been widowed and was now sleeping in a *England* different room. She had terrible nightmares and associated these with the previous occupants. Even more sceptically, I prayed. My Bible fell open at Nehemiah 13. I love that book, but the real action is at the beginning, and I doubted that this could be significant.

My eye noticed '…and came back to Jerusalem. Here I learned about the evil thing Eliashib had done in providing Tobiah a room in the courts of the house of God. I was greatly displeased and threw all Tobiah's household goods out of the room. I gave orders to purify the rooms…' (Neh 13:7-9a), then I asked what I thought was a pretty stupid question, 'Have you any furniture belonging to the previous owners?'

'Yes,' came the reply, 'The carpet and the bedside table.'

We decided that they must go. Eventually the carpet, like Tobiah's furniture was thrown out. My friend slept perfectly!

People, and buildings, are greatly freed by such prayer. Invariably it is very simple – often a renewal of baptismal vows with specific emphasis on 'Do you renounce evil?' is quite sufficient. It can be quite scary – people can be very violent. It can go wrong, especially if we misdiagnose and the problem is chemical not spiritual. It can be very tiring – even if the prayer time is brief. But there is a wonderful sense of freedom, and new light and life, when it is right.

Best of all is when God clears out the problem without us! A man came to see me some years ago. Before his conversion, he had been deeply involved in the occult. He hadn't renounced this involvement, or confessed it, and now he was causing problems – especially to his housegroup and his unconverted wife. Could I help?

I couldn't. I didn't want to pray on my own, and no responsible colleague was available. But we had a big Cathedral healing service two days later. I asked him to come for prayer and anointing with oil. When he arrived, I didn't recognise him. He was quite changed. All the darkness had left the night before! I told his astonished wife on the Cathedral green that she ought to follow Jesus. She joined a confirmation class soon afterwards.

Exorcism and healing are often linked

The healing of society

Faced with the seemingly endless list of insoluble problems, Christians face two temptations. One is to withdraw into a ghetto of Christian activity, supported by Christian households, businesses, and even schools. The other is to become immersed in political and social action to such an extent that there ceases to be anything distinctively Christian about their contribution.

Jesus taught differently. His blunt, but encouraging words in the Sermon on the Mount, 'You are the salt of the earth' … 'You are the light of the world … let your light shine before men, that they may see your good deeds and praise your Father in heaven' (Mt 5:13-16), challenge us to be involved in the world's problems and to be distinctive in our approach to them.

Time was when evangelicals believed that the way to change society was to change each individual. Twentieth-century liberal Christians rejected that way and sought to help the individual by changing the system.

Today there is much greater acceptance of a both-and rather

than an either-or approach.

The epistle of James is characteristically terse: *We are called* 'What good is it, my brothers, if a man claims to have *to be salt and* faith but has no deeds? Can such faith save him? (Jas *light* 2:14). Not much use praying without positive action.

But the same epistle warns us against making plans, without consulting God. 'You ought to say, "If it is the Lord's will, we will live and do this or that"' (Jas 4:15). Not much use making wonderful plans without positive prayer.

We have already seen, in Chapter 2, how prayer undergirded tremendous action in the whole South Africa affair. The same was true in Zambia during the peaceful transition of power in 1991. Prayer can, and often will, be about political matters. The healing of society is a political as well as a spiritual matter.

Anyone who takes the Bible seriously will read a highly political message in the Old Testament. Read Isaiah 58 for instance:

> Is not this the kind of fasting I have chosen: to loose the chains of injustice and untie the cords of the yoke, to set the oppressed free and break every yoke? Is it not to share your food with the hungry and to provide the poor wanderer with shelter – when you see the naked, to clothe him, and not to turn away from your own flesh and blood? Then your light will break forth like the dawn, and your healing will quickly appear, then your righteousness will go before you, and the glory of the LORD will be your rearguard. (Is 58:6-8)

Jesus said much the same. The Lucan beatitudes are desperately challenging to any 'quietist' religion. Here Jesus challenges the conventional virtues of society of riches, food, laughter, and popularity; demanding, instead, very different priorities:

> But woe to you who are rich, for you have already received your comfort. Woe to you who are well fed now, for you will go hungry. Woe to you who laugh now, for you will mourn and weep. Woe to you when all men speak well of you, for that is how their fathers treated the false prophets. (Lk 6:24-26)

The early church cared for widows, children, wives, and slaves. Four very deprived groups! It may not have had the power to challenge the political system, but it certainly preached an alternative lifestyle. Obviously, we cannot be involved everywhere. The important thing is that we, our church and our community, are involved somewhere. That is why I want to offer a number of illustrations of prayerful healing acts, and one burgeoning challenge.

In the 1980's the Church of England issued a timely and challenging report called 'Faith in the City'.[7] It challenged the government, and society, and itself, to recognise the state of our inner cities and to attempt to do something. The church, despite some public attacks on its report, prayed, raised money from individuals and companies, and acted. Many useful projects were founded, and beacons of light shone in dark places. The government, too, acted and brought some massive redevelopment to some deprived areas.

Faith in the city

Meanwhile, another, perhaps deeper malaise, was creeping up on British society. The break up of the traditional family was escalating at an extraordinary rate. One unpleasant result was that many older teenagers felt themselves to be homeless. If mother was into a second or third relationship, they often felt excluded and unwanted – particularly if they were unemployed. As a result, even in small market towns, young people were sleeping rough or on friends' floors. A situation unthinkable a few years earlier.

Shepton Mallet is one such small market town. Some years ago, we did a survey and discovered that young people were sleeping rough in our park. The eventual result, after about five years of prayer and preliminary work was SHAL (the Shepton Housing Association Limited). It is a small lighthouse for the homeless, taking people in for up to two years, with caring professional staff

A home for the homeless

who help them with education, employment, and 'move on' accommodation. It doesn't, as yet, bear much fruit in healing or evangelism. The only resident that I've prayed with, soon afterwards set fire to her room and departed. But it is an important sign, in comfortable England, that the kingdom of God involves hard work and real care for the underprivileged.

SHAL is prayed for regularly, and couldn't have started without the prayerful faith of one of its early leaders (see p 133).

Shepton Prison is an old notorious building. In the war, Americans shot soldiers who misbehaved, and it has a dark, gloomy atmosphere. My curate, Matthew, and his Catholic counterpart, Father Luke, prayed with me and a senior Catholic priest, for the release of the spiritual darkness. Together, *Work in* with others, they present the gospel. There will be fruit, *prison* indeed since writing this much evangelism has taken place. Many people find a real faith and healing in prison. Charles Colson, convicted in the Watergate scandal, is a prime example. Another candidate for the curacy here had been convicted years earlier and sent to prison. He now has a wonderful ministry – full of signs and wonders which began with his conversion in his prison cell.

Some prisoners write movingly to prison chaplains saying that through their work they have discovered the beginnings of a way forward, the start of a better life. Sadly, they are the minority, the system doesn't have the money or the will to spend too much time on rehabilitation.

Jesus had a special ministry to the social outcasts – so must we. We needn't be soft on punishment, but we must present the gospel.

My third example, the only one that I don't know of personally, is from Gerald Coates book *An Intelligent Fire.*[8] He *Costly* described the founding of the Pioneer Trust, and how, *ministry for* out of that, ACET (AIDS Care Education & Training) *the terminally* was born in 1988. Patrick Dixon, a full time doctor *ill* working in terminal care, became its leader. Within two years ACET had thirty staff working in four major centres around the country, providing home care for more men, women, and children suffering from HIV (AIDS) than any other charity. The work spilled over into schools, and in partnership with TEAR Fund, to Uganda. Health authorities and other statutory bodies recognised its unique work and started to fund it.

The Restoration churches, the Ichthus fellowship, and other independent non-denominational churches have a remarkable record for effective social work. Their prophetic awareness in prayer makes them particularly open to God's leading, even when the venture is costly and risky. The full story of the beginning of both the Pioneer Trust and ACET is one of committed Christian men responding, in faith, to challenging prophetic prayer.

The fourth example is the AMANI project in Kenya. In 1986, at the age of sixty, my mother-in-law felt led to go to Kenya. The original invitation from a smooth-talking Kenyan Brethren clergyman seemed crazy – but she felt that it was God's will.

For a number of years she worked in a tiny hut alongside the A1 – a potholed road that is part of the great British dream *It's never too late to start* of a Great North Road from Capetown to Cairo. She organised medical care, spring protection schemes, gave farmers revolving loans and encouraged them to try out new crops – to make better use of their land and to earn some much needed Kenyan shillings.

The Brethren clergyman proved unhelpful, but the local 'chiefs' accepted her. The Anglican Diocese of South Nyanza supported her, Seventh Day Adventists worked for her. There were some disasters – fish ponds with the wrong sized nets to catch the fish, etc. There was much prayer, some personal failures, some successes, and suddenly in 1989 the offer of scrub land on an unused hilltop.

Aided by her architect son, Richard, buildings were designed. A road was built, a large demonstration vegetable plot started, a conference centre opened, tailoring and sewing classes began for women, woodwork, for men, 'Send a Cow' dispatched cows which were looked after and given away with the proviso that the first calf was given to someone else. Bread for the World, a large German charity, provided funds. By 1995 about thirty people were employed, and thousands helped in the 'trickle down' effect of better agriculture and other opportunities. The diocese used the conference centre for a charismatic conference for their clergy (at which I enjoyed speaking).

It was never easy, and when Elizabeth broke her arm badly, there was a period of crisis. But still things went on, and she prays for the right way forward. No small task for a seventy year old!

My fifth example is the Friary at Hilfield. For over fifty years, the Anglican Franciscan movement has flourished, offering the most gracious routine of worship, prayer and service. At a typical meal, about forty people will sit down – eighteen brothers and a mixture of guests. Some people are given permanent employment, some have been in prison, some are on their way there, clergy come in disarray, people come to test a vocation, clergy come to retreat, bishops come anonymously.

The brothers work in the grounds and organise others to help. They help in the kitchen, they lead worship, they visit the sick and those in prison, they help the local *Brothers who help* church, they lead missions, they teach, and they pray! Four services a day occupy about two hours, and they are committed to one hour of private prayer. Some of this is done communally in a deep and powerful silence.

The words from the Song of Songs from their liturgy continue to haunt me (see end of Chapter 5): 'Many waters cannot quench love' (Song 8:7a).

The brothers have not withdrawn from the world – except to live in a distinctive and different way. In a world whose gods seem to be wealth, sex, and freedom, their vows of poverty, chastity, and obedience are peculiarly prophetic. They are very much 'in the world'. Not only supervising the practical running of their buildings and grounds, not only helping those who come with complex and varied problems, but also within the local community. Some of their other houses are in the midst of busy towns and cities.

It is easy to romanticise such work, but it is a costly calling – community life, like family life, is seldom easy. But the quality of prayer and love is such that some who arrive in deep trouble, eventually stay to become brothers.

'Many waters cannot quench love!' In prayer, I picture the Zambezi pouring over the Victoria Falls, overarched by a rainbow. Love of the Franciscans, bound by sacred vows of chastity, poverty, and obedience; love of a seventy-year-old European for the Kenyan people; love of a thriving independent church for the victims of AIDS; love for the prisoners; love for the homeless. That is the Christian gospel. Love flows out of prayer.

A failure and a challenge

In 1994, I was guest at the National Prayer Breakfast. One of the most poignant moments was to hear Michael Schluter (whose mother, Evelyn, lives in Nairobi and is a great support to the

Amani project) telling of how the 'Keep Sunday Special' campaign narrowly failed in Parliament. It made me realise how little we had prayed, and how I had done exactly nothing to help it.

Now, as the great god 'Car Boot Sale' probably has more worshippers than all our churches, I realise that another secular wedge has been driven into our national life. Great campaigns need much more prayer – and sacrificial giving of money and time. Now, with the dawning of the millennium, we face a new challenge by Jubilee 2000. Leviticus 25:10 sets the principle of returning property and sorting out debt in the fiftieth year. What a witness it would be, if the rich West would do something real about the problem of Third World debt. Countries like Zambia are crippled even by paying the interest on their debts. We have profited for years from their land, their natural assets, their people. Isn't it time that we restored the balance?

Jubilee 2000, a great challenge

Jubilee 2000, recently launched by Archbishop Makhuto of Central Africa, Dr Kenneth Kaunda (former president of Zambia) and others, is a vital challenge for justice. Will we pray for it? Will we work for it? It could be the greatest Christian witness for many years, it could help stem the tide of militant Islam, it could even help revive Christianity in the decadent West.

Such a movement, if even partially successful, would be an amazing sign of the kingdom.

How do we pray?

But how do we actually pray for these projects? I think there are three prayer stages – the initial vision, the launching, and the need for sustaining regular prayer.

It is good to dream dreams. Most great Christian enterprises have begun as one person's prayer dream. Think of St Francis, David Wilkerson and Teen Challenge, the Earl of Shaftesbury and Victorian reforms, Jackie Pullinger… the list is endless.

SHAL began with the conviction, held by a small group of persistent people, that God was calling a small parish church, in co-operation with the secular authorities, to tackle a serious social problem. ACET began when a Christian doctor realised that his calling was not, as he had hoped, to lead a fellowship, but first to write about, and then to work in the field of helping those dying of AIDS. Elizabeth Feilden felt an inner restlessness, a sense that God was calling her to something new, and then the opportunity to go to Kenya came, and the Amani project was founded. Back in the 1930's Brother Douglas felt a need to do something to help the tramps. As he prayed, Hilfield was born.

Of course, many visions perish. SHAL might have perished many times, not least without Geoffrey Raymond's leap of faith.[9] Several years' gestation were undergirded by the prayers of the parish and Diocesan officials who helped us on our way. Amani was constantly supported in prayer by supporters in England and workers in Kenya. Many difficult situations were miraculously overcome. The provision of land was an extraordinary answer to prayer.

Praying for social projects

And now, each needs ongoing prayer support, as they seek to discern God's will for the future. Should SHAL expand to include a more 'detached' role among those who wouldn't seek help through a household? Will Shepton prison see the sort of spiritual revival witnessed in some other prisons recently? How will Amani survive Elizabeth's eventual retirement? Should the prophetic Franciscan witness seek to expand and touch new horizons?

Prayer is the key. Through prayer answers have been given and will be given. Probably we, as churches, failed the Keep Sunday Special campaign. We didn't pray, we left it to a small central group. Jubilee 2000 presents a similar challenge. Will we catch the vision? A vision that will need to be sustained by prayer, time and money. Or will we let it perish – a nice, but impractical idea? Time alone will tell.

'Your kingdom come'. To these familiar words we add the kingdom prayer of St Francis:

Lord, make me an instrument of your peace,
Where there is hatred, let me sow love,
Where there is injury, pardon;
Where there is despair, hope;
Where there is darkness, light;
Where there is sadness, joy.
O divine Master, grant that I may not so much seek

To be consoled as to console,
To be understood as to understand,
To be loved, as to love,
    For it is in giving that we receive,
    It is in pardoning that we are pardoned,
    it is in dying that we are born to eternal life.[10]

A prayer which touches evangelism, healing, and the wider healing that society so desperately needs.

Notes

1. Fred Smith's ministry, see Chapter 1, note 9.
2. Church of England, Ministry to the Sick, Authorised Alternative Services, p 29.
3. Francis Macnutt, *Healing* (Ave Maria Press, 1974), is still the one that I would first recommend.
4. See Chapter 5, p 96.
5. See Chapter 8, note 6.
6. SOMA, see Chapter 3, note 1.
7. *Living Faith in the City* (General Synod of the Church of England, 1990).
8. Gerald Coates *An Intelligent Fire* (Kingsway, 1991), p 129ff.
9. See Chapter 6, p 133.
10. As quoted here, *The Oxford Book of Prayer,* (OUP, 1985), p 75.

10

The Upper Room

(Christlikeness and the power of the Spirit)

This chapter looks at the two foci of true Christian life – Christlikeness and the power of the Spirit. We look at what it means to have the mind of Christ, radiate the fragrance of Christ, and to know the friendship of Christ. We look at the work of the Holy Spirit in the lives of the apostles, and today's church. We consider what it means to be filled with the Spirit, and how to pray to be filled.

The Upper Room

Recently, as I was praying, a simple picture came into mind. An ellipse with two foci! An ellipse is a simple curve, drawn by keeping the total distance from two fixed points (the foci) constant. Because of this simple property, wood turners often make tables and mirrors of this shape. Round the edge of the ellipse were written the words 'Evangelism', 'Healing', 'Social Justice'. At the two foci were written 'Christlikeness' and 'the Power of the Spirit'.

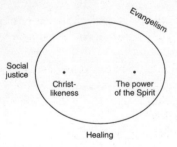

A balanced church, a balanced Christian, needs the double focus. The first expresses our aim to be like Christ – by dying to self, by having the mind of Christ, by releasing the fragrance of Christ, through the friendship of Christ. The second shows our need of the Spirit's power if we are to work effectively in God's kingdom.

Dying to self

When I was at school, if the senior boys wished to punish someone, but couldn't find a specific misdeed, they invariably used the phrase 'general attitude'.

St Paul challenges us, just before writing that great hymn of praise which includes the sentence 'at the name of Jesus every knee should bow', with these words: 'Your attitude should be the same as that of Christ Jesus' (Phil 2:5).

How do you and I treat people? How do we react? Could we ever have the attitude of Jesus to Matthew, to Peter, to Zacchaeus, to the rich young ruler, to Mary Magdalene, to the woman of Samaria, to Judas...? One thing is certain, this doesn't happen overnight. St Paul, after his conversion, went off into the desert for three years (see Gal 1:17,18) and he still had his problems with people.

Watchman Nee[1] tells the story of the Chinese farmer who discovered that a neighbour was diverting his carefully dammed water away from his rice fields to his own. At first he was angry. Then he remembered and applied the text, 'In the same way, count yourselves dead to sin but alive to God in Christ Jesus' (Rom 6:11). If he was dead to sin, then he mustn't be angry. If he was alive to God, he must have a new attitude. Each morning he got up very early and watered his neighbour's rice. His neighbour, when he discovered what was happening, was truly amazed, and eventually became a Christian.

The basis of a disciplined Christian life

As we pray, as we meditate upon Scripture, as we experience the security of Christ's love, gradually it must affect our daily life. Our attitude must change. Self fights very hard, but gradually, in different areas, it is put to death.

A good test is when we are in our car – how do we react when someone cuts in? Drives too slowly? Do we let others out at difficult road junctions? Do we observe speed limits?

If our prayer life is regular, undisturbed, and increasingly Christ-centred (and so much prayer is 'me'-centred – my problem, my family, my church) we will find that our attitude is changing.

The mind of Christ

'We have the mind of Christ' (1 Cor 2:16b). Paul makes this point in a number of ways (see also Rom 12:2; Eph 4:23; and in the Gospels see Jn 15:15). If we have 'the mind of Christ', then as we pray we shall understand his will; we will tend to take right decisions; we will feel and receive inspiration for counselling, sermons... and we will even begin to know and admit when we're wrong.

I remember reading an article by the African evangelist Bishop Festo Kivengere. He had an unresolved argument with his wife. He drove away to address a large meeting. He hadn't gone far when he knew the mind of Christ – he had to turn back, make things up with his wife, and then return to the Lord's work.

Once again, there is no quick fix. A deep knowledge of Scripture helps – particularly if we use a variety of translations, commentaries, go back to the original text, and generally keep our minds fresh. Quiet prayer helps. So does humility!

We often discover Christ's mind through other people – often unexpected people whom perhaps we could easily ignore.

If we are serious about prayer, we must be prepared for God to change our thinking, both in theological and practical matters.

The fragrance of Christ

'Christ loved us and gave himself up for us as a fragrant offering and sacrifice to God' (Eph 5:2).

In spring, as I walk through our garden gate, there is a beautiful fragrance – the glorious scent of our daphne bush. The daphne bush is not much to look at – a low, leafy bush with clusters of tiny pink flowers, but its fragrance is out of this world. It was a gift from a gardener who, years ago, had been churchwarden at Shepton. A man of immense kindness, who didn't take kindly to modern church ways, but who always continued to be courteous and who, behind the scenes, visited and helped many elderly people.

What sort of fragrance do we leave when we visit a home? When we fill up the car with petrol? When someone opposes us publicly? The world watches for our mistakes – just like the leaders of the synagogue watched Jesus (Mk 3:2ff).

I remember visiting an elderly clergyman. He suffered badly from angina, and he was lying down. He was coming to the end of his ministry, having just rescued a church in Winchester from closure (it's now the largest in the city, I think). Although in pain, he gave me his full attention, helping to guide my reluctant mind towards ordination. He had the fragrance of Jesus.

So did an elderly lady in my present church. She had lived a life of prayer and poverty. She had just one possession – her little house – and she wanted to leave it to charity. She was very concerned that she would end her days in a nursing home, and that the value of the house would be spent on her upkeep. She *True Christian lives have a beautiful fragrance* was ill for several years, surviving many misadventures, including a whole night stuck in a bath. Eventually, she did have to go into a nursing home; but she died, peacefully, within a week of her arrival. Her last prayer was answered. Her life had the fragrance of Christ.

Her great friend, from a much more upper class background, did much for her and many others. She visited the sick, took them to hospital, organised meals on wheels for them, quietly kept many charitable ventures alive, supported new Rectors and changing churches – even though they weren't really her scene.

One evening, just after driving the other lady to hospital, she arrived back home, sat down to read a letter, and died. Her life, too, had the fragrance of Christ. (And both would be very cross with me for mentioning them in this book.)

The secret must have been a disciplined life of prayer, worship and service.

The friendship of Christ

'You are my friends if you do what I command. I no longer call you servants... (Jn 15:14). The disciples began to fully understand the friendship of Christ in the Upper Room. What an evening! Apart from the solemnity of a Jewish Passover, Jesus gave so much of himself. First the footwashing and the firm lesson to Peter about obedience. I've only experienced this twice. The first was a disaster when, during a mission which I was leading, the Vicar insisted on washing the feet of his gangling teenage servers. They looked embarrassed, bemused, and finally lapsed into unholy mirth. The second was deeply moving, on Maundy Thursday, before sharing Communion at Hilfield Friary, we washed each other's feet, silently. There was a deep symbol-

Jesus offers us friendship as well as service

ism. The community is a place of service and equality. The footwashing summed it all up.

After his footwashing, Jesus dismissed Judas with a last offer of friendship. Before the dismissal, Jesus shared the bread and the wine. This is the great sacrament for believers. Here we experience Christ's presence in a deeply transforming way.

> Do this in remembrance of me. (1 Cor 11:24)

> Is not the cup of thanksgiving for which we give thanks a participation in the blood of Christ? And is not the bread that we break a participation in the body of Christ? Because there is one loaf, we, who are many, are one body, for we all partake of the one loaf. (1 Cor 10:16,17)

This is a reminder that however good our secret prayer life is, we are part of something far greater – the body of Christ. Isolated, we are of no use to Christ. United, with other friends of his, much can be achieved. The Communion table, with the kiss of peace (1 Cor 16:20), is the place of unity, the place of friendship.

All this began in an Upper Room, and it helps us to understand the first focus – the likeness of Christ. How can we pray for this? In some ways, we can't. It is the experience of a lifetime of discipleship. But a disciplined prayer life, particularly including meditation and prayers of praise and adoration, will help. We, of course, will be unconscious of much progress. Indeed, the lives of the greatest saints often indicate periods of great dissatisfaction with their own spiritual journey. But others may catch a glimpse of something Christlike, and even remark on the fragrance.

The Power of the Spirit

It all continues in an Upper Room (possibly the same one). After the Ascension, the disciples returned for a remarkable prayer meeting:

> Then they returned to Jerusalem from the hill called the Mount of Olives, a Sabbath day's walk from the city. When they arrived, they went upstairs to the room where they were staying. Those present were Peter, John, James and Andrew; Philip and Thomas, Bartholomew and Matthew; James, son of Alphaeus and Simon the Zealot, and Judas son of James. They all joined together constantly in prayer, along with the women and Mary the mother of Jesus, and his brothers. (Acts 1:12-14)

Remarkable because, unlike so many of those whom Jesus had healed (Mk 1:45, for instance), the disciples were doing exactly what they had been told to do.

> On one occasion, while he was eating with them, he gave them this command: 'Do not leave Jerusalem, but wait for the gift my Father promised, which you have heard me speak about. For John baptised with water, but in a few days you will be baptised with the Holy Spirit.' (Acts 1:4-5)

Remarkable because Mary was present, her last mention in Scripture. Even more remarkable, because his previously unbelieving brothers were there.[2] Remarkable because the group of believers had already grown to 120 – quite an improvement since Good Friday. Remarkable because they solved their first practical problem by drawing lots (Acts 1:26)!

Just once I had to preach on St Matthias. During the 1974 miners' strike, I was told on February 25th, St Matthias' day in the old lectionary, to keep preaching until the electricity was restored and the service could end with a hymn. I believe that when I had finished my carefully prepared talk, the lights miraculously came on. My colleagues, especially one whose birthday falls on the Saint's day, had a less kind version: 'After you'd said,

Trusting God means waiting upon him in prayer

"and another thing about St Matthias" for the fourteenth time, the lights came on'!

But more seriously, the drawing of lots, after prayer, indicated a great trust in God's sovereignty – quite different from the soldiers dicing for Jesus' clothes, or British citizens sitting glued to a glitzy TV programme hoping to win a fortune when the right six coloured balls are chosen.

Matthias was chosen, and Joseph called Barsabbas had to be content with his lot. Very few Christians are called to have 'successful' up-front ministries; most of us need, prayerfully, to accept the way of Joseph called Barsabbas with a good grace!

When the day of Pentecost came, they were all together in one place. Suddenly a sound like the blowing of a violent wind came from heaven and filled the whole house where they were sitting. They saw what seemed to be tongues of fire that separated and came to rest on each of them. All of them were filled with the Holy Spirit and began to speak in other tongues as the Spirit enabled them. (Acts 2:1-4)

'All of them were filled with the Holy spirit!' Empowered for evangelism, for healing, for service to a needy world. It happened after ten days of continuous prayer.

Saul of Tarsus experienced something similar after three days *Many different Christians experience being filled with the Holy Spirit* of helpless fasting (Acts 9:9ff). Cornelius and his friends experienced something similar after prayer and a heavenly vision (Acts 10:1-8, 44-48). Twelve Ephesian disciples experienced much the same after Paul's corrective teaching and prayer (Acts 19:1-7).

Martyn Lloyd Jones,[3] expounding Romans 8, sees Romans 8:16 'The Spirit himself testifies with our spirit that we are God's children', as the key experience. He writes of this as the supreme Christian experience on this earth. He describes it in the life of the Wesleys, George Whitefield, Puritan teachers of the 16th and 17th centuries, Jonathan Edwards in America, Charles Spurgeon, and D. L. Moody, as the experience which released them into effective ministry.

For many, it is a deeply mystical experience. I remember

hearing Graham Pulkingham,[4] the early charismatic leader, describing how David Wilkerson[5] prayed for him on a New York street. It is not unlike Mother Julian's shewings,[6] or Teresa of Avila's ecstasy[7] – a happening which bears immense fruit in a person's life and ministry.

God's sovereign choice is apparent! Read the life of Sadhu Sundar Singh, called miraculously from death to be the Apostle of India,[8] or Kagawa,[9] called to be his servant in the slums of Japan, or Bishop Festo Kivengere, escaping from Idi Amin's persecution, to become an amazing evangelist, or David Watson to spearhead evangelism and sacrificial community living in this country, or Jackie Pullinger called to a now world famous work among the drug addicts in Hong Kong.

All of these people were, or became, great people of prayer. We must pray that God will raise up more men and women of this stature. These, perhaps, are people who have received the baptism of the Spirit in the fullest sense. When I was a curate at St Aldate's Oxford in the late 1970's, the late David Watson was a regular visitor. He and Michael Green, in occasional spare moments, would discuss 'the baptism of the Spirit'. Neither was very clear what it meant theologically, but both leaders felt they knew instinctively when people had received it.

I think it is a matter of degree. Few people today would have the sort of experiences of the great leaders that I mentioned in the previous paragraphs – I certainly haven't! But many of us would hope that we have experienced being 'filled with the Spirit'.

What does it mean to be filled with the Spirit?

Paul, in a key passage, taught the Ephesian church that this was a necessity, quite normal!

Be very careful, then, how you live – not as unwise but as wise, making the most of every opportunity, because the days are evil. Therefore do not be foolish, but understand what the Lord's will is. Do not get drunk on wine, which leads to debauchery. Instead, be filled with the Spirit. Speak to one another with psalms, hymns and spiritual songs. Sing and make music in your heart to the Lord, always giving thanks to God the Father for everything, in the name of our

Lord Jesus Christ. Submit to one another out of reverence for Christ. (Eph 5:15-21)

Paul writes about using time sensibly, seeking the Lord's will, worshipping, being thankful, and mutual submission! The key experience is 'being filled with the Spirit'.

Being filled with the Spirit – a command, not an option   Many years ago, I was a substitute speaker at a house party. I wasn't very well, my children were embarrassingly badly behaved, and my teaching on Ephesians pedestrian. One Army officer was particularly bored. When we got to Ephesians 5, the Holy Spirit gave me a nudge. I said, 'Be filled with the Spirit' is not an optional extra, but a military command!' The Major sat up and took notice. Later he received prayer, it was a very important spiritual crossroads for him – and for me. These house parties have been very gracious to my family, and all my children have gained so much spiritually through them. Humanly they have contributed much to my dearest prayer that all my children shall grow up as Christians.

Let me illustrate from nature. When I was a young schoolmaster, Wednesday afternoons were reserved for military activities, or good works in the community. Not being a military person, I avoided the corps and ended up in the relative peace of the school nature reserve. I was given a group of eight idle boys; together we knew almost nothing about nature. Our first task was to mudscoop some stagnant ditches. This seemingly futile operation created a foul smell, foetid mud drenched along the bank wasn't a pleasant sight either, and we left the near stagnant ditches flowing at about 2mm per second instead of the 1mm per second they had managed before.

One fateful afternoon, a friendly pupil said, 'Oh sir!' – always the opening to some rather wild suggestion – 'Why don't we cut through to the main stream, then water could flow into the top ditch and out the other end, back into the stream.' For three fervent afternoons we dug through chalk and marsh, and finally connected with the main stream. We diverted a little water down our channel and waited. There was an explosion of life! Mud swirled away, within a few hours a chalk base to my ditch was revealed, and a trout swam happily up it. Probably the ecology was ruined (but there were plenty of other stagnant ditches, not accessible to the same treatment); but the effect, on the ditch, and the recalcitrant group of unwilling helpers, was electric.

Years later, I realised that it was like the effect of 'being filled with the Spirit.' All the vain effort of futile mud scooping, replaced by the gentle flow of living water. *A parable from nature*

But there is a problem... The Greek text means, 'be *continuously* filled'. In the hot summer of 1995 I visited my former praying partner in Winchester. He, too, had great releasing experiences of the Holy Spirit. A new Pentecost had given him great joy after a period of immense difficulty and spiritual opposition. I insisted on a walk from Fallodon (the nature reserve). I longed to see 'my stream'. I got a horrid shock – it was almost dry, reduced to a few stagnant puddles. The stream which flowed, and the edge was also dry – the canal, the ultimate source of Falladon's water, was being dredged! What a parable! If we wander away from the source, if we cease daily to be filled, and prayer is the main source for this filling, even the brightest spiritual stream can dry up.

Seeking prayer to be filled with the Spirit

It seems good to ask for help. The Samaritan woman (John 4) eventually asked Jesus for the living water. Jesus promised that it would be poured out for those who believe.

> On the last and greatest day of the Feast, Jesus stood and said in a loud voice, 'If anyone is thirsty, let him come to me and drink. Whoever believes in me, as the Scripture has said, streams of living water will flow from within him.' By this he meant the Spirit, whom those who believed in him were later to receive. Up to that time the Spirit had not been given, since Jesus had not yet been glorified. (Jn 7:37-39)

We may, indeed we ought, to pray for such a 'filling'. I described my own experience when Tom Smail prayed for me. The eventual result was a conviction that I should get involved in the healing ministry, confirmed when, to my amazement, I saw people being healed. I also had some very significant Saturday nights. My colleagues seemed more successful at being invited out to dinner, and I spent many Saturday nights alone. They became very special. Meeting times with the Lord. I read, I prayed, I listened to Graham Pulkingham's Fisherfolk on record, I sang (when nobody could hear my tuneless voice), I prayed in tongues. Like many others, I doubted the genuineness of the tongues.

Gifts of the Holy Spirit experienced

Two years later, confronted by a witch screeching in a demonic tongue, which sounded like Latin backwards emerging from a machine gun, my Rector (Michael Green of St Aldate's, and later of Springboard) ordered me to pray in tongues. Like the Major, I obeyed! To my amazement, and hers, the witch shut up. Although diagnosed by a psychiatrist as having an incurable personality disorder, she was baptised, healed, and went on to live a normal life – not least due to the loving discipling and friendship offered by Michael's wife Rosemary.

How do we pray?

During a Diocesan Renewal evening held at Shepton,[10] Peter Hancock[11] gave a powerful talk on being filled with the Spirit. People came forward for prayer. The ever-cautious Rector (me) gave out a 'government health warning'. 'You may fall over if Peter prays for you. It isn't especially spiritually significant – but come and be prayed for by me if you want to be safe'. You can guess what happened. I only had to look at someone, and they staggered on to the floor under the power of the Spirit. Anne[12] gives a testimony to the Holy Spirit's work on that evening:

'Some years earlier our family had moved to Somerset. It was not a success! We bought a property which I never liked, and felt had an oppressive atmosphere. The family was in disarray. My husband, normally rational and competent, became the reverse; my musically gifted son was being bullied at school and professionally neglected; my daughter, who had dropped out of school, spent her time like a pale little ghost in the stables; and I was prone to outbursts of uncontrollable temper.

One day, drawing on the convictions of my Anglo-Catholic background for help, I called out for help. A few days later, I discovered that a local rector had written a book which included a chapter on dealing with the occult – which seemed relevant to our house and situation.

'We met, and during a time of prayer I remember the extraordinary sensation of golden liquid light flooding through me as he laid hands upon me. I don't know how long it lasted, but I remember feeling complete freedom from the fear which for months had dominated my life. *A testimony to the work of the Spirit* Difficulties remained, but I felt energised, calm, and able to cope.

'Some years later, back in a period of deep depression, I went, accompanied by my teenage son, to an evening service in the church. Peter Hancock was preaching and then praying for people. I felt deeply suspicious of the phenomenon of people 'falling over the Spirit'. I sought prayer from John – which was likely to be safer and more restrained.

'Standing in the side chapel, prayed for by John and one other member of the church, I quickly felt dizzy. Swaying and struggling to stay on my feet, I heard John say, 'Don't fight it Anne!' to which I replied, 'Oh, I will!' The next thing that I knew was that I was flat on the floor with my head under the Communion rail – laughing. My first reaction, on eventually getting up, was to tell others! I first sought out my rather staid solicitor, and then various others. My depression lifted, and my son and daughter were both intrigued and glad. For some days, I continued to experience the same feeling of calm energy.'

I believe we can pray, and lay hands on, or near someone's head, and ask God to fill them with his Spirit. It is important to check that they are clear of any occult past, committed to Christ, and genuinely seeking go forward in the Spirit. What happens is up to God! We cannot, and must not, predict gifts, experiences, phenomena... that is one great blessing of the Toronto approach, 'Come, Holy Spirit...'; the bane (if I may use that critical word) is lack of objectivity. If the Holy *Praying for others* Spirit comes with power, there may be collision. People with spiritual or psychological disorders may be in deep trouble, and the least we can do is to recognise this and seek prayerfully to help.

Sometimes people ask for prayer for particular gifts – tongues, healing, knowledge. I think this is fine, but we must remember 1 Corinthians 12:11: 'He gives them (the gifts) to each one, *just as he determines*'.

I described at the end of Chapter 3, God's 'no' to me. A few months later I tried again. This time, one of the other candidates handed out his books on the Holy Spirit. Normally, I would have been very angry, but on this occasion I read them while waiting for the negative result (which was a relief on this occasion!). They opened my eyes to the value of the 'Come, Holy Spirit prayer', and I experienced great encouragement in Shepton next Pentecost, nearby on a mission, and later in Zambia. Reading the books started a chain of events which led to considerable healing, guidance and blessing.

There is a danger that this prayer, too, can become a technique. We must wait on the Lord and use whatever prayer seems appropriate. It is good to invoke the Holy Spirit's presence, but we will be led differently according to the situation in which we are praying.

The double focus

In the end, God is calling us to respond to the double focus. We need that balance between interior discipline (Christlikeness) and exterior fire (empowered by the Spirit). The perfect model would be a circle – found only in Jesus' life.

I want to conclude with an encounter that I witnessed between two men who surely both understood the double focus. Dr Billy Graham was leading a 'small' mission to Oxford University in the early 1980's. He arrived in great pain – he had slipped in the shower and cracked, or bruised, several ribs. His programme was curtailed and the whole enterprise was in great doubt. I was present at several anxious staff meetings. We were all immensely moved by Dr Graham's demeanour. Although obviously in pain, his only concern was not to let people down. Michael Green suggested getting hold of Fred Smith[13] to pray. Dr Graham, not quite into healing, agreed – a little nervously.

Fragrant Christians filled with the Spirit

Fred, a former policeman who discovered he had a remarkable

gift of healing, was tending his bonfire in nearby Abingdon. He heard the Lord speak (and he often did speak to Fred): 'Today you will pray with Billy Graham!' Fred, moving in rather different theological streams, hadn't even heard of Billy Graham's mission to Oxford. A little while later, Michael Green phoned. Later that day, Fred and I went to the Randolph Hotel and eventually reached Dr Graham's suite. The two men laughed, discussed theology, and prayed. It would be nice to record a miracle – certainly Dr Graham's health improved enough for him to fulfil his programme. After their brief meeting, Fred returned to his garden.,

Two men, surely baptised by the Spirit, had met and prayed. One, a world famous evangelist continuing his amazing work with ever-increasing fervour, despite Parkinson's disease. Thousands, humanly, owe their conversion to his preaching. The other, with whom I've been present when some amazing and instantaneous healings have taken place, died quite suddenly just when his failing health was beginning to hinder his work.

One anonymous, 'Only God could use a man with a name like Fred Smith', he used to joke; the other world famous. Both deeply Christlike, both deeply anointed by the Spirit, both deep men of prayer. Both men who knew what it was like to have their feet washed in the Upper Room, and to receive the empowering of the Spirit.

If the world is to be changed, if the kingdom signs are to increase, we must pray that many more people understand the need for the double focus. And we had best begin with ourselves.

Notes

1. *Sit, Walk, Stand,* Watchman Nee, (Kingsway 1962), p 26.
2. Cf Mark 3:21; 2:31-35; John 7:5, with 1 Corinthians 15:7. The conversion of James and the presence of Jesus' brothers at this prayer meeting is remarkable evidence for the Resurrection.
3. Martyn Lloyd Jones, *Romans: Expositions of Chapter 8:5-17*

(Banner of Truth 1974), chapters 23-30.

4. Graham Pulkingham's leadership of the 'Church of the Redeemer' in Houston received many blessings – not least the music of the Fisherfolk.

5. See Chapter 6, note 12.

6. See Chapter 4, note 6.

7. Shirley du Boulay, *Teresa of Avila,* (Hodder & Stoughton, 1991), especially Chapter 5.

8. Many biographies of this remarkable saint are available.

9. See *Torches for Teachers,* (see Chapter 7, notes 2 & 3).

10. The Bath & Wells Diocesan Renewal Group runs a six week course each autumn in four or five different centres. 600-800 usually attend, culminating with a joining together for Advent Praise in the Cathedral.

11. Peter Hancock, see Chapter 6, note 4.

12. Anne Goode, see also Chapter 9, p 201.

13. Fred Smith, see Chapter 1, note 9, and elsewhere.

11

A Call to Prayer

(Why do we find it so hard to pray together?)

The final chapter faces up to some of the difficulties of praying together, looks at the 'prayer of agreement', and the many advantages and encouragements that flow from a strong determined prayer life.

A Call to Prayer

Despite all that has been said, written, or preached about prayer, we find it difficult to pray, especially in groups. It seems to require a considerable personal or national crisis to motivate people to pray together. Frequently, when we set out to pray, we end up spending much time in worthy conversation, finishing with a few cursory words of prayer. Yet the Scriptures are full of promises, and encouragements, to challenge and inspire us. Well known examples include:

> If my people, who are called by my name, will humble themselves and pray and seek my face and turn from their wicked ways, then will I hear from heaven and will forgive their sin and will heal their land. (2 Chron 7:14)

> For this reason I kneel before the Father, from whom the whole family in heaven and on earth derives its name. I pray that out of his glorious riches he may strengthen you with power through his Spirit in your inner being, so that Christ may dwell in your hearts through faith. And I pray that you, being rooted and established in love, may have power, together with all the saints, to grasp how wide and long and high and deep is the love of Christ, and to know this love that surpasses knowledge – that you may be filled to the measure of all the fulness of God.
>
> Now to him who is able to do immeasurably more than all we ask

or imagine, according to his power that is at work within us, to him be glory in the church and in Christ Jesus throughout all generations, for ever and ever! Amen. (Eph 3:14-21)

Again, I tell you that if two of you on earth agree about anything you ask for, it will be done for you by my Father in heaven. For where two or three come together in my name, there am I with them. (Mt 18:19-20)

Three breathtaking promises about prayer. The first encourages a nation to pray; in the second Paul, a great man of prayer, prays for his Ephesian friends that together they 'may be filled to the measure of all the fulness of God'; in the third, Jesus quite simply guarantees his presence at each small prayer meeting and underwrites a meeting between any two who come in agreement.

We all know that these statements are true. Occasionally, we've seen a nation at prayer: possibly this country in the darkest days of the Second World War, certainly South Africa before her recent historic elections. Most of us have been present at small gatherings of prayer where extraordinary things have taken place – I've cited many examples in the preceding pages.

A reluctant people

Yet there is still a strange reluctance to pray. You know it, I know it. Local and national prayer initiatives struggle. Husbands and wives know that it is important to pray together, yet somehow they don't manage it very often. In Britain, faithful Lydia[1] groups of praying women battle on; adherents of Noon and Crosswinds pray for the nation – but the going is hard, the *Difficulty of* response quite small. Occasionally, a Diocese or *getting people* some other large organisation, launches a prayer *to pray* initiative, but only the keenest climb aboard. In 1993 Springboard[2] organised a prayer initiative around the Cathedrals of England. The meeting at Wells was scheduled for 6 a.m. The vergers put out a few chairs in the Lady Chapel. By the time the meeting was underway, half the nave was full. That was a rare response, due humanly mainly to a vast effort by the Renewal Group. Sadly, this response was exceptional.

Leadership needed

When Nehemiah realised the state of his nation, he turned to fervent prayer. He mourned and fasted. When given an opportunity to do something he prayed to the God of heaven. When opposed by Sanballat, Tobiah and Geshem, he prophesied success. When insulted (quite entertainingly by Tobiah), he sought God in prayer. When faced with social injustice, the work stopped, the matter was sorted out, and the people said 'Amen'. When Sanballat tried to trick Nehemiah into making a fatal visit to see him, Nehemiah prayed for strength. When Shemaiah came with pious words and tried to get Nehemiah to the refuge in the Temple, Nehemiah, with great spiritual insight, sent him packing. When the wall was completed there was a great service of dedication and praise. The book concludes with another run in with Tobiah and the author's prayer, 'Remember me with favour, O my God'.

Nehemiah gave practical leadership, undergirded by his personal prayer life, unafraid to call the people to prayer.

It is much harder for our leaders to call us to prayer. But if South Africa, torn and divided, could do it in 1994, why can't we? Doesn't Northern Ireland merit at least a day of prayer and fasting? Doesn't the lack of vocations to the ministry in all the mainline churches merit a public call to prayer? Couldn't synods take a leaf out of the Franciscans' way, and have half-an-hour of communal quiet prayer – perhaps then they would find a way through various thorny issues.

Prayer of agreement

'If two of you ... agree ... it will be done' (Mt 18:19). This holy agreement is very powerful, and very rare. It seems to happen when two people, often no natural spiritual allies, come together to pray.

I remember a powerful story told by John Hutchinson of the Good News Crusade at Blaithwaite in 1980. At one meeting, a while earlier, someone steeped in the occult had made an appointment for prayer. Normally such a session could have been lengthy, disturbed, and very tiring. Two leaders made a 'prayer of agreement'. They met the person, and to her astonishment they announced that God had heard their prayer and that she was free (see also Mt 18:18)! She was. A dramatic deliverance, leading to real discipleship, took place 'at a word'! God's promises are powerful – if we believe them. Of course this doesn't give us a 'recipe' for deliverance sessions – there were particular reasons why God allowed this prayer session to be so brief; but, it does suggest that a great deal of time and effort could be saved if we'd learn to pray and listen first, and act second.

A few times, I have experienced this sense of agreement. Once it occurred before the extraordinary revival (see Chapter 8) at the school at which I was chaplain. Two of us, at that time not particularly close, prayed for the whole school by name. It was a mammoth task – but it felt real, it seemed important. Now, twenty years on, when we pray there is a deep and natural agreement. *United prayer is effective*

On another occasion, two of us prayed for someone else's marriage. Again we weren't that close spiritually; we spanned the house church - Anglican divide. But we felt 'an agreement', and felt confident that the marriage would survive. It has more than survived, it has flourished.

We can never know how much difference our prayers make – what is quite clear is that there is a strange correlation between prayer, where there is that deep sense of faith and holy agreement, and surprising results. As a mathematician, I know that unlikely events happen – people do get struck by lightning! But as a Christian, I know that the most remarkable events that I've witnessed have always been undergirded by prayer.

I was once out to dinner with a schoolmaster contact. We had met because of the death of a colleague of his. This man had come for prayer for motor-neurone disease. Our prayers hadn't helped him physically, but he had experienced a great spiritual change. After dinner, imagining that I was 'off duty', I relaxed. Suddenly, a distressing story of crippling early morning migraines emerged. I noticed a Bible sitting beside a decanter of port. The Lord said, 'Read Habakkuk 3, verse 4'. Struggling to find the right page, I read it out: 'His splendour was like the sunrise; rays flashed from his hand.' I realised it was 'out of context', but I asked my new

232 THINKING CLEARLY ABOUT PRAYER

friend if that's what his migraines felt like – flashing rays! He nodded. I said, 'We must pray – I don't think you'll ever have another one.' To the best of my knowledge, he hasn't.

Such a healing by itself would be quite remarkable, such a Bible reference has an almost zero probability of being relevant (my only knowledge at that time of the book of Habakkuk was limited to a tiresome schoolboy who answered every question on the Old Testament with the word 'Habakkuk' – until I made him write out the whole book several times!), the two together combined to give a powerful sign.

The greatest prayer meeting

> In the church at Antioch there were prophets and teachers. Barnabas, Simeon called Niger, Lucius of Cyrene, Manaen (who had been brought up with Herod the tetrarch) and Saul. While they were worshipping the Lord and fasting, the Holy Spirit said, 'Set apart for me Barnabas and Saul for the work to which I have called them.' So after they had fasted and prayed, they placed their hands on them and sent them off. (Acts 13:1-3)

Antioch was a great church, well led by Saul and Barnabas. It had a shared leadership team of prophets and teachers. It was generous – they had organised the first ever 'Christian Aid' mission for the starving brethren in Jerusalem (Acts 11:27ff). It was significant – they became so numerous that they acquired the nickname of Christians (Acts 11:26). It was prayerful.

There was a long period of prayer and fasting. What did the

After prayer a clear message

Lord want? Where was the next church plant to be? Who was to lead it? Suddenly the Holy Spirit spoke. We are not told how – it may have been a direct voice, it may have been a prophecy, it may have been an inner certainty – but the leaders recognised the voice, and obeyed it.

The message was remarkable – remove the leaders and send them off on a new mission. We can imagine the response of today's synods or church councils. 'Lord, we can't afford it!'; 'Lord, who will chair the committees?'; 'Lord, give us time to think about it – these things must be planned properly.' But the church at Antioch returned to prayer, continued in faith, and sent off Saul and Barnabas with the laying on of hands.

The result of this prayer meeting was felt in the Roman province of Asia, and then in Greece. It was the first of the great missions by the world's greatest missionary.

It wasn't all beautiful. Not only was there fierce opposition from without (to be expected), there was deep unease at Jerusalem (Acts 15:1ff). But worse still there were broken relationships, caused by Mark's defection. A few years later, at the start of the next missionary journey, Paul and Barnabas parted. Barnabas defended, and then discipled his young cousin Mark – and thereby paved the way for the writing of the oldest Gospel! Paul chose Silas, discipled and trained young Timothy, and continued his work. Eventually they were reconciled, meanwhile two different missions spring out of one.

The prophetic truth of that great prayer meeting in Antioch wasn't undermined because of subsequent human failings.

'Brothers, pray for us' (1 Thess 5:25); 'Pray also for me' (Eph 6:19) writes St Paul. 'I thank my God every time I remember you. In all my prayers for all of you…' (Phil 1:3,4).

Paul knows that leaders and churches need prayer. Leaders are vulnerable, but vital to the expansion of God's kingdom. Today there seems to be a dual need – for Spirit-led leaders, men like the late Archbishop Bill Burnett and Bishop Ban It Chiu, who saw their dioceses in Capetown and Singapore transformed by the power of the Holy Spirit; and for Spirit-led local churches like those of Philippi and Colossae. The results of prayer can be quite extraordinary. Scientists sometimes say that the flutter of a butterfly's wings can change the weather pattern miles away (mercifully they don't usually!). Prayer, rather more frequently, brings unforeseen changes of great consequence.

In 1854, a young Victorian clergyman, aged thirty-four, lay dying. His parishioners sat up all night to pray. Alfred Christopher[3] recovered. Five years later, he was appointed, the notable first evangelical incumbent, to the living of St Aldate's Oxford. His life's work, which continued past the turn of the century, included building St Matthew's Church in Grandpont in the south of the parish; missionary work, with much prayer support

The consequences of fruitful prayer are far-reaching

for CMS, and regular contact with missionaries; and student work. He was involved with the setting up of the Oxford Pastorate.

St Matthew's flourished, became independent, then decayed almost to the point of extinction in the early 1970's. A few determined ladies prayed, and years later a recovery began. For a while St Matthew's returned to St Aldate's, and now flourishing as never before, has become, once again, an independent parish.

Missionary support has remained a great feature of the St Aldate's ministry. Judging by Christopher's memorial window, we may assume that this included support and prayer for the young James Hannington, newly appointed missionary Bishop of East Equatorial Africa.

Bishop Hannington, and many young Ugandan converts were soon to die under the fierce persecution of the Kabaka of Uganda. Their blood produced much fruit, and, sadly, more persecution in later generations.

The student work, especially when relaunched in the 1950's under Keith de Berry, produced many conversions and ordinands.

I write as one, first impressed, and then converted through the student ministry. Later discipled by Keith, I heard, reluctantly, a call to ordination via his holiday preaching. Working at a St Aldate's student party, I met Jane, my future wife. Some years later, asked by Michael Green, the incumbent of the late 1970's, to be curate there, I discovered the beginnings of a healing gift, and looked after St Matthew's – which had already begun to turn its long spiritual corner. At St Aldate's, Jane's mother (see Chapter 9) made the initial Kenyan contact which led her to found the Amani project.

Thousands of others can be similarly grateful to the ancient church dwarfed by Christ Church and Pembroke College. Prayer didn't protect Bishop Hannington from the Kabaka's evil wrath, but his sacrifice paved the way for the future. Prayer did restore Alfred Christopher, and this enabled him to begin the great work at St Aldate's. Such is the inescapable paradox: 'The Spirit intercedes for the saints in accordance with God's will' (Romans 8:27b).

We, imperfect humans, cannot know the will of God. Occasionally, usually in prayer, we are given glimpses of the Father's plans. That is when our prayer becomes really effective, and when that happens, mountains move, strongholds crumble, and signs of the kingdom follow.

What to others is coincidence, to believers is confirmation. We slowly learn that prayer is vital to our relationship with God. Without prayer, we soon lose our spiritual vitality; with little prayer, we make feeble prayers and become discouraged; with prayer inspired by the Spirit, there is no limit as to what can be achieved and experienced.

Butterflies may flutter their wings, sceptics may laugh, mathematicians may calculate probabilities, but Christians, in faith, know.

Notes

1. Lydia, Noon and Crosswinds are three interdenominational national prayer groups whose aim is effective prayer for the nation. Details can be obtained from The Parish Office, Holy Trinity, Nailsea, Bristol, BS19 2NG, and elsewhere.
2. Springboard is the Archbishop of Canterbury's initiative on Evangelism. Martin Cavender, see Chapter 3, is their administrative director.
3. John Reynolds, *Canon Christopher of St Aldate's Oxford* (Abbey Press, Abingdon, 1967), pp 59-60.

Appendix

Suggestions for Prayer, Alone and in Small Groups

(With exercises related to each chapter)

Unless in the first waking moment of the day you learn to fling the door wide back and let God in, you will work on a wrong level all day; but swing the door wide open and pray to your Father in secret, and every public thing will be stamped with the presence of God.[1]

Introduction

It is important to find somewhere quiet and undisturbed. Jesus, himself, regularly withdrew to quiet places. You may find it helpful to start or continue, a prayer diary. The purpose of this is to record some of the experiences that we receive in prayer, which can strengthen our faith in the future, to ask some serious questions, and to write some of our intercessions for other people.

The prayer exercises are suggestions, which may be adopted or discarded to suit our own situations. Their purpose is to widen our experience. One of the biggest difficulties in prayer is that it quickly becomes mere repetition – we need to pray that the Holy Spirit will intercede for us in sighs too deep for words (Rom 8:26 RSV). There are also some similar suggestions suitable for a house group, or for use with a friend.

Chapter 1

Diary. Write down some of your greatest encouragements in prayer. What have you learnt about God and about yourself, and other people, from them? Record a few of the disappointments and difficulties that you experienced. What did you learn from them? What is your greatest prayer challenge today?

Meditation. Imagine yourself, briefly, to be one of the characters in this chapter. Write a prayer that Dr Dodd, Patrascanu, St Polycarp, or one of the others might have written. Imagine yourself to be in their situation. How did they experience God's grace?

Group question. What makes prayer difficult – unbelief, past disappointments, lack of encouragement, lack of discipline, lack of teaching, lack of expectation?

Group exercise. Share anything from your diary that seems important and appropriate to share.

Read aloud either Revelation 22:1-5 or Luke 22:39-53 and meditate on the text for ten minutes silently. You might choose, if reading Luke, to be one of the characters in the Garden.

At the end, you may wish to share briefly some experience, or you may prefer to close with a general prayer.

Chapter 2

Diary. Consider the story of the five birds. Add one or two more of your own.

Question. What do you find it hardest/easiest to pray about – national matters? Missions overseas? The local church? Family? Friends? Social problems? The sick?

Meditation. Try to spend twenty minutes in quiet, unhurried prayer. Use a visual aid if it helps – a cross, a candle, a vase of flowers, a picture, the scent of flowers, the sound of music, a beautiful place. Don't intercede, just try to 'be' in the presence of God and to listen. (Ps 46:1)

Group. Share anything from your private meditation that seems important. Is it easier to pray in a group about some things? Are there things you cannot pray about in a group?

Read the poem *Come Follow Me*. Keep silence.

Read Luke 18:9-14. Are you like the Pharisee? How do we pray like the Publican, without false humility?

Planning for next meeting. Plan a group meditation. Think carefully about a suitable place, a passage of Scripture, visual aids or music, length of time, seating.

Try to ensure that the group comes already prepared, and on time!

Chapter 3

Diary. Write down a brief description of any recent wilderness experience(s) that you have had. Was it a place of failure, testing, learning – or a bit of each?

Has God spoken to you in the sort of way I've described with the angel at Mutwe, or in the L shaped field? Record any such recent experiences. What do you believe about angels – people's experiences today? (I personally think that the 'fruit' of such an experience is the overall test as to its genuineness).

Question. Do you have any special places where you find it a pleasure to pray? Could you create (or improve) such a place?

Do you find silence difficult?

Group. Do the prepared meditation (see Chapter 2).

Debrief carefully. It may be easier for people, if they want to, to write down a few reactions. An important question, for the individual and the group: is there anything we should be doing as a result of what we've experienced?

Preparation. An Emmaus Walk.[2] The 'Emmaus' walk as described by Brother Ramon is very simple. A pair of people meet, read a passage of Scripture, set out on a walk of 1-1½ hours which, ideally, is 'there and back', but could be circular. For the first half there is discussion about the passage of Scripture and anything that flows out of it. The return journey is silent. Back at home, there is a quick debrief, some light refreshment, and a parting prayer.

A group could enjoy the same experience. A suggested timetable:

7.00 meet and read the Scriptures. Split into pairs (non-walkers could do the exercise at home and prepare the refreshments!).

By 7.30 arrive at a suitable starting place. (A circular walk would be best.) Set off in pairs at suitable distances apart – faster walkers in front! Aim to return home by 9.00 for a simple, shared meal, debrief, pray together.

If this is not practical, follow the alternative suggestion at the end of the next chapter.

Chapter 4

Diary. Write down how you visualise God.

Question. What was (is) your relationship with your parents? Does it affect your ability to relate to God as Father? If you have a problem in this area, it is important to talk and pray it through with an experienced person. Many people's ability to pray, and to live (!), is seriously hampered by bad relationships with parents.

Meditation. Read Frank Houghton's poem *Thick Darkness* and also Psalm 139: 1-18. (If you are disturbed by vv19-22, read C. S. Lewis[3] on the Psalms).

You may also find it helpful to acquire the tape by Reg East.[4]

Group. Do planned Emmaus Walk. If defeated by (English) weather, or group inertia (!), discuss how the group could be more disciplined in prayer, how you could be more open to each other and to God, and whether a half-day/full day/weekend away would help the group.

Chapter 5

Diary. Write down, in brief, as many things as possible that you can give God thanks for. Put an asterisk beside the really important ones. Write down things that you have learnt/are learning to be thankful for. Write down the things for which you are not thankful, put a † beside the really troublesome ones, and ask God what you should do about them. Compose a prayer of praise. Let the words flow – don't worry too much about order or structure.

Spend time in adoration of God. You may find it helpful to meditate upon some well known Scripture verses (any part of John, chapters 14-16, the parables of Luke 15, Psalm 103...), to listen to some music, to sit quietly in a beautiful church, to go for a walk (but if so, don't be too distracted by the wonders of nature). You may like to attempt to be completely silent. (If you find this difficult, and most of us do, seek out someone who can teach you about 'contemplative' prayer.)

Group. Aim to spend thirty to forty minutes in prayer! Explain to the group the structure. A suggestion would be ten minutes of verbal thanksgiving, beginning with the reading of Philippians 4:4-7. When the leader feels it right to move on, read Philippians 4:8-9 and have a time of praise. This may include choruses, reading of poems, Scripture. This section should last ten to twenty minutes.

Then read John 17:20-26, or some other appropriate text, and have a time of silent adoration. Encourage people to get comfortable first, legs uncrossed, body relaxed, with plenty of space (three on a sofa is not a good idea). As an alternative, use the Reg East tape mentioned in the previous Prayer Exercises. Aim to spend ten to twenty minutes; the leader should use his discretion as to how long the group can engage for. Even ten minutes can seem a very long time, if you are not experienced in this approach to prayer.

Don't debrief! Let people leave quietly, or have a drink. Any debrief could take place later, or in pairs. Warn the group that the next session is on Intercession.

Chapter 6

Diary. Pray and write out, in rough at first, a prayer matrix. Here is an example (mine while still on Sabbatical, May 1996). You may well want to be more specific, you may want more columns, but don't make it too burdensome... Make a copy (see over!)

Mon.	Jane	SM Church & Congregation	Godchildren	Amani (Elizabeth)
Tues.	Rachel	SM Church leaders	Children's godparents	Chipili & Zambia
Wed.	Susie	Dt Church & other churches in SM	Friends & Marriages	Missionaries
Thurs.	Tim	Cr Church & SM Prison	Healing Ministry & Sick	Writing
Fri.	Katy	Diocese (especially DHAG/ DRG/ZOG	Social needs (esp. SHAL)	My return!
Sat.	Wider family	National Church	Evangelism	Jubilee 2000

Brief explanation – SM, Dt, Cr, my three parishes: Shepton Mallet (c.8000), Doulting (c.600), Cranmore (c.600). DHAG = Diocesan Healing Group, DRG = Diocesan Renewal Group, ZOG = Zambia & Overseas Group, SHAL = Shepton Mallet Housing Association Limited (see Chapter 10), Amani (Mother-in-law's project in Kenya, see Chapter 10), Chipili and Zambia (see Chapters 3 and 6), Jubilee 2000 (see Chapter 10).

Group. Have a time of structured intercession. By that, I mean, the leader gently directs the group into broad areas of intercession. It is usually easiest to start at home and work outwards! The reverse is probably more theological, but in practice much more difficult.

If you are feeling brave, share your prayer matrix with someone else and ask them to pray it through over a period (week/fortnight). It's a useful way of getting to know someone at a deeper level.

Chapter 7

Remember forgiveness – receiving and giving – is a difficult business. If it were not, Jesus wouldn't have spent so much time teaching about it.

Diary. Write a brief account of God's forgiveness to you – both the total forgiveness won by Jesus on the cross, and the ongoing forgiveness that we need to experience day by day.

Write a brief prayer expressing your gratitude for God's forgiveness, expressing your penitence for things that are wrong now, and asking for guidance about forgiving others.

Consider. Do you feel like Jonathan Edwards, a growing sense of sin despite much time spent in serious discipleship? Where are the ongoing areas of spiritual battle in your life?

Read. Romans 8:12-17.

Write. A list of people that you need to forgive (don't rake up the past unnecessarily. If you've forgiven someone, then leave well alone). (a) People who have died, (b) people with whom you have lost contact, (c) people for whom it would be embarrassing, or difficult to contact, (d) people you see regularly.

Pray about what you should do, or not do, in each case.

Add to the list people who need to forgive you. (e) People you have lost contact with, (f) people you have asked to forgive you, but haven't, (g) people you need to ask to forgive you.

Pray for them and consider what action you need to take.

Group. Do a short Bible study on Romans 8:12-17.

Bring a list of people in categories a-d. Pray (silently!) for them, and symbolically tear the list up. (A cross, and a good fire are useful aids). Be prepared to pray and comfort one another, and to seek pastoral help if anyone is clearly out of their depth spiritually or emotionally.

Pray to experience 'the Spirit of sonship' and 'assurance' which makes the whole matter of forgiveness so much easier.

Chapter 8

Diary. Write down some of your experiences of evangelism. Learn 1 Peter 3:15. Record your own account 'of the hope that is in you' – who was praying for you?

Have you ever shared your faith with anyone else? Have you ever prayed with anyone who was on the brink of commitment to Jesus? (I was asked this question at the only really searching interview that I had when looking at four Anglican Theological Colleges before starting ordination training.)

Prayer. Give thanks for all those you know who have apparently been converted in the last year. Ask the Lord whom you should especially pray for (it is likely to be a short list), and pray for an opportunity to speak with them.

Group. Read 1 Peter 3:15 and the parable of the great banquet (Luke 14:15-24). What could the group do? Organise a supper party and a speaker? Run an Alpha course? Help with Sunday School or Youth Work?

Prepare, for next time, a faith sharing role play. (The group splits into three's. One rôle plays their preconversion state, a second tries to lead them to faith, a third observes. This role play, although artificial, really shows if we understand the gospel, and several times, to my knowledge, has led to the conversion of one of the participants!)

Chapter 9

Question. What do you think about healing in today's church? (a) Not for today's church – causes too many disappointments. Use medicine, and pray! (b) An important sign of the kingdom – but not your scene. (c) Important. I'd like to be involved, but I feel unworthy and don't know how to get started (a very saintly bishop once told me that when someone has healed, after he had prayed for them, he felt too unworthy to see such things. An interesting reaction, in sharp contrast, to some of the triumphalism of today). (d) Important – I am involved, but would love to be more effective.

Prayer. Write a prayer reflecting each of these attitudes. (This will probably show you what you really believe).

Question. If you substitute evangelism for healing, are your answers any different? Why?

Meditation. Consider the social projects mentioned in this chapter: The Church Urban Fund, SHAL, Prison, ACET, Amani, Hilfield, Keep Sunday Special, Jubilee 2000. Focus on one of them. Try to imagine what it is like to be in need of such help and to be a helper.

Group. Do the role play prepared last week.

Read Acts 28:7-10. Does this sort of thing happen today? Consider getting an experienced speaker to talk to the group, going to a conference... Pray that God, if he is calling you to be involved, will show you whom to pray with (they may well be present!).

Read Acts 6:1-7. What were the qualifications to be a deacon? What is your church doing about the problems – of its members and those outside? What could the group be doing? (Be realistic!)

Chapter 10

Diary & Action. Read John 15:1-5 (RSV). Try to spend a day 'abiding in Christ' – thinking how he would act. What he would say, believing that he is both in you and guiding you through the Holy Spirit. Record your experience.

Question. What are the situations where you, often, fail to be Christlike? Can you avoid them? Change your attitude? Welcome them!? What are the situations in which you succeed.

Diary. Read Acts 10. Write down what it felt like to be Cornelius and Peter.

Question. How you have seen (or experienced) anything like Acts 10:44-48?

Prayer. Read John 7:37-39. Pray to be thirsty and to drink!

Group. Study John 15:1-5. What Christlike qualities do we observe in other people?

Are we thirsting for a deeper experience of the Holy Spirit? What are we going to do about it?

Possible suggestions – Have a time of prayer, ask the Holy Spirit to come, and wait and see what happens. Organise a speaker with experience to visit the group. Have a day away. Split into pairs and pray for one another.

Chapter 11

Diary. Re-read what you've written in the last few weeks. What has been

good? What prayers have been asnwered? Where has the struggle been?
Question. What now?

Meditation. Bishop Hannington and Canon Christopher affected the spiritual life of Uganda and Oxford for many years. Meditate upon your spiritual goals – for your church, your family, yourself. 'Dream a few dreams'. Would you like to do 'Something beautiful for God'. Tell God your hopes, your longing, the deepest things in your mind.

Group. Read Psalm 37:3-11.

Have a time of prayer, focusing on the way ahead for the group, the local church, the wider church, the nation.

Notes

1. Oswald Chambers, *My utmost for his Highest* (Marshall Morgan & Scott, 1927), p 237.
2. Brother Ramon, SSF, *A Hidden Fire – exploring the deeper reaches of prayer* (Marshall, Morgan & Scott, 1985), p 99ff.
3. C. S. Lewis, *Reflections on the Psalms* (Collins, 1961), see Chapter 3.
4. Reg East's tape 'Relaxing with Prayer' available from the Revd Reg East, Shepherds Cottage, Whatcombe, Nr Blandford Forum, Dorset.

Biblical Index